THE
S♥UL
MILLIONAIRE

by David Scarlett

PRAISE FOR THE SOUL MILLIONAIRE

"David Scarlett changes the way you see the link between money and emotional maturity. If you're struggling with financial self-sabotage and want to make a difference in the world, you'd be mad not to buy this book today. A great read and so easy to apply! Destined to be a bestseller."

**David Hyner, Director,
Stretch Development Ltd and GiS Sales Club Ltd**

"Not only is the information in this book insightful, but David's method of imparting it is inspired. I absolutely couldn't put it down. Read it, and be prepared for the story to touch your soul. A classic is born."

**Maria Davies, www.speakinginstilettos.com,
International speaker, entrepreneur, property investor**

"If you're looking to truly understand the magic of making and keeping wealth (not just money) then look no further than The Soul Millionaire. *You'll be reading practical instantly useable ideas you'll want to share with everyone for whom you care. Better still . . . get them a copy too."*

**Peter Thomson, Peter Thomson International plc,
www.peterthomson.com**

"Rather than present Laws of The Soul Millionaire as a Dogma, David encourages you to question what you're doing, and try these approaches out for yourself. This book will surely be a classic."

Neil Davidson,
Managing Director, WellBeing Network

"When you are a) eager to get your knowledge across, b) enthusiastic about communicating and c) have earned the right to tell others . . . then you have created a powerful message. David has managed all three conditions in this book."

Will Kintish,
Professional Speaker and Trainer

"A refreshingly different view on achieving financial freedom, this book is a very special gift."

Andrea J. Lee, Founder, Multiple Streams of Coaching Income, Creator, www.TheMoneyAndMeaningMovie.com

"This book is truly superior. Brimming with simple, yet thought-provoking strategies that anyone can use to build a life of real abundance and financial maturity. A gem!"

Lesley Everett,
Executive Branding Coach & International Speaker

"The principles in this book work. The story is persuasive, yet so effective. I knew there had to be a better way to create financial freedom, whilst building a life of real purpose and value. There is – The Way of The Soul Millionaire!"

Karl George (MBE),
Business Mentor,
Director Andersons KBS Ltd

"A must-read for anyone who's ever been frustrated by the 'you-can-have-it-all' blockbusters that leave you feeling ignorant and confused. A veritable antidote to the hype and psychobabble that proliferates the popular bookshelves. The one book on financial transformation, and becoming rich in the truest sense, that I'd have if I could have just one. A truly excellent book."

Jonathan Jay, Founder,
The Coaching Academy,
Business Expert, Author and Self-Made Multimillionaire

"It's rare to find such insightful, usable, advice in one place. As I read through this amazing book, I sensed the power that would come into my life if I could convert these principles into practice. I can say that I'm doing that right now . . . and I urge you to do it too! It's not often that a book has that sort of effect on you."

Gary Outrageous,
www.GaryOutrageous.com

"The Soul Millionaire *is a compelling read. It is written in a style that makes it easy to learn the core messages that tell you how to build an abundant life for yourself and the people you care about. Key lessons are conveniently captured at the end of each chapter and I would recommend this book as a must-have volume for anyone who is serious about being a master of their life and their finances."*

Tony Burgess, Director,
Academy of High Achievers Ltd (Aha!)

"A beautiful, inspiring, moving book. A compelling tale written with finely crafted language, wonderful story-telling, and the authority of the best self-help writers of our times. For those seeking financial and life success, this book is right up there with the classics of the genre."

Andrew Walsh, Property Developer
and Business Turn-round Specialist

"David does a fantastic job of providing inspirational, uncomplicated laws that get real results. Immerse yourself in this parable, if you're struggling with the practicalities of attaining financial freedom. You'll emerge feeling that there is a way forward, a step-by-step plan, and a radiant future at the end of the tunnel."

Huzefa Dungarwalla,
Investment Company Director

"A unique way of looking at personal and financial responsibility. I was committed to reading the entire book by the time I reached paragraph four on page three of the story. I believe that anyone who reads The Soul Millionaire *will not fail to 'connect' with it. They'll see themselves reflected in some way . . . at some point in their lives. And they'll want to change!"*

Clive Gott,
Inspirational Speaker

David J Scarlett

To the courage,
determination and devotion
of my greatest champions –
my ever-believing Mum and 'Pa Bear' Dad.

Their lives have shown me that
dreams really can come true.

David J Scarlett

Acknowledgements

As I consider the generosity of those who have helped me give birth to the concept of The Soul Millionaire™ brand, and now this novel . . .

. . . I am left somewhat overwhelmed.

I'm going to break protocol with an increasingly secular UK market and give thanks first to God.

It is He that has enabled this journey called Life, has moved people and situations into my path, and has endowed me with the faith to develop whatever talents and gifts I have to offer. As I look back calmly over the peaks and valleys of my life, I can only describe the whole process as a miracle.

Next, Wendy, my wife. What can I say that is sufficient about My Eternal Companion, guide, guardian angel and helpmeet? She who has endured my moods, strengthened me and hauled me through moments of doubt; providing me with an abundance of common sense and insight into what works and what doesn't …and love. She is the heroine depicted in this novel, and I consider myself fortunate to be surrounded by women as gifted as she is.

I owe such a debt of gratitude to our dear friends David and Lesley Bridgstock, whose family is the model for this novel. They allowed me to traipse around their home and grounds for hours, doing research for many of the scenes. Their children and grandchildren shaped much of the conversations and ideas that lead the hero along his path.

Then, my family. Particularly Briony and Lauren, my girls, who have provided the substance of many tips and ideas expressed in this and other publications. And let me not forget the support and encouragement from sons Adrian and Matthew. At each step and turn, God has presented me with yet another skilled and talented spirit to guide my steps as an author, speaker and business coach.

First amongst these professionals must be Jo Parfitt, 'The Book Cook', editor, author, journalist and speaker, and proprietor of Summertime Publishing. Without her patience, expertise, experience, clear-thinking, straight-talking and creative hand-holding this story would not have taken form in the way it has.

From John Eggen of Mission Marketing Mentors has come tens of hours of coaching in the power of the written word to open doors to millions of lives. To him I owe my place amongst co-authors like Mark Victor Hansen, Brian Tracy, Robert G Allen and Bob Proctor.

Meanwhile, insightful entrepreneur, Andrew Walsh has been a mentor and sounding board throughout all of my writing, coaching and speaking ventures. It is his ongoing mental, emotional and spiritual support that has helped my business develop the capacity to get behind the launch of the 2nd edition of *The Soul Millionaire*.

Kind words, encouragement and masses of practical support have come from directors and club leaders of the Ecademy network who have shown me a new world of courageous entrepreneurs.

I must express a massive thank you also to my wonderful financial planning and coaching clients who have allowed me into their lives and permitted me to use them as models for my stories.

And finally my parents, my patient, ever-believing parents; my courageous, determined, self-sacrificing Mum and my huggable, beloved, faithful Dad. They keep pouring their generous praise upon me, declaring every effort, article, newsletter, book and report as a work of sheer genius. How can you falter or fail when those you love believe in you so deeply?

Thank you.

David J Scarlett

David J Scarlett

Contents

David J Scarlett

Preface

When you combine the experiences of 20 years as an Independent Financial Adviser and Financial Planner with 25 years of Christian Ministry, you emerge with a deep insight into people's feelings, thoughts and behaviour. This insight applies not just to their behaviour with money, but to their response to life.

After more than 3,500 searching interviews it doesn't take a genius to appreciate that life is a struggle for most people in a western culture that is supposedly overflowing with pleasure, leisure and riches.

The sad fact is that there is very little true richness in far too many lives. Too many people toil through years of emptiness and quiet desperation.

If you're one of the fortunate few who enjoy peace, balance, fulfilment and are buoyed up by loving relationships . . . congratulations! You deserve it!

If your bank account remains consistently healthy and you can get by without credit cards, then I know this: you'll be only too prepared to confirm that your situation did not come about by luck or happenstance.

From that position of understanding, you'll recognise that:

There is confusion . . . in the midst of a plethora of knowledge.

There is overwhelm . . . in the midst of shiploads of information and education.

There is frustration and pain . . . in the midst of supposed freedom of choice and independence.

There is isolation . . . in the midst of noise and crowd.

In essence, folk today feel trapped.

And one of the most suffocating traps of all is the daily wrestle with money.

There always seems too little to meet all of the demands and enticements that modern existence places upon us.

Debt is rampant and sucks the energy and hope from us.

Relationships are burdened and torn apart by it.

What can we do?

The good news is that there is an answer!

The answer lies in the recognition that the state of our bank balance and our relationships are a pretty accurate reflection of what's going on inside our hearts and minds.

How we view and value life is reflected in the choices we make. Those views and values play themselves out in the way we treat both people and money.

What you're about to read will place before you a different way to view both.

You'll learn about ten Principles that – if learned and adopted – will lift your life to a level where you can declare that you are truly rich!

- For the first time you will be given the strategies and tools to evolve, step-by-step, from Debt Slave to Money Master.
- This transformation will also play itself out in the way that you see your purpose in life. You really do have a unique and magnificent purpose!
- With that recognition you will begin to clarify what things in your life you truly value – and you'll invariably discover that they're not things.
- Your vision will clear, your intellect will sharpen, your resolve will strengthen.
- This clarity and strength will move you forward towards goals that are meaningful whilst enjoying the journey each day.

- You'll find yourself with the wisdom and capacity to live life On Purpose rather than reacting to people and events around you.
- You'll reduce your levels of stress and discover how to become staggeringly productive and effective, measurably progressing in those things that are important to you.
- You'll find yourself able to give more generously to others whilst constantly being recharged and renewed yourself.
- You'll increase the power of your hope and faith in a better future for you and those you love.
- Frankly, you'll be happier.

And that's my promise to you!

How do I know that these ten Principles will bring about such profound changes?

Because what you're about to read is based on a True Story; in fact, a combination of True Stories.

I've rearranged times and timescales. Some of the characters might have been merged and mixed. But the people and places do exist.

You'll find a hero and heroine based on reality. You'll be introduced to a family modelled on real, wonderful, vibrant people. You'll be taken into the privacy of their home and their lives. If they seem too amazing to be true, that's because fact is sometimes more astonishing than fiction.

And I believe you'll be deeply influenced by meeting them and walking with them through this adventure.

In the final analysis you'll be presented with the opportunity to be far happier – on purpose; to understand the true meaning of Joy.

This I know for certain, because . . .

This is my story!

David J Scarlett

Chapter 1
East View Mansion

Saturday, 14th April

"Can you explain again why we're doing this?" I asked warily.

"I thought it would be fun for you to meet my sisters. That's all. Don't tell me Mr Cool is getting nervous?"

"Look, Naomi, your sisters don't bother me. But I assume that your parents are going to be home, and frankly, I'm not into the 'meet my folks' scene right now."

"Oh lighten up, Jonathan! Nobody's going to eat you. And I'm not setting you up for a pre-nuptial interview with 'Papa'. Give me some credit, pleeeease!"

It was the Easter weekend. Naomi was on holiday from University and excited about chilling out with her family in the country.

I, on the other hand, was still in the process of dodging angry creditors and trying to hold down my new job, with some difficulty.

Anticipating her two-week visit had helped me to get through the last miserable threads of winter. But I hadn't figured on meeting her family after such a short time. In fact, I hadn't considered meeting them at all.

"Ah, here we are." She sounded relieved. "Home is next left."

She slowed and turned her red Peugeot into a wide drive, and I was greeted by a polished brass sign announcing 'East View Mansion'.

I thought the name sounded a bit pretentious. But within ten yards the thought was swallowed up by my widening eyes as the drive swept before me, flanked by large fields as far as I could see.

Dozens of rabbits scurried away as we slowly drove by. After 50 yards I could still merely glimpse the roof of an approaching building through some oak trees. It wasn't until we swung right and came around the low branches that I first caught sight of East View in all its glory.

"Wow!" I exclaimed. My jaw dropped open so wide that Naomi tapped it back shut again with her fingers.

She chuckled. "It's just a house, silly. C'mon, out you get. We'll miss Saturday breakfast."

Before I could pull her aside, she was bounding up the smooth steps to the double front doors of what was little less than a stately home. I was left staring to the left and right, trying to figure out how many windows, roofs and chimneys overshadowed me.

An assortment of shouting and laughter brought my gaze back to door level as I watched Naomi being engulfed in a flurry of arms.

I guessed her sisters had to be amongst that mêlée.

"Come on, Jonathan, over here!" Naomi beckoned.

I ambled up the steps as nonchalantly as I could, to be greeted by a handshake and an unabashed hug from a complete stranger, which quite took me aback. Holding me at arms' length for a moment, the hugger proclaimed, "Well, Naomi, he's not that bad!"

Through my embarrassment I was met by the gentle gaze, finely shaped face and striking raven hair of Corrin: every whit as beautiful as Naomi.

"Do come in," she encouraged. "But let me introduce you to Jessica first."

Jessica was no less arresting than her sister, though slightly taller, and with a more direct, matter-of-fact stare. The astonishing jet-black hair obviously ran in the family. Only Naomi's flaming auburn set her apart from the pattern.

I was ushered inside, stripped of my coat and left to stand in the hall whilst the girls disappeared into the woodwork like hobbits.

I noticed rows of shoes at the door, so I slipped off my own and immediately noticed how warm the floor was.

I stared at the panelling and staircase. I took in the soft plum carpet, which spread everywhere. The rich colour was echoed in subtle touches against the cream walls and décor. To my left an open door displayed part of a seemingly huge kitchen. Despite its vastness I had the feeling that I had only glimpsed a tiny portion of East View.

"Well, Jonathan, nice to meet you."

Startled out of my reverie, I spun around to be greeted by an outstretched hand and a tall, undeniably handsome man; his greying beard neatly trimmed. Amusement played in his eyes, and a warm smile settled on his face.

Clearly, I still looked confused.

"Naomi's dad," he announced.

"Mr Lambert. Hello," I replied, relaxing a little. He didn't look too threatening.

"Call me Andrew," he said, moving towards an open door. "The small lounge is through here."

Obediently, I trotted in behind him. In my stockinged feet I felt compelled to ask him about the warm floor, but as I entered the room I noticed a glorious log fire filling the hearth, the warmth of which made me forget about the floor.

"Just relax in one of the armchairs," he signalled with a wave of his arm. "The girls are going to, well, do whatever girls do when they arrive. So don't count the minutes. I'll go and check with the head chef when she expects us for breakfast."

For a moment I believed him about the head chef. Then I smiled in complicity. I guessed he was referring to his wife.

A grandfather clock set the pace and calm of the atmosphere, its gilded pendulum clicking back and forth like a metronome.

I quickly scanned the portrait photographs on the wall, searching for Naomi. It was tough to spot her amongst such an array of beauty. Then my gaze fell on the undeniably attractive woman in the centre of a family gathering, taken when the girls were younger. There was that same remarkable, dark hair and the commanding gaze.

Andrew peeked around the doorframe, startling me again. "Well, seems as if we're ready, Jonathan. Breakfast is being served. Hungry?"

"Famished," I replied.

Within seconds, a cacophony of stamping feet, raucous laughter and shouting announced the family gathering in the spacious dining room. The head chef, who was busying herself flitting from oven to dining room table, halted only enough to smile and usher me to my chair.

This was she: the striking figure in the photograph. In the flesh she was no less regal despite the passing of years. One glance confirmed that this was a woman to be reckoned with.

Two men about my age had joined us, persuading children into their places and hugging two of the sisters. From Naomi's description I guessed that they must be Daniel and Nathan, Jessica's and Corrin's husbands.

I counted twelve of us there. With the mass of dishes, we overwhelmed the long table, spilling over onto a second smaller one, where four small children now rattled their cutlery and tapped their feet.

Just as I was settling into my comfortable chair beside Nathan, he grasped my left hand. I was stunned, and glanced at him only to find him ignoring me with his head bowed.

Looking around the table I found that everybody was in the same posture, and a child's voice started a prayer at the same instant that my right hand was engulfed by Daniel's palm.

I writhed in the midst of this alien scene and was still staring when heads were raised and attention was turned immediately to the stacked dishes awaiting us.

That shock over, my eyes strayed constantly to Naomi throughout breakfast. But it wasn't long before she was hauled into conversation from all angles.

As my senses grew used to the traffic of conversation and laughter, I noticed the glances and rapport between the girls and their father. They chuckled with him. They sought his opinion. They groaned in sympathy as he laughed at his own jokes.

Hardly had we stopped to hold our stomachs in appreciation, than the table was being cleared and passing thanks tossed to the head chef, whom I now knew to be called Louise. The family's over-filled bodies began to disappear as magically as they had arrived.

As I stood in mild confusion, Naomi bounded back into the kitchen. "Dad, I have some catching up to do with Mum. Why don't you show Jon around?"

Clapping me on the shoulder he nodded. "Jonathan, are you fit for a quick tour outside?"

"My legs are fine. But I'm not sure if my belly will keep up." I rubbed my stomach and puffed out my cheeks.

He laughed. "That clinches it. The only cure is to walk it off." And he shepherded me towards the front hall, where the softly gusting April air greeted us through the open door.

Together we strolled out onto the gravel driveway, heading right, across the front of the house.

With a sweep of his arm, Andrew took in the magnitude that the vast south-facing frontage presented to our view. Extensive windows and mahogany cladding took up much of the space on the ground floor. Urns dripped with early wallflowers and pansies. Daffodils nodded in profusion from the slim beds that lay beneath every window. Wordsworth would have been impressed.

"Would you believe that this was merely a hunting lodge; part of an estate of at least 1,000 acres?" he commented, sounding awed by the statement.

I let out a low whistle – I knew how to behave.

"We couldn't resist the challenge of rebuilding 'the old mansion', as we call it. It was completely derelict. Empty for a decade and originally built by the Champernon family back in the 1890's."

"Oh . . ." was as much as I managed as I glimpsed the side of 'the mansion' and the other buildings, which now came into view.

"As you can imagine, it's a pure money pit, and I daren't think how much we've spent on it. Probably as much as we sold our previous home for – and more. But Louise fell in love with it." He rolled his eyes to the heavens and shrugged his shoulders helplessly.

"How could you say no?" I empathised. "Round her little finger, eh?"

"Extravagant, I admit. But what an opportunity to bring the whole family together! What grandparent wouldn't give their right arm to have their grandchildren constantly at hand yet not under their feet? When you see the cousins growing up and playing together, well . . ."

He pointed ahead and explained that his eldest daughter Jessica and her husband Daniel had renovated the large wing to the rear of the main house. Over many months they'd completely gutted and restructured the interior, doing most of the work themselves.

As we walked along the side of the house, Andrew pointed out the door to his office – previously the gunroom – and another glass door that led into what used to be the gardeners' storeroom. Between the two doors was a long porch.

I halted to point at a rope hanging from a hole in the porch roof.

He responded by pointing higher. "If you look up there, you'll see that's our excuse for a bell-tower. Oh, the bell works. Three times for meals or continuously should there be an emergency. Gathering the whole family in a hurry isn't easy across ten acres! Fortunately, we've only ever needed three rings."

Following the gravel around to the right, we came to a paved quadrangle in front of Daniel and Jessica's impressive north wing. I craned my neck to take in the height of the roofs surrounding me.

As we retraced our steps, he pointed to the long, low building now standing to our right, away from the rest of the house.

"On the other hand, Corrin and Nathan have made the converted cow parlour and barns into their home." It looked spacious and enjoyed an expansive mass of windows. "They love it, and the children have oodles of room to play."

Before I had a chance to take in much more, it arrived: the anticipated, and dreaded 'Well–Jonathan–tell–me–about–yourself'.

By now we were standing again in the middle of the front hallway, alone.

Not waiting for me to answer, he nodded towards the kitchen. I followed him to the cushioned seats, facing each other, and fitted cosily inside the square of the kitchen's large front bay window.

And so it was that, in spite of having prepared my thoughts days before, I found myself opening up to this enigmatic man, spilling scenes and fears and events that I had sworn would remain hidden.

It wasn't an impressive story.

I told him of my years after leaving college, enjoying great success in sales but sliding into increasingly frequent evenings of gambling.

There was the recruitment business I had started – and promptly demolished two years later. I had let the expansion into two offices – The West End of London and Croydon in Surrey – go to my head. That ego trip was accompanied by the flat in Battersea, near the river, and – of course – the BMW 6-series convertible.

I described how the constant clubbing, together with nights at the roulette table, had forced me into heavy overdraft and a wallet full of credit cards, 'maxed' to the limit.

Finally, having eventually lost everything, there were the nights trudging around London, looking for somewhere to sleep before eventually crawling, humiliated, back to my parents in London. From there I had managed to find myself a new job and gone back to the rank of an employee in a recruitment consultancy.

With merely an occasional nod and soft sounds of encouragement, Naomi's father came to hear my sad and sorry tale.

"And Naomi?" he prompted.

I explained how I had met her friend Megan before I had started my own company. Megan had persuaded me to join her at a huge Valentine's Ball held by her church, near South Kensington in London. It was there that Naomi had first left my senses reeling.

I'm not sure how long we sat, bathed by the morning light. But, attentive and patient, he waited until I had nothing more to tell.

Then he asked, "Do you like music?" It was as if he hadn't been listening to a word I had said.

Standing up Andrew nodded towards the kitchen door. "Why don't we head up to my music room? I have something to show you that I think you'll find interesting."

From the hall he bounded noiselessly up the wide staircase with me trailing close behind. Turning right I followed him along the first floor corridor, flanked by open doors displaying huge bedrooms. Each spoke of elegant comfort and understated opulence.

Climbing an ornate, white circular staircase, we emerged into an attic room furnished with a small, green, two-seater Dralon sofa, a stool and a keyboard in the midst of wires and recording equipment. Against one wall was a desk.

An assortment of children's photos were interspersed with awards, certificates and framed silver discs, which – at a brief glance – suggested a musical career. More curious was the row of half a dozen portraits with each person proudly holding a medallion hanging from a ribbon draped around their neck.

"Do you play?" he asked as he gestured to me to sit down on the sofa.

"Not really. A few chords on the piano." Now I was really confused. I wasn't sure whether I was about to receive a lecture or a one-man concert.

Andrew sat opposite me on the stool in front of a microphone, momentarily closing his eyes; his fingers caressing a pale cream guitar across his lap.

Gradually I noticed that the random chords ran together to form a haunting tune. His humming changed as his lips formed a barely audible melody.

"I composed this for the girls a year ago," he said.

As I witnessed a father's feelings for his children captured in song, I instinctively lowered myself to the uneven floorboards. In the last verse he sang of Naomi, and his voice became noticeably husky. The words spoke of his farewell to her in the days before she had left for University.

The last notes drifted away as he stopped playing and hugged the guitar closer to his chest.

"See that desk next to you?" Without opening his eyes he nodded towards a smart, chrome-handled beech desk. "In the centre; tell me, what do you see?"

"A small maroon box. It looks like a ring box," I answered, my throat feeling tight.

"Please, open it," he quietly commanded.

Reverently, I lifted the soft leather box and prised it open. I whistled softly.

There on the blue velvet lay an exquisite gold ring which held in its clasp the largest diamond I had ever seen. A blue-white diamond.

Now, I know little about precious stones, but my gambling had allowed me to witness affluence at close hand. I recalled being educated about the fire and brilliance that erupts when a diamond's facets and central face are perfectly balanced.

To my simple view this square-cut gem was breathtaking.

His eyes snapped open. "Before East View that was the most valuable item we possessed. It's been in Louise's family for, I'd say, 90 years or so."

He shifted his gaze back to his guitar.

"But you're right if you've guessed that it should belong in a safe. It does. I've taken it out to show you today." Without raising his head, he moved his eyes back to me . . . challengingly.

"Would you like to keep it for a while? You know, borrow it until you fancy bringing it back?"

"What? Are you serious? This is worth a fortune!" I was alarmed.

"Do I look as if I'm joking?" He didn't sound amused.

"Well no. But Mr Lambert – Andrew – I mean, you hardly know me!"

"Oh," he said, frowning and looking slightly bemused. "That's right. And yet, you know, I have entertained a whole line of young men across the years who've wanted to borrow my daughters for a while, wondering if I minded. Tell me, Jonathan, what do you think they're worth to me?"

I felt trapped; I mumbled something about their worth being more than all his possessions, including the mansion.

"You'd be right. You'd be absolutely right. But you'd like to 'borrow' my Naomi for a while, wouldn't you? And you're right again Jonathan, I hardly know you."

At this he laid his guitar down and stood up, his hands behind his back, his eyes squarely on me.

I started to rise, holding onto a dark oaken pillar beside me. "I'm not sure what you want me to say. It must be obvious that I'm really attracted to her. Who wouldn't be? Frankly, I have to admit that I'm totally besotted. And, yes, I would like to spend more time with her, to 'borrow her' as you call it."

I turned slightly to snap shut the box and slide it into the centre of the desk away from me. Then I continued.

"Look Andrew, I don't want to steal your ring, and I don't want to harm your daughter. If you ask her, she'll tell you that I've treated her with respect."

"Hmm." He looked at me, and the room went silent. I could hear my own heart thudding loudly near my throat. From somewhere below I thought I heard a cuckoo announcing an early summer. He turned away to place his guitar carefully against the wall.

"You owe £300,000 you say?"

I was thrown by this change of direction and summoned up a slight cough and a nod of agreement before I dared to voice a quiet, 'yes, sir'.

He turned to sit down again. "What are you planning to do about that, Jonathan?"

"I'm about to declare bankruptcy. It seems the cleanest way to deal with it."

"Oh. Really?" He raised his eyebrows rather condescendingly. "Tell me Jonathan, if you could pay it back, would you?"

"Look Andrew, I simply don't see how I could do that." I stood up and let my gaze wander to the glass door to my right.

"But if you could . . ?" I could feel his eyes fixed on me, unwavering.

"What's the point?" I walked to the door feeling more uncomfortable than ever. I turned and shrugged, my arms folding. I could feel the tension building across my neck.

I continued, my tone rising a little. "Why not wipe the slate clean and give myself a chance to start afresh?" I had started pacing the floor and gesturing heatedly. "I'd rather that than drag out the pain."

"I see. And what about the creditors whose businesses you're damaging?"

I held out my hands. "Surely they know the score! Everybody does it nowadays. Business is a risk, isn't it?"

"Yes it is. But I'm not sure that everybody else should pay the price of your ill-considered habits and incompetent business management, should they?" By now, his voice had an edge to it.

I was stung by this comment.

However, he hadn't finished pushing the point home. "There's a morality at stake here, Jonathan. If there's the remotest possibility of repaying a debt that you've incurred, then integrity demands that you grasp that possibility."

His finger was pointing and prodding the air, his words becoming almost staccato. "You entered some transactions. People gave you value, goods and service, trusting you to pay back what you owed. To then walk away, because you've lost control, smacks to me of cowardice!"

I felt myself back up against the wall, almost nauseous.

For long moments we looked at each other.

His eyes never left my face. "Look. I'm going to make a suggestion – perhaps a better solution. Are you ready to hear this?"

I folded my arms again and tried to sound casual. "Go on."

He sat back onto his stool, put his forefingers together and tapped his chin lightly. "Let's say that you could find a way out of this. Let's say that I could show you how to arrange the debt so that you could pay it off quickly, maybe in a couple of years. If we could find a way together, would you be willing to try that?

Oh, and before you answer, I'll add some spice to the riddle. Let's say at the end of that time, I helped you to discover a way to become a millionaire. What would you think of that?"

How could he switch from flaying me to jesting so quickly? "What? Are you serious? A millionaire?"

"Well, young man – are you interested or not?"

Feeling a little weak at the knees, I collapsed onto the green sofa. "I'd be mad to say 'no'. But how on earth . . ?"

"Uh-uh. No questions, Jonathan. Just answer me: 'yes' or 'no'."

I stared at the floor, trying to understand what was going on. I ran my hands through my hair, looked up and caught his eye.

"Yes, okay. I'm up for it," I blurted. "So what do I have to do?"

He clapped his hands together, stood up and came towards me. "Let's see. Naomi returns to university next week. Why not drive down here next Saturday, the day after she leaves? I'd like to introduce you to someone you'll find helpful."

He held his hand out for me to grasp and pulled me up onto my feet.

I hesitated, embarrassed. "Drive? Erm . . ."

"Oh, sorry. I forgot. You no longer have a car, of course. If you phone me from Croydon station, I'll meet you at the local station here. How's that?"

I took his offered hand and felt the sincerity of his grip.

"Good. That's settled then." He waved me towards the spiral staircase.

"Oh, and Jonathan . . ."

I looked over my shoulder, my hand on the railing.

"Not a word of this to Naomi. Right?"

"Right." I grinned.

JONATHAN'S NOTES

- What a strange day this has been. Yet I sense instinctively that something important is happening. It's as if I'm standing on the edge of a chasm.
- Somehow I know that I have to write this down. If I don't and it does turn out to be a dream, then I know that when I wake up, it will be too easy to forget the detail.
- I found this old diary in my bedside drawer and it seems appropriate that I start using it. So here we go:

LESSONS LEARNED

- To Andrew Lambert having a big house and lots of money is not a definition of success. Being happy is;
- Families that eat together regularly are relaxed and happy in each other's company;
- Functional families are a tremendous source of strength;
- Andrew's most important asset is his relationships with his family, not his wealth;
- Integrity is more important than simply being free of debt.

PROGRESS TRACKER

- I've been in my new job for two months now;
- Naomi leaves again for university next week.

David J Scarlett

Chapter 2
The Three Challenges

*"J*onathan, let me introduce you to Chris Charles. Chris, meet Jonathan Broom – budding entrepreneur."

It was mid April. I was back at East View and standing at the doorway of Andrew's office. He stood beside me with his hand on my shoulder.

Seated at Andrew's elegant desk was a somewhat stout if not corpulent man whose huge hands looked large enough to span a football. He looked from Andrew to me, his broad, welcoming smile showing a row of perfect white teeth. With surprising speed he raised himself to greet me, and I noticed the heavy gold watch that emerged from blue and white striped cuffs on his outstretched arm.

My hand engulfed by his palm, I was surprised to find his handshake both warm and gentle. I laughed feebly. "Correction, I think you'll find that's 'failed entrepreneur'. Nice to meet you, Mr Charles."

As we settled into the comfortable high-backed chairs, Andrew responded with a wagging finger. "Come on, Jonathan. You've not failed until you've surrendered – given up. So let's forget such language in our discussions. Shall we?"

I put both hands up in defence. "Okay, okay."

Andrew continued. "Jonathan, Chris is one of our most trusted advisers on matters to do with accountancy, tax and business disposal.

He has a proposal that I think you should listen to. It might help you get through this without losing the goodwill of all your creditors."

Chris started by discussing the implications of bankruptcy. His version was naturally more technical than Andrew's comments. But I was left in no doubt as to his view regarding the morality of my options.

For the next ten minutes, scribbling furiously on the desk-pad, he went on to explain the workings of an Individual Voluntary Arrangement. It was this option that he encouraged me to take.

The plan was for Chris's practice, Stafford Charles, to negotiate with all the creditors. His suggestion was that they might accept an offer to pay 33 pence in every pound with the payment spread over four years. Then I would only have to pay a regular amount to one creditor – Stafford Charles.

"Believe me, Jonathan." Chris concluded. "When you deal with creditors in this way, they tend to have far more respect for you in the long term. I have seen business relationships continue without ill-feeling, simply because there is evidence that the debtor is doing all he can."

I quickly worked through the figures in my head. "That amounts to £100,000 over four years, doesn't it?" I queried. "What's that? About £2,000 per month?"

"Well, do you think you could handle that?" he challenged.

I stood up, hands in pockets, and began to pace across the warm floorboards, becoming aware that I had started chewing my lip.

"I just don't see how I can, Chris. I'm currently only on a basic salary of £30,000, and I'm lucky, because my parents are supporting me right now. But unless I instantly start to hit my sales targets – and that's pretty tough in a new job – I just don't see how I could manage."

"I have an idea," said Chris, sounding hopeful. "What we could do is arrange for an easier schedule for the first year: let's say £1,000 per month. Then we simply load the balance onto the remaining years. But that does mean that in subsequent years the monthly figure jumps to £2,500 per month."

"I have to warn you," he said, his voice becoming suddenly serious. "If you default for more than three consecutive months, we will have to declare you bankrupt."

I looked at Andrew, who nodded his head.

"I'll take the thousand now, then," I said at last hoping that within a year or two I'd be hitting my targets easily. I held out my hand to Chris. The deal was done and had been surprisingly painless.

"That's great. I'll send the paperwork to Andrew this week. Good to meet you, Jon."

Then turning to Andrew, he briskly shook his hand too. "Look, I must dash now. I'm joining my family for a birthday treat. We're off to the theatre to see 'The Lion King'." He grinned and left the room with Andrew following close behind. I guessed they needed a private word together.

For a few minutes I sat alone in the office, slowly shaking my head. A 'grand' a month – that was a lot of money. Andrew returned, and I looked up.

"I've worked with Chris for some eleven years now," he said, "and this is not the first time that he has helped a friend through a difficult time. Technically he's superb, one of the best. He's done some excellent work for my companies. I recommend that you seriously consider his suggestion."

"Look, Andrew," I said, "this has been a confusing day for me. But I want you to know, I'm grateful for what you're trying to do. Having said that, what I don't understand is why you're doing this for me? You know nothing about me, well nothing good at least. I can't believe you are just being generous? And I can't help but feel guilty to be taking so much of your time."

He turned away from me, bowed his head and walked over to the window before looking up and facing me again. "Well, Jonathan, it's a long story, and one you will come to understand better as time goes on, but in a nutshell, I suppose I just like doing this for people. It's also something to do with showing gratitude for what I have."

Then he slowly moved back to the desk and sat down opposite me once more, fixing me with his brown eyes. "A few years ago I realised that we had more than enough money and talked to Louise endlessly about ways of giving back to society. We talked of setting up charities and scholarships and all sorts of plans. Perhaps we'll do those things eventually. But nothing felt right at the time. Then we realised that the greatest gift we could offer was our time and our knowledge to those who would benefit most."

"Well, you sure found someone who could do with some benefit here, didn't you?" I butted in. "Sorry Mr Lambert, I didn't mean to interrupt. Go on."

"Thank you! And you can just stick to Andrew! I suppose what we're doing is a kind of coaching but much more than that. You'll find out as time progresses." He paused.

"Sort of a mentoring service for budding millionaires, then?" I asked, intrigued.

But he waved away the rest of my thoughts and shifted the subject in that easy, maddening way that I was coming to recognise.

"Tell me more about you and Naomi," he asked.

I got up and started pacing the length of his office. "Well you already know how I feel about her. Having said that, I have to admit that I find her frustratingly different from anybody I've ever met before. I don't know, she doesn't play the games that I'm used to. You know what I mean?"

He relaxed into his own chair at the desk. "Go on," he insisted.

"Well, I have to say that her strong religious views throw me a little; a lot actually, if I'm going to be brutally honest. Frankly, I find them a bit prudish, even ridiculously outdated. I'm sorry to be so rude."

"No, not at all."

"Anyway. I'd like to keep on seeing her."

I looked at him as I waited for a response.

"Jonathan, there are no conditions attached to the help Chris will give you regarding your debt. I want you to understand that."

"That's very kind of you. I'm still not sure what to say," I said, but I could sense a 'but' coming.

"Hear me out first," he said, holding up his hand, "because you may have a lot to say when I'm finished."

"Oh, I see," I said quietly.

"No, I don't think you do, Jonathan – I'll hand it to you. You're a nice guy, a real charmer."

I shifted uncomfortably in my seat.

"Yet," and he hesitated, stroking his beard. "As I've listened to you, I'm pretty sure that what it boils down to is that you've just wasted years of your young life on a major ego trip, with you as the glorious centre of your universe."

I turned feeling my face flushing, but I was determined not to be browbeaten like the time he showed me the diamond. "Look, er, Andrew."

"No," he said, raising his right hand in a swift motion. "Bear with me for a couple more minutes, Jonathan, and then you can curse me all you like.

"You suggest that you've stopped gambling, but listening to you, it seems to me you've developed habits that, left unchecked, will only reappear elsewhere in your life and bring you down again.

"Now, you don't have to listen to a word I say if you don't want to. You can see my daughter without my knowledge or permission, and there's absolutely nothing I could do about it. Right?

"But I believe you're both worth more than that. I know Naomi is. Far more.

"So . . ." at this he paused and looked at me thoughtfully before nodding.

"So, he continued, "I have a deal to put to you. An agreement. A pact, if you will."

I was intrigued although I sensed that he had something up his sleeve that I wasn't going to like.

He continued, gesturing me to take a seat. "Let me explain what I mean. Then when I've finished, you can tell me, what shall I say, where to 'stick it', if I remember the language correctly. Okay?"

I pulled a chair away from the wall and sat to face him, but at a distance. "Possibly. I'm ready to listen." Then I leaned back and waited.

"Good. Before I proceed let me warn you that what you're about to hear might sound audacious." He hesitated, pushing out his bottom lip in thought before continuing. "You might feel that the challenge stretches beyond what you can handle. Are you with me so far?"

I sat stony-faced knowing that he wasn't expecting an answer. Then he raised his right hand and held up three fingers.

"Our agreement comes as a package; a challenge with three parts," he said, "and here's the first part.

Challenge Number One is this: that you aim to pay your creditors back in twelve months."

I started to lean forward in my chair. "That's madness! You heard the figures from Chris. You know my basic income. How the heck do you expect me to do that?"

"Answer me this," he retorted. "Do you imagine that, financially, I have achieved a few things that most folks haven't?"

I could feel my temper rising in response. "Perhaps, yes. But this isn't about you," I countered.

"No. This is about you trusting somebody who can see what you can't." His answer flew back instantly.

That shut me up. I couldn't string together a coherent response quickly enough. There was a strained silence as he continued.

"**Challenge Number Two** is this: you are to create a way to communicate with one million people, and your communication must aim to help them change their lives for the better. This too must be done in twelve months.

That's part of becoming a Soul Millionaire."

"A what?"

"A Soul Millionaire."

"I thought you said you'd teach me how to become a real millionaire. What's all this 'Soul Millionaire' business?"

"Who said I won't? But before you can create what I have created, you need to travel the road I have travelled, and that requires learning how to think differently about money.

When you've proved you can do that, you become what we call 'A Soul Millionaire'."

I sensed the hairs on the back of my neck lifting. Against my cynicism my instinct told me that, whatever a Soul Millionaire was, I needed to discover more about it. Much more.

"Look, I really don't know what you're talking about, but if it can help me create a mass of wealth – like you – then I'll have a bash at your 'Soul Millionaire' thing. I hope to goodness the next challenge is a little less extreme."

He paused, his features hardening as he stared at me. I wasn't comfortable in the silence.

"I'm afraid I can't grant your wish, Jonathan. You see, **Challenge Number Three** is the toughest one of all. You suggest that you love my daughter. Yet what I observe isn't true love at all."

"What are you talking about?" I burst out. I didn't recall telling him exactly how I felt about Naomi. But he was right: my feelings for her were running deeper with each passing week.

Unmoved by my reaction, he continued without missing a beat. "The way I see it, true love is doing all in your power for the emotional well-being and spiritual growth of the one you love. Frankly, Jonathan, I'm not convinced that's what's going on here."

I could feel my fists clenching and my breath becoming shallow.

So The Third Challenge is this: that you promise not to communicate with Naomi, in any way, for those twelve months."

"What?" I shouted, as I leapt to my feet. "You can't tell me what to do with Naomi! I'll damn well see her if I want!"

And he rose slowly, his arms held out in pleading. "No, Jonathan. I can't tell you anything. But I can ask you."

"No, don't ask me!" I was close to shouting now. "Because I don't want to hear any more. I'll tell you what this is all about. Your help with my debts, getting Naomi to bring me down here, these stupid challenges, this Soul Millionaire rubbish. This is just emotional blackmail so that I'll leave your precious daughter alone. And I bet you want to try and ram your religion down my throat at the same time."

By now I was hot and shaking with anger, pacing aimlessly around the room. I stumbled over my overturned chair and cursed before continuing.

"And d'you want to know something else? Being a millionaire like you doesn't interest me that much. I don't need your damned help. I can do this on my own!"

I threw myself blindly towards the nearest door, tearing angrily at the handle and throwing it open.

Finding myself at the side of the house, I turned instinctively onto the gravel, heading left towards the drive.

Within seconds I was striding towards the main gate, bracing myself against the rain and half expecting Andrew to come running after me. But I heard nothing except the wind.

And my anger.

I stopped at the wide entrance looking right and left at the empty road. Where to now? Ask the directions to the nearest station?

But I didn't. Minutes later I was still standing with my hands deep in my jacket pockets, rain running down the back of my neck.

Looking to my left inside the hedged boundary of East View, I recalled seeing a wooded area. I'd shelter there for a while until the rain eased off.

My shoes were soaked and muddy by the time I reached the protection of the trees. But it was warmer there. And even in my misery, I could recognise the charm of early bluebells that carpeted the woodland floor.

There I stayed as the sun broke through and moved across the broken sky. Pacing and talking to myself, I was besieged by memories as sharp and as poignant as I could bear.

As these pictures from the past haunted me, I found myself staring fearfully into the future and wondering.

Shuffling out of the leafy canopy, I stood in the brief rays of the sun, lifted my face to the sky and croaked, "I'm thirty years old. I'm a mess. If there's anybody up there, for God's sake, help me!"

I was so confused that I no longer knew whether I was cold or plain unhappy. Hunger came and passed. The sky darkened and cleared again only to reveal the sun disappearing behind the trees.

The edge of dusk found me walking slowly onto the drive, staring at the approaching chimneys and the wide, lofty silhouette of East View.

For long moments I leaned my forehead against the glass of the great outer front doors. Then standing back I reached for the large brass knocker. I waited.

He was there as the inner door opened.

Silently we stood staring at each other until I spoke first.

"Okay, Andrew, what is it you want me to do?"

LESSONS LEARNED

- There is an alternative to bankruptcy – an Individual Voluntary Arrangement (IVA);
- I've finally woken up to the fact that I don't have all the answers about relationships, about money, about life;
- It's possible that I'm learning about love for the first time in my life, even if taking the first steps on this path hurts more than I could have imagined;
- I've encountered gratitude in action and have come face to face with a person who is 'giving something back';
- There are times when something just feels right in your heart even if it doesn't make any sense to your mind;
- Because I can't see what's possible, it doesn't mean that somebody else can't;
- I guess faith means believing in something when you have no evidence of the outcome;
- When I tell Naomi, she'll think I've gone mad. More to the point – I think I'm mad!

PROGRESS TRACKER

- Naomi returned to university this week.

Chapter 3
Law One : Develop The Mind of a Soul Millionaire

Saturday, 19th May

A month had passed since that painful day at East View. I was back: this time without Naomi.

"Jonathan, let's stroll to that bench over there. It's warm enough to sit outside."

The dew still lay thick and there was a blanket of mist inches above the tips of the grass. I followed Andrew as he walked towards the low morning sun, passing a tall fir and skirting a gnarled oak then over to a bench settled in its shade. Stopping, I bent down to pick up a long thin twig and recalled how often I had done so as a boy. The memory brought a smile to my face.

With a long, satisfied sigh, he settled onto the sturdy bench.

I ambled towards him and eased myself down leaving space between us on the bench.

"That was great news last week, about the creditors' meeting, I mean," Andrew began.

"Yes." I smiled. "I have exactly four years to pay back £100,000, just as Chris promised. You can imagine how amused he was, a little cynical even when I mentioned our goal."

Gazing beyond the yew hedges, holly and laurel trees that bordered their land, he spoke slowly, almost savouring the words.

"Apart from the music room, this is my favourite place to sit and ponder. Louise calls it my 'Thinking Bench'. I like that. So, Jonathan, tell me the worst."

Caught off guard by the question, I turned my head and met his gaze. I wanted him to talk first. But he wasn't about to back off. His dark brown eyes pierced right through me.

"Naomi, you mean?" I leaned back and tapped my outstretched legs with the end of the twig.

I let the words tumble out as I thought back to the previous weekend. "I confess it took me four weeks to summon up courage to keep my promise. I'm still not sure why I did it, but I phoned her last Sunday. I can tell you now that I silently cursed you as I heard the emotion in her voice, particularly when I told her what I had agreed to do. I can't imagine you're her favourite person right now."

He grunted.

I carried on, "What threw me was that by the end of the conversation she sounded so brave. I suppose I had expected a bigger scene than that. To be honest, after a few minutes she seemed ridiculously calm about the whole thing. She even said that she 'knew it was the right thing'. How she could possibly know that beats me."

He sounded as if he were humming. "Our Naomi has some surprising qualities," he said, "perceptive and farsighted would just about sum her up."

I folded my arms, leaned my head back and, closing my eyes briefly, wondered again what the day would bring.

"Jonathan, I'm ready to start our adventure. How about you?" He had been reading my mind again

I opened my eyes, squinting at the sky. "I'm here aren't I? So I guess I'm as committed as I can be. But one thing before we start. I can't see how you expect me to create £100,000, after tax, in a mere twelve months."

"Giving up already?" he jibed.

"No, that's not the point." I shot back at him. "It's just that, well, twelve months!"

"Right," he said, seeming to ignore me. "The first lesson in becoming a Soul Millionaire is this:"

At this I was jolted out of my comfortable lounging.

"A Soul Millionaire is someone who is resolved to touching one million souls – people that is – here and here." And with that he leaned over, putting one hand on my chest and the other on my forehead.

"Does that make sense?" he asked.

"Yeah, I think so . . ."

"Are you ready to try that challenge, Jonathan?" he asked, brushing aside my wavering.

I responded as pompously as I could, "Try? What was it Yoda said in Star Wars? 'Do or not do. There is no 'try'!'"

"Hah! Touché!" he exclaimed rocking back and laughing at the sky.

"We're going to work through Ten Laws. We'll call them '**the Ten Laws of a Soul Millionaire**'.

This is how we'll do it. You'll take each law and . . ." then he went on to explain how during the next ten months I would be taught a new law each month.

Having learned each law, I would then need to set clear goals to help me to put each law into practice.

Within that same month I would have to demonstrate that law in action, to prove myself, if you like.

Meanwhile, I would commit to making a written record every evening, logging my progress towards my goals.

I could call him if I was struggling.

Finally, we would meet at the beginning of each month to review my progress towards the three goals – 'The Three Big Challenges' as he called them – paying the debt off early, touching one million people and not communicating with Naomi.

Both of us had brought along a pad of paper, and I concentrated hard on taking notes.

"Recording the date is important. The seasons too. Are you ready for the First Law?" he asked.

I nodded, pen at the ready.

"Right! **Law Number One** is this:

"**Develop the mind of a Soul Millionaire.**"

He looked at my face contorting with the struggle to understand. Then he continued:

"A Soul Millionaire recognises a number of truths. There are many, but today we're only going to touch on four.

"The First Truth is this: We can achieve extraordinary things when we give our lives to a purpose much bigger than ourselves."

Again, I looked towards him in confusion.

He continued as if anticipating this, "Most people live out their existence meeting their immediate wants and needs, satisfying their most obvious appetites and desires. Often that stretches to satisfying the wants and needs of their family.

"That's fine, it's necessary, even noble, to meet those basic needs, and admittedly, this is our primary responsibility."

I was nodding in agreement. Isn't that what my parents had struggled with all their lives?

His voice warmed with passion. "But if that's all that drives us, it doesn't have the power to satisfy the yearning we all have. The soul-deep hunger to live with a sense of purpose, a sense that our lives have meant something."

He paused, and his brow knitted just a little.

"So they settle," he said, slowing his pace considerably. "They pass through their fretful hours doing whatever satisfies their comfort today. There is a hollowness in their soul that they try to fill with running to and fro. They work and they drink and they party and they holiday in quiet desperation. In the rear window of their life is a sign that says 'Are we happy yet?'"

At this sadness crossed his face. "I meet them all the time," he said. "They approach the end of their working lives and wonder, 'Is that all there is?'"

He paused and pointed to a fox, hiding in some large bushes, now boldly trotting across our line of vision.

Slapping the arm of the bench, he broke the spell and became excited again. "Now, let us suppose that you could see a huge purpose for your life, a purpose that is not about your personal comfort. Suppose this requires an effort so grand, so mighty that the work needed to reach this goal would continue far beyond your lifetime. Yet, in the process of pursuing it you sensed you could bring happiness to hundreds, maybe even hundreds of thousands of lives, including the lives of those you love."

The passion in his voice rose. "If this magnificent purpose was also something that rang true to your heart, wouldn't that have some kind of gravitational pull?" I knew he wasn't waiting for me to answer.

"When you are striving to rise above the tiny circle of personal life, when you are drawn to something extraordinary and without limits, can you see that this would lend you the strength, the courage and the determination to fulfil your mission?"

Again he stopped and turned, presumably gauging my reaction. I had forgotten to write, mesmerised by his excitement.

"Are you ready to move on?" he asked, pointing at my pad.

I smiled and nodded.

"Let's see," he said. "Ah yes, The Second Truth."

"The Second Truth is this: A Soul Millionaire uses wealth to lift lives."

I turned to a fresh page in my notepad.

"To do this they first learn to recognise that whilst this beautiful world blesses our lives, its resources are not ours to possess."

He must have caught my raised eyebrows . . .

"Don't you see? If we view the world through those eyes, we become grabbing and possessive, caught up in the ruthless pursuit of self-interest.

"We discover that such a course doesn't result in long-term happiness."

My eyes dropped to study my shoelaces intensely. I tapped the end of my 'trainers' with my stick.

He could see my discomfort. "I'm not digging at you intentionally," he said more gently. "But it is important that you recognise both cause and consequence in what has happened to you."

I dug my stick into the layers of leaf-mould around me.

"Jonathan, think of everything that you see and acquire as your stewardship. It's like a gift, but a gift with responsibility. The measure of a person then becomes not what they acquire, but how they use those possessions to bless the lives of others."

He paused just as a nearby rabbit stopped nibbling and looked up nervously, possibly sensing the fox.

I wanted to make sure I was following his thread. "Yeah, I think I understand," I muttered. "Sounds to me what you're saying is that the possessions we own don't make us who we are. It's the way we use those things to help others. Have I got it right?"

"That's about it," he answered, nodding in agreement.

"Well, thank goodness I'm getting something right," I grumbled, brushing away the small cloud of gnats that was gathering in the shade of the oak.

He grunted in response and went on. "There is one rule that you seemed to have learned instinctively."

He had my attention again. "Oh, what's that?" I asked.

"Ah!" he said, with an edge of mockery in his voice. "That's **Truth Number Three: Take Responsibility**."

"Responsibility for what?" By now the few gnats that were still around had started to settle in my hair making me itch furiously. It took a few seconds to whip off my baseball cap and clear the air sufficiently to settle down again.

"When you've quite finished," retorted Andrew, offering no sympathy whatsoever. "I was about to say that I meet many people who refuse to take responsibility for their financial situation. They blame the government, the stock market, their parents, their lack of education, the price of houses.

Typically, you'll find that they don't insure themselves to protect their families and never get around to saving for the future. They won't invest in books, seminars, courses or other means of improving their financial knowledge. Not surprisingly they tend to be continually trapped in debt and in jobs they hate.

In a society like this where information, education, luxury and opportunity abound, we take for granted what we have and ignore what we could achieve.

At least you tried to take responsibility for your destiny when you started your own business."

"Hey, do I hear a hint of praise from you, Master?" I said, still smarting from all that implied criticism.

I caught a hint of a smile as he tried to retain his composure.

"Humph. Very droll," he said moving on. "**Now, we come to the Fourth Truth. And that is this: A Soul Millionaire learns to understand and respect money**.

"As we work together you'll learn that money comes with laws attached. Learn those laws and you can create a great deal from a very little. Break them and, frankly, they'll break you.

"You'll learn why it's important to value money and respect its power.

"You'll also learn laws that few people understand. Then you can make them work hard – very hard – for you and those you love.

"Your business is a classic example of putting ego before a healthy respect for the laws of money." He paused and looked at me for a moment while I pondered. "Go on, tell me I'm wrong," he added.

My huddled silence was enough answer for both of us.

"I know you think I'm being tough. But imagine what you could achieve if you learned to think differently."

He paused to let the point sink in.

"How do you start respecting money and valuing it?" Again, his question was rhetorical. "Surely, a basic step is to recognise that – like most things – money feels sweeter when it has been earned. A Soul Millionaire expects to work and give great value before expecting wealth in return."

He pointed towards me. "Since I know that you're capable of working hard, I know that you already have that principle ingrained in you. It's the other steps that are not in place."

"Such as?" I did not much like what I was hearing but couldn't help myself from becoming intrigued.

"We'll get to that during the months ahead, I promise," he answered.

I felt frustrated hearing that. First he was suggesting great things, giving me tantalising clues, and then leaving me dangling on the line.

"So what's the next step?" I asked.

"First you need to record what we've discussed in a quality hardcover journal. You do keep a journal or diary I presume?"

"But of course," I began sarcastically. "Doesn't everyone? Actually I thought that was for teenage girls." I hesitated. "But since it's part of the programme then I guess I'd better get one, right?"

I paused. "Hey, actually, I have just started writing a few thoughts down in an old diary every time I see you. Is that the kind of thing?" I felt rather proud of myself for a change.

"That's it. I recommend keeping one daily," he responded, stressing the last word. "Merely making entries every time you see me is not enough, but I admit it's a start. Oh, and one other thing, before you go, I want you to take this." He tore a page from his pad.

"I've created a list of books and other resources that we'll be using during the coming months. I could have bought them for you, but you need to make that effort yourself. Here are the first two titles."

I looked at the list. This was like going back to school. I had things to learn, homework and now books to read too. I started reading the titles out loud. "*The Courage To Be Rich* by Suze Orman. Okay. *Rich Dad's Cashflow Quadrant* by Robert T. Kiyoo... Kiyoo..."

"Ki–yo–sa–ki"

"Yes, him," I continued, mockingly.

Ignoring my tone, he continued, "Your task is to read both books by our next meeting, the first Saturday in June. That's one book a week. If you need to discuss any ideas you come across, call me."

I was feeling overwhelmed by now and more than a little out of my depth. There seemed to be so much involved in becoming a Soul Millionaire I couldn't imagine doing it alone.

I sighed. "I will, don't worry. But Andrew, before I go can I ask one more favour?" I must have looked at him with a worried expression.

He clapped me on the shoulder. "Sure thing. I'll let her know you're doing well and still look lovelorn."

"Thanks. That means a lot," I said.

A soft chime reached our ears.

"That's three rings to say lunch will be just about ready."

LESSONS LEARNED

- This Saturday I started learning about the Ten Laws of The Soul Millionaire. The First Law is 'Developing The Mind(set) of A Soul Millionaire';
- Truth No. 1: I need to have a purpose in life which is bigger than my own personal wants and needs;
- Truth No. 2: There's a different feeling in deciding to create wealth in order to benefit other people, not just myself. And I'm already beginning to like that feeling;
- Truth No. 3: I need to take responsibility for my financial destiny and be prepared to invest in it;
- Truth No. 4: Apparently, I don't have enough respect for money, which is why it slips through my fingers.

PROGRESS TRACKER

- This is the third month in my new job;
- Things are going well at work, but I'm still flat broke;
- The first payment of the Individual Voluntary Arrangement (IVA) starts 1st June;
- It's been a difficult week having said 'goodbye' to Naomi last weekend;
- I'm soaking up Andrew's Soul Millionaire's Laws as if I were parched.

David J Scarlett

Chapter 4
Law Two : Create The Big Picture

Saturday, 2nd June

*N*ormally, the first Friday in the month would have been my evening with the team from the office. The City Peddler pub tended to be our first stop.

But awakening to an early June morning in the depths of West Sussex was enticing, and I had succumbed to the invitation to travel down to East View on the Friday night. I had also grown to relish the weekend breakfasts with 'The Clan', as they called themselves.

Glancing around the spacious bedroom as I awoke, I estimated that our family's lounge and dining room would fit comfortably inside it.

Rising early, in the half-light of dawn, I walked alone circling the estate and stopping only to skim stones across the fenced pond stocked with golden Koi.

Strolling across the tamed meadow, kicking showers of dew as I went, I wasn't surprised when I found myself standing at 'the Thinking Bench'. It seemed a natural place to quieten my whirlwind of thoughts. Almost ritually, I lowered myself onto the bench, my notepad on my lap, and allowed my lids to droop.

I didn't hear his arrival, but I became aware of Andrew beside me. Opening my eyes, I greeted him with a smile. Peacefully, we murmured a little between us, waiting and watching as the June sun rose.

"So tell me, Jonathan. Have you made any progress?" His invitation was soft and encouraging.

I began to shake my head in disbelief as I took a deep breath and recounted the shifting of my routine.

I admitted that the habit of keeping a journal of each day's events had been hard, almost artificial at first. More surprising had been the ease with which I had swapped an hour or so of my usual glazed television viewing for quiet reading.

I described my fascination with the books he had recommended. Handing him my notepad, I pointed to the pages full of comments and intended actions gleaned from twice reading *Rich Dad's Cashflow Quadrant*. I also mentioned my confusion that some of the advice from Kiyosaki seemed to contradict the recommendations by Suze Orman – both of them highly successful authors.

He felt the same, commenting that Orman seemed to take a different and more cautious view of business and investment risk.

"They're interesting and instructive views," he said, "not universal truths."

Continuing my report, I realised that I was finding increasing enjoyment in my work and had completed a pretty good month in terms of sales revenue.

On the other hand, my paycheque didn't yet reflect that achievement. Even with the promise of increased earnings, I still didn't see how I could clear £100,000 from my net income in the next eleven months.

I left the question hanging in the air.

There was a brief silence which I eventually broke by saying, "I wrote to Naomi this week."

From the corner of my eye, I saw him turn towards me frowning.

"But I didn't post it." I couldn't help chuckling in mischievous triumph. Thankfully, his sense of humour got the better of him and he joined me. After a few moments of silence, I felt compelled to carry on.

"So, what lesson comes next?" I asked succumbing to my eagerness.

"Next? Oh yes, next," replied Andrew reaching for his pen and flicking through a few pages of his pad.

"Ah! Now we come to the next law. **The Second Law is this: Create The Big Picture**."

If he saw my puzzled look, he didn't show it.

"The Big Picture has three elements to it," he continued.

I glanced over to see him circling a large '1' in the margin of his page so I did the same.

"Element number one is a question: How huge and audacious is the task or goal you have set for yourself?

"As we discussed last month, the task you've accepted is huge. In fact, it's hardly about you at all. It's about one million other people. And its effect will be evident long after you are gone.

"The task is audacious because you can hardly believe it yourself. But you sense that if you don't do it, perhaps somebody else will,which raises the teasing question, 'Why not me'?"

I flicked away the spider that had floated down from the oak and had started walking across my subheading 'Huge and Audacious Goal'.

"Element number two: Describe your three-year vision.

"This requires some creative talent. You need to be able to describe your life as it would ideally be in three years. The secret is to paint it with strongly descriptive words. Try portraying precisely what would be happening around you, to you, within you, when we meet for lunch three years from today."

Rising from the bench, bending his back to stretch, he then half-closed his eyes for emphasis. "The picture needs to be vivid."

"Hmmm. That's all well and good," I interjected, "but it sounds as if I need to have the skills of a poet and I'm still struggling to create decent business letters. This may be a bit beyond me."

He thought for a moment. "Maybe so. But, Jonathan, if you are to succeed in business, you need to understand the power of the written word."

Signalling with his finger for me to wait, he walked out of my line of vision. Within seconds he ambled back, rubbing something between his fingers.

Holding his hand near my face, he waited until I had inhaled.

"Lavender." I sighed.

"Powerful, isn't it?" he said. "Your words need to evoke emotions as strongly as that tiny flower."

Reaching to the sky to stretch one final time, he took up his pad and lowered himself beside me once more.

He continued. "Let's look at your vision of life in three years, and I'll suggest some points to add power to the process."

I grabbed my pencil as the words tumbled from his mouth.

"You need to write as if you're enticing someone you love to join you. You weave in lots of detail to describe where you are, who is there with you, more about the surrounding scenery, the style of home you're in, the weather, the smells and sounds of the garden, the plans for the day.

"Do you get the picture?"

"I think I do, yes," I said at last, for a moment absorbed in the thought that while I loved the sound of the house and life he had just described; it seemed rather a pipedream right now. "And you call this 'The Big Picture'?"

"Yes. You paint it and sculpt it and craft it with such passion that, were I the director creating a film of your life, the description would give me all I needed to produce a breathtaking scene."

"Next – and this is **Element number three – you write it in the present tense**. For example, 'it's Sunday, in June, and I'm taking my morning cup of coffee in my conservatory. Out of the window I can see a pheasant walk across the lawn, which is studded with buttercups. I hear my wife calling that breakfast is ready. I walk over to the door and as I open it, the smell of bacon hits my nostrils . . .' That sort of thing."

He hesitated, looking at me to see if I had grasped the process.

"I get it," I said, standing and rubbing my thighs. "But what on earth will all that help me to achieve?" I asked.

"It's where the magic starts!" He turned towards me and leaned forward, his eyes widening. "When you have involved your heart and your emotions in a process like that your mind begins to believe that it really will come true.

"From that moment your feelings and thoughts will start seeking out ways to make the vision evolve into reality."

"Almost like a radar system scanning the skies," I was beginning to understand.

Just then the third chime for breakfast broke through the intensity of our discussion and Andrew clapped me on the back.

"Looks like the more lofty things of life will need to wait for our appetites."

It didn't surprise me when he signalled me to join him after breakfast.

Outside the morning sun had dried the dew. This time we headed down the path that ran along the east side of Daniel and Jessica's wing and came to an abrupt halt at an elaborately wrought, iron gate.

He resumed as if there had been no pause in our conversation at all. "I'll warn you now," he said, "it will seem as if forces are combining in an effort to destroy your three-year vision. I call them 'Exocet missiles'. They can come in the guise of people or events. But if you know they're coming, you can prepare for them. When you are warned and ready for these 'missiles', you're not so vulnerable, and it's easier to keep that vision intact."

Leaning against the gate and staring at the Jersey cattle grazing in the next field, I mused for a while before answering.

"What's worrying me is that the process you described sounds a bit implausible. I'm going to have to take your word for it that it works."

Andrew stopped studying the cows, and stared at me. "Why do that?" he said. "Why not experiment yourself? Involve all of your faculties: the sense of touch – through writing; sight – perhaps through sketching a little; smell, taste; whatever it takes to make it real.

"I'm asking you to exercise a tiny particle of faith." And here he held up his index finger and thumb as if holding a tiny invisible object.

"When you've started, you won't need to trust me. You'll discover the power of The Big Picture yourself."

I nodded, and then stood looking sightlessly towards the horizon for a long time.

"Andrew, just one thing . . ." I began. "Look, I can sense the possible power of this Big Picture process. But I have one problem."

Struggling with the words, I tried to explain that, grand as they sounded, the goals that I had agreed to didn't excite me, didn't inspire me. I pointed out that the goals I was working towards weren't *my* goals. In fact, it seemed to me that Andrew and Chris, the creditors and even Naomi had set them for me.

I hesitated, fumbling for words. "They're not based on the things that I'm passionate about right now – the things that I want to do." I thought for a moment about the flat and the BMW I had once felt epitomised success.

His response surprised me. "Great insight. I was worried that you'd discover that too far into the process and fizzle out. So tell me," he asked, "what would rouse your passion to make it *your* Big Picture?"

We moved away from the gate and began to walk in the shade of the bordering holly and American maple trees.

"Well, I was thinking," I began, pulling a handful of leaves from the nearest branch.

"Finding a way to reach one million people is pretty audacious and noble and all that, but, how shall I put it . . . I'd like to add some spice to it. You know, some personal interest?"

He looked at me with those piercing eyes.

I faltered. "Don't look at me like that, Andrew. I just want to make it more daring, that's all."

Despite my obvious discomfort, he still held my eyes. I felt embarrassed laughter bubbling in my chest, in spite of myself.

"I'm sure you'll moan at me," I continued, "but I've been thinking. This is the goal I'd rather go for: in the process of communicating with one million people, we should create one million pounds. Sterling, that is."

My mentor's mouth twitched, his eyes started to twinkle. Then his mirth exploded. I found myself joining in with him, relieved.

Slapping me on the shoulder, he proclaimed:

"Let's do it! I can see that we have some serious business planning to carry out. What I suggest we do is . . ."

His words faltered as his face froze. It was no more than a second before I realised what was wrong.

We strained to make sure our ears weren't deceiving us. There was no mistake. It was the bell. Not only was it nowhere near time for lunch, but . . .

. . . it had now rung far more than three times.

He turned immediately and started to run back across the grass just as Jessica came into view.

We reached her together as she ran into Andrew's outstretched arms. She was shaking and breathing quickly, her face streaked with tears.

"Dad, it's Naomi. She's been rushed to hospital!"

That June morning as we rushed into the quiet elegance of the drawing room at East View, I expected to join a scene that matched my own state of turmoil. Instead, I walked into an atmosphere of such calm that I felt as if I had intruded on sacred ground.

The whole family was on their knees, children and adults, and they all held hands in a circle; the padded cream chairs and glass-centred table pushed to the wall. When Andrew had finished on the phone, he fell down beside Louise, and the circle was complete.

Every head bowed. And there was silence.

I hesitated, frozen in the doorway from the hall. I could feel the sweat prickling my upper lip. My fingers were moist and clammy.

I had no place here. The scene was so foreign to me that it seemed ridiculous – laughable even. Yet I was bound to them by a bond of pain that threatened to burst my heart. I knew it – and so did they.

An arm was raised towards me. It was Daniel. His hand slowly opened and closed, willing me to grasp it.

Uncomfortable as it felt, I dropped to my knees and became part of the circle. Staring at the carpet, I tried not to disturb the prevailing reverence. Somehow I managed to rein in the words that screamed for release from deep inside me.

In the moments that followed, Andrew and Louise pleaded in prayer for the life of their child.

Eventually the room was still. Yet no one rose immediately. I looked up to see Andrew tenderly kiss Louise's fingers. Every face in the circle turned towards him waiting for him to speak.

"Naomi has been rushed to an intensive care unit near Cardiff. They suspect meningitis. There's no denying that they're worried. But I feel certain that she will recover. Mum and I will drive to see her today. For now my advice is that you go about your daily routine and keep a prayer in your heart."

Then turning to me he continued, "We have no need to fear. I sense that everything will be well. If we all have faith she'll be fine, I promise."

In the days that followed, I was torn by emotions that threatened to derail all of my efforts to succeed at work, or to keep my promises to Andrew and myself.

LESSONS LEARNED

- The thought of losing Naomi has thrown me into a state of helplessness and confusion;
- The Lamberts seem to have more courage and calm in an emergency than any group of people I've ever seen;
- There's an inner strength which seems to come from all of them, and I find myself leaning on that almost unwillingly;
- I'll think twice in future about laughing at the thought of people kneeling to pray;
- Someone is trying to teach me something; and it's not Andrew Lambert!
- When planning for the future:
    1. make the vision Big and Audacious;
    2. give the picture clarity and power by creating a three year vision;
    3. make the description of the vision so vivid you can almost touch it, smell it, see it;
    4. describe your vision in the present tense.

PROGRESS TRACKER

- I have been away from Naomi less than one month, and the possibility is that I might never see her again!
- I started paying my IVA on 1st June, £1,000 per month;
- I'm in the fourth month of my new job.

David J Scarlett

Chapter 5
Law Three : Take the Leap of Faith

Saturday, 7th July

Naomi was indeed diagnosed with meningitis. By itself that was frightening and unusual in the summer. What terrified me was the news that her case was part of a cluster. One of her university friends had died within hours of Naomi reaching hospital.

Even before this trauma, waking up every day had been a painful experience accompanied by a dull ache deep in the pit of my stomach. It was as if I was deep in mourning.

But the thought that I could lose her forever: that seemed unbearable. Fortunately for me Andrew had patiently explained Naomi's condition each time I called. I was intrigued when he described how he, Daniel and Nathan had laid their hands upon her as she lay sleeping, giving her a blessing of healing. I had heard about such things but had always dismissed them, treating them with caution and suspicion. Now, what had previously sounded like a meaningless ritual became a matter of hope.

By the end of the second week she was out of danger and was moved to a private hospital to convalesce.

What also made life more bearable was the increased effort made by Naomi's friends to remain regularly in contact with me. They made a point of inviting me to every dance, volleyball game, concert and just-jump-in-the-car-and-go trip that arose.

I was grateful.

Another small victory was buying a roadworthy Fiat. So pulling into East View under my own steam on that first Saturday in July, I welcomed a feeling of independence.

I was a little late, however, and swore I could smell breakfast as I slowly wound my way down the drive, watching for playing children. I'd missed the bell.

"Hey, Jonathan!" Nathan called out from an open window. And before I knew it, Daniel was at the door of my car, opening it before I had even had a chance to turn off the ignition, dragging me through to the kitchen.

As I entered the long, green dining room, Nathan tapped the chair reserved for me, and the chaos settled as we expressed gratitude for the delicious spread with heads bowed.

"Jonathan, looks like you're settling in as one of the family!" Nathan announced.

I must have blushed because the men laughed teasingly. But Corrin came to my rescue.

"That's unfair, Nathan. Jon is cooking up some business deals with the Professor. Right Dad?"

I must have looked puzzled and started to mouth 'The Profess . . .' when Daniel broke in.

"Yeah, Andrew has always loved teaching and harbours dreams of lecturing at university. He hasn't done that yet because of the time taken to rebuild the house. But we started calling him 'The Professor', and it seemed to stick."

Andrew didn't look up from his plate immediately but smiled slightly as he reached for some toast.

Then Louise took me by surprise. "Tell us about the good news in your life, Jonathan."

"Well, Louise, to be honest, I'm a little bemused by all that's happening to me; I've had two pieces of good news in the last week." I paused, partly for effect and to relish the chance of catching all eyes fixed on me, but also because I was rather proud of myself. "Firstly, I was promoted to UK sales manager for the Communications Recruitment Team."

This brought some cheers and spoon-banging on the table, which stopped abruptly at a quick glance from Louise.

"Secondly, I won a rather large recruitment contract to supply thirty people to the Middle East for at least twelve months."

Here, a low whistle from Andrew confirmed his grasp of the value of that to me and of the amounts involved.

Corrin took up my torch again, "I say a toast to Jon for some big wins. Come on everyone!" She glanced round the large mahogany table, catching everyone's eye in turn.

Glasses were raised and used to wash down the stacks of pancakes we had consumed. A chorus of satisfied sighs preceded the clearing of dishes and the usual exchange of 'See ya laters' as everybody went their way.

As if joined by an invisible thread, I sauntered with Andrew through the vast, modern kitchen, picking at the remaining rashers of bacon as we went.

Making our way to the front porch, he pointed to the thick line of trees running along the edge of the estate. Nathan joined us as we strode under the budding pink and cream horse chestnuts and headed towards the entrance to the woods that had sheltered me back in April.

"We're going to take a leap in the dark today," Andrew announced. "I've asked Nathan to join us to share some experiences as we walk through the spinney. I hope you don't mind?"

I realised then that this millionaire mentoring thing was involving more than just Andrew. It seemed that the whole family was joining in. But I wasn't complaining.

Moving out of the rising July heat, we entered the welcome shade of the trees. Noiselessly, we trod the ancient carpet of leaf mould.

"So tell me, Jon," began Nathan, "how are you getting on with all these things the Prof is teaching you?"

"Hmmm. I'm glad you asked," I responded, stopping to scratch my leg as I brushed past some nettles – maybe wearing shorts had not been such a clever idea. "Actually, I'm starting to feel a little bewildered. I'm beginning to produce some surprising results at work. Frankly, I find them alarming considering the struggle I used to have pulling myself out of bed in the morning."

I noticed the corners of Andrew's mouth drawing down, but I was now fully in my stride. "But, even with the build-up of commission and living at home with my parents, I'm still only meeting the minimum obligation of the IVA: £1,000 per month.

"The arrangement started on 1st June, so I've managed to pay back a paltry £2,000."

Here I turned fully to Andrew. "Your challenge says 'Pay back my creditors in twelve months'. That's £98,000 in the next ten months. Prof, can I call you 'Prof'? I just don't know how I'm going to manage."

"Jonathan, Jonathan," Andrew cut in, "you seem to be forgetting how far you've come in the last three months."

"How do you mean?" I queried, ducking just in time to avoid a broken holly branch.

"Why don't you tell us about the changes in your life since mid-April, whatever their magnitude?" We walked on, the dappled sunlight dancing across our bodies.

"Well, there are the changes in my business life. As you can imagine, becoming a mere employee is a pretty humbling experience after having owned my own company. That's been the biggest strain on my pride.

"Then there's my promotion, which took me by surprise. After all, I've only been in this job for four months.

"And hard on the heels of that came the big coup last week winning that new contract."

Nathan nodded. "They sound pretty significant changes to me."

"Maybe," I continued. "But, without question, the most painful change of all is not seeing Naomi. Just being able to hear her voice would help ease the pain a little. I can't believe that I'm putting myself through this."

Suddenly, I halted realising how self-absorbed I sounded when the family had been carrying a grief much greater than mine.

"I'm so sorry," I blurted out. "That sounds appalling. I guess I'm still wrapped up with . . ."

"Over here," interrupted Nathan. "Let's sit in this clearing. It looks dry enough."

We settled down on a small patch of grass, which looked fresh and completely untrodden.

"Is there anything else you're feeling?" prompted Andrew

"Yes there is. I've been inspired by reading those books on money and prosperity. They've turned my ideas about money upside down. I feel almost shell-shocked by the new concepts I've learned. And they ring so true!"

"They are persuasive, aren't they?" enthused Nathan, leaning back against a springy bough so that his weight pushed it right down to the ground.

"Yes," I continued. "I can't believe how far away I was from the Millionaire Mindset described in some of the books in spite of having run my own business. As for becoming a Soul Millionaire," I paused, not quite sure if I wanted to share my true thoughts on this matter.

"Anything else?" Andrew asked hugging his legs.

"There is one thing," I replied. "At first I was shaken by that experience with prayer when we heard about Naomi. Now, I find myself sitting on the edge of my bed every night thinking about what's happening and asking for help from, well, I'm not sure where from. But you know what I mean."

"Yes," said Nathan, slowly. "I know exactly what you mean."

"Oh, and there's my journal. That's been a battle not having recorded private thoughts like that before."

"So are you managing to write in it daily?" asked Nathan.

"Yes, I am," I replied, picking up a mouldy acorn which had been peeking out from a pile of leaves and tossing it into a blackberry bush.

"I had the same problem with creating my Big Picture. It took me days and days to even start writing. It's hard work, I can tell you. I now appreciate how fiction writers feel when they sit staring at a blank page."

"You mean your Big Picture is fiction?" queried Andrew, smiling.

"You know what I mean," I reacted. "It's all so new."

"But, after Naomi, do you know the biggest struggle of all? It's wondering how on earth I'm supposed to talk to one million people and persuade them to act on my say so."

"Aaaah! Now there's a question," mused Andrew staring up through the branches as I sensed his mind drifting off towards the possibilities. "Fear not, adventurer. The ideas will come. The ideas will definitely come."

There was a comfortable pause.

Andrew continued turning towards Nathan. "Jon, I've invited Nathan here because we are moving to the next step in your Great Challenge.

"It's time for **Law Number Three**. The title of this law is '**Take the Leap of Faith**'.

"Aside from missing Naomi, I believe this will be your next biggest challenge."

A brief glance passed between them.

"I'm going to challenge you to take a leap of faith and begin practising something we call 'tithing'," he said.

"What on earth is that?" I queried suspiciously.

Turning to Nathan he said, "Why don't you help out here?"

"I'd be happy to," smiled Nathan.

"Jonathan, what I'm about to share with you changed my life. It's one of the most powerful and practical principles you'll ever learn about money. Yet it hardly makes sense unless you're willing to learn and experiment."

"I think I'm ready," I replied.

What followed was an account of disaster-recovery that made my problems seem feeble in comparison.

I heard a tale of regular drunken stupor; of hopeless debt from student loans and constant overspending; about his initial friendship with Corrin at university. The tale wound from one town and job to another and ended in squalor in a bed-sit somewhere in Essex.

I heard how Corrin had sought him out with the help of friends, believing, as women do so well, in the goodness she had glimpsed in their student days.

Finally, I heard how he had experienced what he called 'an awakening' when he tried and tested a few simple physical and spiritual principles. The first step had been to start praying. Next, he had managed to stop drinking. After praying for help for some two months, he had awoken one morning with no desire whatsoever to drink again!

But, it seemed, the habit that had made the most impact on him and his finances was this thing he called 'tithing'. He told of the months after he had started to pay a tithe when everything he tried turned to success: job applications, debt clearance, even his relationship with Corrin.

Eventually, he had joined the same church as Corrin and had travelled overseas to fulfil a self-financed church mission for two years.

When he returned, he was a completely changed man and ready to ask Corrin to marry him. It was quite a saga.

As the shafts of sunlight reached us through the gap in branches, Nathan explained exactly what this thing called 'tithing' was.

The principle, he said, was as old as time and was essentially spiritual. It meant to give a tenth of your increase in goods to God. In practical terms that meant to the Church. And an 'increase in goods' applied to anything from livestock to cash.

I could feel a sense of panic rising.

"Whoa! Hang on a minute Nathan! You two have pushed me to my limits already and you know my views on religion. I'm certainly not a member of your church or any church for that matter. And I've no intention of giving one-tenth of my income to your church whilst I still owe £100,000."

"You're right, Jonathan," said Andrew. "Besides, not being a member of our church you couldn't pay tithing to it anyway."

"Right. That's agreed then," I snorted.

"But what you can do is let the power of tithing work in your life to create the miracle you need," Nathan added.

"I'm sorry, Nathan. Now you're talking in riddles."

"Let me quote some words which I've committed to memory," he continued.

Then he clasped his hands together, closed his eyes and spoke slowly, as if savouring every word.

" *'Will a man rob God? Yet ye have robbed me.*
But ye say, wherein have we robbed thee?
In tithes and offerings . . .
. . . Bring ye all the tithes into the storehouse, that there may be meat in mine house, and prove me now herewith, saith the Lord of hosts, if I will not open you the windows of heaven, and pour you out a blessing, that there shall not be room enough to receive it.'"

He stopped. But, keeping his eyes closed, he repeated one line, this time with more emphasis.

" '*. . . and prove me now herewith . . . if I will not open you the windows of heaven, and pour you out a blessing, that there shall not be room enough to receive it.'"*

He opened his eyes.

"Can you grasp what is being said here?"

Then, he raised his right hand and used his fingers to count off what he was saying.

"Firstly, you're being thrown a challenge to put God, the Universe, whatever you like to call it, to the test; to make Him *prove* what He is saying.

"Secondly, if you *test* Him with honest intent, He'll open up the windows of heaven so that blessings will pour out upon you."

By now his voice was falling to a whisper and his eyes were fixed on me. I shifted uncomfortably.

"Finally, what you'll receive will be so overwhelming that you'll hardly be able to contain or deal with it."

He watched me as I unfolded my legs and stood up rubbing my calves to soothe my pins and needles. I walked away for a few feet, putting out my hands to lean against a thick oak. I studied the rough bark, unable to meet Nathan's eyes.

Then he asked, "Jon, what have I possibly got to gain by recommending that you try out this promise called tithing?"

"Well, let's see," I mused. "You could make your church awfully rich by persuading people to give this tithing thing to them."

He smiled. "You heard what The Prof said. You're not a member of our church."

"Well no. But . . ."

"You could start by depositing your tithe into a savings account until you're sure which church or charity you wish to give it to. It's the spiritual intent that counts."

"Well, how about this intent," I responded. "Once I have cleared my debt and increased my earnings, surely I can give far more to a church or charity than when I'm flat broke."

"You're missing the point, Jon," he said.

"The point is, God is asking you to trust Him, test Him out. Only when you've had the strength and courage to do that, will you receive an outpouring.

"Are you trying to tell me that you can easily get through the next year without that type of help?"

I heard my voice rise. "Come on, Nathan. You're talking ten percent of my income! That simply doesn't compute!"

"No Jon, it doesn't," interjected Andrew, "and it never will do if you apply normal accounting logic.

"But we're talking here about powers of the Universe that we hardly comprehend. We're talking about benefits of all kinds – financial, emotional, physical, spiritual – that are yours for the taking if you'll just have the courage to experiment."

I sighed and stood up, shuffling away from them towards the shadows of the trees.

Turning slowly I looked back at them sitting there expectantly. It seemed that none of us was breathing.

Shaking my head, I lowered my gaze and kicked at the few tufts of grass.

Then looking up, I firmed my jaw.

"Ten percent you said? Gross income?"

Nathan broke into a grin as he stood up and held his hand out hauling Andrew to his feet.

Walking between us with his hands on our shoulders, Andrew steered us along the path to the other end of the spinney. As we emerged, we looked around us at the darkening sky. Thunder rolled in the distance.

"So," I asked, as we quickened our pace. "Whatever happens to this tithing your church collects?"

Andrew parried this question to Nathan nodding in his direction.

"Well, if you were to visit church headquarters, you would see a remarkable enterprise devoted to preparing goods for both local welfare needs and for shipping across the globe.

"There are farms, canning factories and supermarkets. Thousands of wheelchairs, blankets, tents, medical kits, toys, school kits and other supplies are shipped annually.

"How am I doing so far?"

"Sounds pretty impressive," murmured Andrew as large, warm raindrops began to fall upon us.

Nathan continued. "There are teachers and business leaders donating months of their time to serve communities in other countries. Where there is more urgent need, we have the resources to send emergency teams, construction teams, nurses, doctors and surgeons. There are universities, radio and satellite facilities to run . . ."

By now we were drenched but determined not to be bowed or hurried.

"That, Jon, is the power of tithing.

"No complex tax system. One-tenth. Even the smallest child can remember that."

Just then the darkening clouds lit up as lightning forked in front of us and thunder exploded almost immediately overhead.

We looked at each other, our eyes wide.

Andrew was the first to move. "Last one back gets to inspect the cesspit after lunch."

As Nathan bolted after him, I lifted my leaden feet, making a determined note to do something serious about my lack of fitness.

LESSONS LEARNED

- There are some universal laws which don't appeal to Western logic;
- However, without having received any proof, I have a sense that the Law of Tithing is one of those laws that can simply work (I think!);
- The influence of the goodness of a woman can smooth away the coarseness and shortsightedness of a man;
- It seems that miracles are possible, even in this cynical and so-called scientific age.

PROGRESS TRACKER

- 1st July was the second month of the IVA, and I've only paid £2,000;
- This is my fifth month in my job;
- Although my income is already improving, my finances still remain very tight;
- It's nearly two months since I said 'goodbye' to Naomi. Waking every morning remains painful knowing that I might still never see her again although her life is now out of danger.

Chapter 6

Law Four : Create Freedom Not Wealth

Saturday, 4th August

Still sleepy and regretting the lack of breakfast, I phoned Andrew from the tiny, empty station forecourt. Six o'clock on a Saturday morning was an inhuman hour to be meeting, but with no traffic around he would be with me in less than ten minutes.

As I strolled lazily from my trusty Fiat, I marvelled at the August sky, cloudless apart from the streaks of gold and purple on the horizon. This was turning out to be a glorious summer.

There was every reason to feel light of heart except for the sickness gnawing from deep within me. Here I was, newly thirty-years-old, with very few pleasures in life that I hadn't already tasted, feeling like a lovesick teenager.

The very thought that just a few miles away Naomi was home for the summer holidays and sleeping at East View tore me apart.

The blast of a car horn lifted me physically into the air as I instinctively leapt back onto the kerb.

"Good morning, young man. You awake yet?" Andrew called through the open window.

"Scaring a bloke like that at this indecent hour," I muttered approaching his car. "Awake and flipping starving!" I called back.

"Come along then, jump in your wagon and follow me. A morning of indulgence awaits us."

It wasn't long before we were cooling off at the local sports centre, relishing the freshness and pleasure of almost total possession of the pool.

As I floated and rolled, life felt beautifully uncomplicated. I was a boy again.

We chatted and joked as we showered and dressed. Listening to myself I realised I hadn't laughed with such abandon since Naomi's illness.

We didn't need to drive far to order a generous breakfast amongst the lavender, honeysuckle and willow trees that divided the manicured lawns of The Peacock's Parade – an immaculately preserved centuries-old inn.

The air was languid but not heavy. The smell of summer earth was intoxicating. The sky was filled with the incessant song of meadow birds and the droning of bees heavy with their burden. I remembered a time when I would not have noticed.

While we waited for our order, conversation was lazy and relaxed.

"Andrew, I'm curious. I never did ask you how you created your wealth."

"Hah! I wondered when you would get round to that."

I should have known that his notepad would be on the table, and he scribbled as he spoke. "First let me prepare you by pointing out the obvious. It wasn't always like this. Not even remotely so. During the first few years of our marriage, life was difficult and money was very tight.

"We also wanted a large family. Families and children; to us, they are the very core and purpose of life. Not a popular view today, I imagine."

"So, what happened to change your financial position?" I asked.

He answered slowly and carefully. As he spoke, it became clear that there had been no single event or achievement. Rather, he pointed to a number of experiences, lessons and habits that he had combined over the years. As he recounted them, I realised that I was in the process of being taught those same lessons.

He went on to explain that the Ten Laws, which I was now learning, had been gleaned from events and thoughts recorded meticulously in his journals.

Then he hinted at a law which had been behind his enormous success in building a thriving financial planning practice.

"Oh! I didn't know you were a financial planner!" I said, surprised.

"Yes," he said. "When I first started out I hated it. I was no more than a life assurance salesman. Friends started avoiding us; it was difficult and embarrassing. But very soon I discovered that I was pretty good at what I was doing. I studied hard and realised I had an aptitude for more complex aspects of financial planning."

As usual, I was intrigued at Andrew's ability to visually capture the essence of what he was saying, thanks to the subheadings, lines and circles on his pad.

"Soon my skills attracted some influential and wealthy clients as well as lucrative corporate business."

Just then breakfast arrived, and the disarmingly vivacious waitress bustled around ensuring that we had all that we had ordered. Tucking into his ham and tomatoes Andrew continued.

"It wasn't long, about four years I guess, before I broke out on my own and formed an independent practice.

"Then one day I attended a seminar by a chap called Clive Ferrer. The seminar was entitled 'Wealth Strategies: A Better Way'. I remembered thinking that it was expensive – about £800 for two days. But I'm forever grateful that I went. His genius inspired me and helped me to reshape the whole of my business. More than that it helped Louise and me to reshape our family's financial future."

This sounded important, and I started writing keenly between forkfuls of sausage and scrambled eggs.

"What I heard was a clear explanation describing the difference between wealth and true financial freedom," he continued.

He paused long enough to glance at my puzzled face before smiling and continuing the attack on his rapidly emptying plate.

He described how the speaker had challenged the seminar delegates with the statement that, '**achieving financial and time freedom was so much more powerful than gaining wealth**'.

Ferrer had asked his audience to picture all of the high-earning entrepreneurs and corporate executives, including themselves, who enjoyed any freedom at all. Generally, they were trapped by their own lifestyle.

He had then pointed out that if those people stopped working themselves stupid, their financial support would have collapsed like a pack of cards. Meanwhile their relationships – those that should be deep, loving and meaningful – hung by a thread because their business stole all the time and energy available.

To cap it all, he concluded that many of them died unnecessarily early, their health being sacrificed on the altar of a 60 to 70 hour week.

I brushed crumbs of toast from the table into the crisp white napkin on my lap. "I can't argue with the evidence Prof. But, I'm still wondering about this Financial Freedom. What exactly does it mean?"

"Stay with me. All will become clear."

He signalled to the waitress and ordered some more sparkling water plus a coffee for me.

"The conclusion I had come to long before that seminar," he continued, "was that those who pursue the goal of wealth are often doomed to lose that part of their lives which is most precious: their close relationships. Financial Freedom on the other hand is designed to support living in such a way that we can choose . . ."

And scribbling on his pad, he listed the benefits that could become ours. We could choose:
- What sort of fulfilling work we do
- Where we do it
- When we do it
- Whom we spend our time with, and
- How we spend it together.

For a while we debated these aspects of freedom, our opinions bouncing back and forth.

Eventually he summarised. "To me, such freedom means being able to come and go as I choose living according to my cherished principles and values".

He leaned forward a little, his face becoming more animated.

"Now, what followed next in this seminar changed the whole purpose of my financial planning activities. I found myself having to erase many of the opinions that I had formed over long years." He paused to take a sip of water.

"I was shaken, I can tell you. Ferrer made an incredible statement." He stopped for a moment. "You know, Jon, I have remembered it word for word all these years. It made such an impact on me, and yet I never even wrote it down. Didn't need to."

He paused again. I could hardly bear the agony of waiting and leaned forward in my chair, my coffee now stone cold in the cup. I held my breath and had my pen poised.

"Jon, this is what he said that day: '***Don't yearn to amass a large pot of money. Instead, learn to create sufficient streams of income.***'"

I sat back feeling deflated. Was that it?

My ignorance didn't weaken his passion. "As you can imagine, I was stunned!" he went on. "What he was saying to the average income earner and to professionals like me was this:

"Firstly, you don't need to win the lottery; and secondly, you're unlikely to become free if all you're doing is saving in your personal pension, your deposit account, your unit trust or mutual fund.

"The most painful thing about that comment was that I specialised in pensions at the time so I wasn't immediately overjoyed at his comments."

"Does that mean that I shouldn't invest in savings and pension schemes?" I interrupted.

"Not at all. But Ferrer was asking financial planners and the public to think more clearly, be more realistic. He was also giving them the key to a life of tremendous hope.

"Look, let's just mop up this breakfast, and I'll sketch some facts for you on my pad."

By now I was eager to understand more clearly, so it didn't take long to polish off the last of my toast, gulp down some fresh orange juice, and wait, pencil in hand, with all other thoughts suspended.

"Incidentally," he asked, changing tack completely in that annoying way of his, "how are you feeling after our last discussion?"

Irritated but rising to the opportunity to prove my progress, I recounted how I had surprised myself by walking into a building society on Baker Street and opening a savings account. It had been the week after learning about tithing.

I could see he was duly impressed.

I then went on to explain how two weeks later I had landed another international recruitment contract in France, which would push my earnings to the monthly equivalent of £70,000 per annum.

Finally, I admitted that his fitness had goaded me to start jogging each morning although my lungs and feeble legs couldn't quite carry me for a complete mile.

He laid his pen down to offer a patter of applause, to which I bowed my head in response.

Suddenly, I felt the strength of the sun on the back of my neck and was surprised how hot I had become. Getting up, I moved around the table to join him in the shade of a spreading chestnut tree some yards away. I noted the green pods forming meaning that autumn – and games of conkers – were a real promise now.

The heavy perfume of August wrapped itself around us.

Sketching once more, he continued. "Look, let's take the creation of your pension fund. How big do you think that fund should be for you to enjoy a dignified life at retirement?"

I shrugged.

He wasn't waiting for my answer. "I'll tell you. Right now, to provide an income of just £1,000 per month, a sixty-year-old would need a pension fund of a little over £200,000.

"Not an outrageous figure, you say. But hold on! That's if you were retiring today. Build an inflation factor into that and . . ."

Within a few minutes I could see that someone of my age would need to save about £850,000 to enjoy an income equivalent to £1,000 per month. I was shocked. If it hadn't been Andrew explaining the logic, I would have struggled to believe the figures in front of me.

"Blimey!" I said. "Most of us wouldn't contemplate paying back a mortgage of even half that size."

"Exactly. And that's to provide an income in today's terms of £1,000 per month. Don't you think some people might want a lifestyle requiring somewhat more than that? Say, twice as much, perhaps?"

I looked at him, scratching my head. "So, how on earth will people manage?"

"The truth is," he responded, "far too many won't!"

We both paused to take in the enormity of that fact.

"The answer," he continued slightly melodramatically, "is in the memorable phrase that I learned that day: '***Instead, learn to create sufficient streams of income.***'

"Those eight words completely changed the way that I saw the world of money. That degree of change is known in science and business as a 'Paradigm Shift'. It shifted me, I can tell you!"

"A para-what?" I asked, not sure if I had heard correctly whilst trying to shoo away a persistent wasp.

His voice dropped almost in conspiracy. "The intelligent way to create Financial Freedom is to stop trying to build a fund of £800,000 or £1 million or more. Instead, start seeking ways to create streams of income worth £1,000 per month."

Then he repeated himself, this time more slowly.

"The intelligent way to create Financial Freedom.... is to start seeking ways to create streams of income. That, Jonathan," he said, beginning to stab his pen into his pad emphatically, "is the golden secret that can separate you financially from the rest of struggling society today."

He stopped, beaming, and looked towards me, his face filled with satisfaction. He then looked at his page of figures, arrows and circles, carefully tore it out of his notebook and handed it to me.

By now our breakfast was over. I could see him getting ready to rise, and yet the lesson seemed only half complete.

"Come on then, Prof. You've given me a clue about what not to do. You've even suggested how we can be financially free. But, how exactly did you make it work for you? And how can I do it?"

"Ah, yes. We must come to that, mustn't we? But first we need to prepare you carefully to handle that process. Which we shall start doing . . ."

I groaned before he finished his sentence.

". . . early in September."

LESSONS LEARNED

- Having wealth is not the same as being financially free;
- Rather than try to create large lumps of cash, create streams of income to provide Financial Freedom.

PROGRESS TRACKER

- 1st August was the third month of the IVA. I have paid £3,000 so far;
- This is my sixth month in my job;
- It's nearly three months since I said 'goodbye' to Naomi;
- I'm enjoying these monthly meetings with Andrew. In each one I feel more relaxed than before. Laughter is returning to my life;
- I can barely jog one mile. But I'm blowed if I'll let Andrew be fitter than me!

David J Scarlett

Chapter 7

Law Five : Become the Financial Master

"*H*old it hard against your shoulder. Yes, that's it. Now, I'll call for you. Pull!" he bellowed.

Mesmerised by the flying disc, I tried to remember and coordinate all that my instructor had patiently taught me as I swung the barrel and pulled the trigger.

"Ahaaa! Great shot!" he called. "Now keep the barrel up. There's another one to come. Okay. Pull!"

I was getting the hang of this as another black disc disintegrated to my childish satisfaction.

"Well done!" he shouted as I pulled out my earplugs. "I think that's enough for today, don't you?"

"Yeah," I said. "My shoulder feels like it's been kicked by a mule."

Andrew strode over as the instructor took the gun from me. "You think it hurts today?" he said. "Wait until you see the colour of it tomorrow."

As we strolled back past the clubhouse and across the car park, I looked at the crisp September sky. I was grateful for a morning when I could forget all the pressures upon me. I was also grateful that Andrew had agreed to see me, bearing in mind that Naomi was still at home and not due back at uni for another two weeks.

To meet Andrew's friends at the exclusive shooting club, he had collected me from the same station as last month. Together we had travelled some way from East View through tiny West Sussex villages along winding lanes burrowing into woods and floating past small farms that defied time.

Now we headed back with the scenery whispering at the centuries of history that lay in the fields. Eventually we pulled up outside an impressive 19th century coaching inn. The historic façade had been well maintained with swirls of late flowering honeysuckle adding to its charm.

As I followed Andrew into the elegant, calming lobby, I made a mental note that our days together had been measured by the constant rhythm of enjoyable mealtimes.

The restaurant was French and the service prompt and courteous, enticing us to order Brie with avocado to start followed by a delicious sounding red snapper: mine in garlic sauce, his with basil and tomato.

We gulped our much-needed, ice-cool drinks following our morning's exertions. Andrew produced his notepad.

As he reached inside his shooting jacket and brought out his pen, I anticipated the start of another lesson. Before he could begin, I stepped in.

"Andrew, I couldn't stop thinking about what we discussed last time and would love to discuss ways to create those income streams you mentioned."

Our avocado and Brie arrived, and we tucked in gratefully. My eyes were raised to his in anticipation of the answer I had been awaiting for a month. For a while he said nothing, so I took the initiative.

"I understand that if I can start automated income flowing from different sources, then I'll eventually be free to choose what I do with my time, right?" I began.

Andrew nodded. "Ah! There's the problem," he replied. "You yearn for the outcome, but you're attempting to build a financial structure with no foundation."

"I'm sorry, Prof. You've lost me. What foundation are we talking about now?"

"Jonathan," he continued. "Before we can talk about creating streams of income, you first need to go back to a rule within the First

Law of a Soul Millionaire. You need to develop a foundation of respect and mastery."

"I don't understand," I replied. "Respect? Who for? Mastery of what?"

"Respect for money," he said, "respect and mastery of money."

"Achieving both of these is the purpose of the **Fifth Law: Become The Financial Master**."

I had now opened my own notepad and was busy scrawling the Fifth Law in a bold heading. To be honest, I hadn't the faintest idea what he was talking about.

"To move from Apprentice to Master requires not just knowledge; it requires skills, practice, and gradual improvement over time. In this case it also requires a healthy respect for the power of money."

"Apprentice . . . Master?" I murmured. The penny was starting to drop. "So, you're saying I should become a Master Craftsman with this thing called money?"

In response he waved his fork at me. "If you want to make it your servant and fashion a life of freedom and generosity, then, yes."

Andrew was now in full flow, sketching diagrams of income and expenditure linked to the creation of assets.

"Jonathan, right now you're a skilled apprentice – you're pretty good at creating income, earned income."

"Er, yes. Is there something wrong with that?" I asked.

"As a starting point, no," he said, "but if all you do is increase your income, you'll discover that there's definitely something wrong with that. There are four steps to becoming a Financial Master, ready?"

Then he introduced me to **Step Number One in becoming a Financial Master: Learning To Value Money**.

He explained how many people had come to him throughout the years still financially stressed no matter how much their income increased. He had shown them that the core of their problems was not being short of money but their unwillingness to value, respect and manage it.

Next, he introduced a concept that was new to me: valuing money not as something tangible but as an idea that has the capacity to multiply and propagate itself.

He explained that I needed to appreciate the main routes to creating money other than working for earned income as an employee. In his view these routes were:

- Investments
- Property
- Marketing: which included running your own business and using the Internet.

I was pleased to learn that by investigating Internet marketing, as I had done the previous week, I had stumbled across one of the right routes.

We were interrupted by the sweeping gestures of our waiter delighting us with our main course.

Andrew climbed to his crescendo. "When you value it, respect it and learn how to wield it as a tool, money will unleash its power as a servant under your control.

"But . . ." and his face hardened a little. "If you treat it casually and carelessly, it will slip from your grasp, enslave you and finally crush you."

I sat quietly, stunned by the fierceness of his comments. Memories of gambling and drinking hovered at the edge of my mind.

His voice brought me back to our lunch. "There's a specific aspect of valuing money," he said, his voice now more even, "that you need to understand."

He raised an eyebrow as a signal to the waiter who moved quickly and smoothly to refill our glasses.

"Which is?" I asked.

"For every pound you spend," he continued, "ask yourself this: how long did it take me to earn that money? When you calculate how many hours you've worked to receive that income and pay tax on it, you'll get a nasty shock!"

"Oh, I think I see what you're saying," I responded hesitantly, working through the figures in my mind. "I need to put a monetary value on my time?"

"That's it," he said. "But it's more than that. It's not simply time you're giving away, it's chunks of your life, Jonathan."

This was all impassioned and stirring stuff. But I was still a little confused.

Drawing a large question mark in the centre of a fresh page, I shrugged.

"Look, I hear what you're saying, Andrew, but you spoke about 'respecting it'. I'm not sure about how to show respect to lumps of cash."

Quickly, he drew the outline of what looked like a football pitch.

"You show it by the careful attention you pay to it.

"Look, let's examine the world of sports to understand about paying attention.

"Have you ever watched a cliff-hanger of a football match where the scores are even and just five minutes to go to the whistle?

"You know what I mean. Your hands are trembling, you feel sick in your stomach and you wonder if your team's facing disaster or victory." His voice rose with the drama that he was painting. "Tell me, why is the game so tense at this point?"

"I guess because the scores are even," I responded weakly.

"But how do you know that?" he urged.

I laughed in amazement at the question. "For goodness sake! The crowd have eyes in their head! And there's a scoreboard!"

"Exactly!" And he slammed his hand down, shaking the cutlery around us. "The scoreboard tells the story. The game's progress is being carefully monitored. Not just by the crowd, but by the coaches, trainers, managers, every darned journalist and TV reporter. Everybody is tracking every move."

"Well? So what?" I had stopped eating as I tried to grasp his point.

By now he was almost pleading at my lack of understanding.

"Don't you see, Jonathan?" he questioned, his voice rising by an octave. "Everybody knows precisely what needs to be done to win the game. The energy of the players and crowd is more focused because of that knowledge."

I thought that was it, but like an encore he repeated: "Tracking. That's what does it. Tracking. So that everybody knows exactly where they are. Tracking can put you on the winning team!

"And that's **Step Number Two in becoming a Financial Master: Tracking Every Item.**"

Then he challenged me.

"Tell me, how many people track the score with their personal finances? How many people do you know track exactly where they spend every single penny, every day?

"So, there they all are, treating money with an abandon, a casual attitude, a lack of respect that would destroy any small business or large corporation.

"They simply don't value money enough to care about the state of their game. And they couldn't tell you whether they're winning or losing. Why? Because they haven't a clue."

By now I had grasped the first two steps.

"So the shift of mind," I said, "is to '**Value It**'. Then the first practical step of mastery is to '**Track It**'."

"Precisely," he beamed looking every inch like Henry Higgins in "My Fair Lady" when Eliza Doolittle 'got it'.

I was relieved. "But what is the best way of tracking it?" I asked.

"Two simple exercises will give you all that you need."

From his Mary Poppins-like pocket he pulled a small notebook and waved it.

"First, carry a pocket notebook with you and record every single penny you spend. Do this for a month – thirty days, that's all – and you'll begin to see a pattern unfold."

Handing me the tiny notebook, he carried on. "When I asked financial planning clients to do this they discovered two truths:

• Their spending pattern shocked them!

• Simply by monitoring, or 'tracking,' their behaviour, that behaviour started to change."

Then he opened the notebook to reveal a folded sheet, which he carefully spread out on the table.

"The second tool is an expenditure spreadsheet on your PC. With that created you can log and categorise every item that appears on your bank statements across a full twelve months."

He pointed at the rows and columns. "Look how certain patterns of spending behaviour show up clearly."

Then he made a comment that I shall never forget. "The old leadership maxim holds true: *'when behaviour is monitored and reported, behaviour changes'*."

"Hmmm. Sounds logical to me. But I must tell you that the practice of 'tracking' sounds more than a little boring, Prof."

"Tedious? Perhaps. Basic to learning personal control? Definitely!" he retorted.

He supported his comment by observing how many potentially successful people live in a financial shambles. That was a painful reminder of my own experience of the last twelve months. I nodded in agreement as it dawned on me that no matter how many streams of income I created, my life would still be a mess if I didn't control my expenditure.

"I can't argue with that," I said. "So, you're saying that once I've learned to 'Track It', I can then create *streams* of 'It'?"

"Sorry, not quite," he replied, wagging his finger. "We've worked together long enough. You should know me by now."

Just then the mango torte and ice cream arrived with a flourish. So we gave ourselves over to the serious business of devouring every scrap.

He was right. I should have known better. We had spent a great deal of time together: time that he could otherwise have devoted to his family and his business interests. I began to understand why his children intuitively looked to him for guidance.

"Jonathan. Are you still with me?" his voice broke through my thoughts.

"Yes, yes. Please, go on," I murmured.

"I know you're eager to start creating those enticing streams of income. But first you need to rein in your habits."

I sighed and folded my arms as he continued.

"With a good tracking system, you'll find it much easier to **'Trim Back'**."

He turned to a fresh page in his pad and wrote the heading **'Trim Back'**.

"By that I mean targeting those areas of your life where money dribbles through your fingers merely to satisfy a whim, an urgency or an emotional need."

"Such as?" I asked.

"Well, we all know how some people splurge out on buying things when they are either in a particularly good or horribly miserable mood."

"Oh, right. You're talking about being driven by wants versus needs?"

"Exactly. But once '**Tracking It**' becomes a habit, you'll begin to begrudge throwing away your resources on 'stuff' or emotional knee-jerk behaviour.

"You'll also begin to find areas of expense where cutting back will not affect your ability to live a dignified lifestyle. Become a Master of Trimming and you'll stop giving away tomorrow's prosperity for mere 'stuff' today.

"When you've done that, you'll see through the general belief that 'I'll be richer and freer when I increase my income.'

"The truth is: It's not what you EARN that makes you free and prosperous, it's what you KEEP.

"So, that's **Step Number Three in becoming a Financial Master: Trimming Back.**"

His message certainly wasn't lost on me, and a silence sat between us.

I broke the spell with a sigh, absent-mindedly rubbed my sore shoulder and tried to recapture what he had taught so well.

"Let me see if I've got this right," I said, writing as I spoke.

"Step One, I have to Value It. Give money the respect that it's due.

"Step Two, I have to Track It. Be clear where my hard-earned income is disappearing.

"Finally, Step Three, I need to Trim Back. Cut back on gratification today so that I can enjoy freedom tomorrow."

He drummed the table in applause.

"That's it then! Tummy is full, shoulder is sore, and I'm much wiser. Thanks Prof."

"Hang about! Not so fast!" he said looking up from signing the bill. "We haven't reached the interesting part yet."

"Which is?" I asked.

In response he nodded his head towards the doorway, and we walked out into the afternoon sun.

Lingering a while longer, we strolled around the immaculately tended gardens to the rear of the hotel.

Seated on a bench, we watched as two children earnestly concentrated on learning the sedate game of croquet from their grandparents.

Andrew turned to me. "**Keeping It**. Deciding how much you're going to give away and how much you're going to keep: that is **Step Number Four in becoming a Financial Master**."

I was curious. "Frankly, Prof, I thought I'd achieved that when I started paying tithing. At the time I was giving away more than I could logically cope with."

"But that's the point," he said. "You've now become too generous."

I stared at him in disbelief.

He continued. "You're giving away your income to others. And you're giving it to them first."

"Sorry, Prof," I replied bemused. "My full belly must be clouding my brain; you've completely lost me."

"With every bill you pay," he said, "with every purchase you make, you're swapping your hard-earned cash for something that you feel you need or want this month."

"Right." I agreed but still couldn't see where this was leading.

He went on. "The problem is this," he went on, "everybody else gets paid first, and you get what's left. Usually, for most people that's little or nothing."

We stopped to applaud as the little girl started jumping on the spot having finally rolled her ball through the croquet hoop.

"But surely, if there's a finite amount of money," I continued, "then that's all that can be done?"

"You'd think so, wouldn't you?" he smiled.

"But ask yourself this. Suppose that your income was cut by 10%.

Would life become a disaster? No, generally not. People tend to adjust their life to meet their income."

"Oh, I see. So why not determine to give that 10% to yourself first."

"That's it!" he said rising from the bench. "Save it. Set it aside. Invest it. Whatever you do, make sure it works for your benefit.

"Then let the Miracle of Compounding work for you."

"The Miracle..?" I stammered. We were off again, and I loved it.

He tapped his temple teasingly and headed around to the front entrance with me kicking stones in petulance behind him.

Sitting beside him in the car, I couldn't stop myself from bursting into laughter.

"Come on. Out with it," I demanded.

We quickly nipped out in front of an approaching tractor and purred along the winding roads. As I looked across the fields to my left, I marvelled at the bright profusion of blood-red poppies that still carried their drooping petals.

Finally, he succumbed to my determined stare.

"Einstein declared that one of the miraculous laws to most benefit mankind was the mathematical law of compound interest: the law whereby a few pounds or dollars per day can grow – compound – into hundreds of thousands, if not millions.

"That is one of the laws that separates the two groups of people who exist side by side in the western world: those who earn interest and those who pay it."

He waited while I digested that thought. "Just a minute!" I burst out. "Today has been fascinating and an education; really it has. But I seem to remember that my first question was: 'How do I create streams of income?'"

Then he laughed in that maddening way of his and prodded the stereo system.

"I was thinking about that, and I'm going to arrange for us to meet a good friend of mine. She specialises in property investment – one of those routes to financial freedom."

Then he turned up the volume on the stereo, and I was left to wonder at the incongruous tastes of this man beside me as 'The Best of The Beach Boys' started to assail my ears.

LESSONS LEARNED

- Financial mastery isn't complex, but it does take discipline and insight;
- Step One in financial mastery is Valuing It. Value how much time it takes to create your money. Then value that money and how much of your life it represents;
- Step Two is Tracking It: keeping track of every penny of expenditure;
- Step Three is Trimming It: trimming back every expenditure that does not contribute to what you feel is truly important in your life;
- Step Four is Keeping It: retaining and paying yourself a percentage of what you earn, before you spend it on what everybody else is tempting you to spend it on.

PROGRESS TRACKER

- 1st September was the 4th month of the IVA. I have paid £4,000 so far;
- Following my discussion with Andrew and Nathan, I have started to pay tithing – 10% of my gross income – into a building society account;
- This is my seventh month in my job. My recent promotion has increased the pressure on me, but I'm thoroughly enjoying the leadership and business responsibility;
- It's nearly four months since I last had contact with Naomi. I never thought I'd last this long.

Chapter 8
Cheering on My Progress

Wednesday, 19th September

I had never seen my mother move so fast.

She whirled around as I entered the kitchen. "Oh, hello darling." She flashed a smile whilst replacing the phone. "Are you joining us for dinner tonight?"

"Yes, I'd like that. Did I interrupt something?" I slid the door shut behind me. "Mum, I'm a big boy now. You don't have to drop everything you're doing, the moment I get home!" I gave her a kiss on the cheek and she blushed.

"Alright, I know that, you cheeky young blighter! Anyway, I'd just finished." She sounded flustered. "You know how I like to catch up with family gossip. News from Florida. But don't worry; everything is fine, just fine."

I sat down at the table noting the familiar plastic cloth. "Why should I be worried? Are you sure there's no bad news that you're keeping from me?"

"No, just the opposite!" She laughed nervously as she brushed a greying curl from her forehead. "Your Aunt Myrtle has been signed off, clear of cancer. And would you believe that your brother has been nominated for an ER Nurse of The Year award."

"Well, that's great! I'll give him a call later in the week." I noticed the cutlery and napkins, carefully set. "How soon's dinner Super Cook?"

It still felt strange eating around the family table, seated with the same people (apart from my brother, Ray, now settled into his medical career across the Atlantic) with whom I had fought and from whom I had longed to escape as a teenager.

There sat Dad throughout the whole meal staring intently at his plate as if it would escape should he dare lift his eyes.

Mum flitted backwards and forwards hardly relaxing between forkfuls fretting about what was missing on our plates.

"So tell me, honey," she said, pulling off her apron, "what secrets have you been getting up to in your room? I've seen you coming in and out, up and down with boxes of things and spending hours up there until late at night."

"Oh that? That's computer equipment. I'm learning about the Internet and trying to develop a few ideas that'll help me fulfil these darned promises I've made to Andrew Lambert. But boy, am I struggling. What I need right now is a miracle."

"Yes, I remember you talking about something the two of you were planning to do."

She took my half-empty plate and piled it with more curried chicken.

"Yes, I've got some ideas that could be quite exciting if I could only get them down on paper fast enough. It's as if something is bubbling inside of me, and if I don't write it down, I'll explode."

"Like writing a book, you mean?" she asked, casually.

"Yes, possibly. Anyway, two or three ideas have been haunting me recently so that I can hardly sleep. But the thoughts are like pieces of jelly, squidging through my fingers whenever I try to get hold of them."

"You know, Jon, I'm confident you'll work this through." She looked at me with a pride that only a mother possesses. "I can tell you're excited about what you're doing. I've noticed you missing out on the soaps on TV, which is not like you. And you're spending so much time in your bedroom with that computer. You've certainly got the bit between your teeth at the moment!"

"That's sweet of you, Mum. But the challenge ends after twelve months. Here I am at the end of month four and not even a coherent idea."

"Hey! Don't beat yourself up, son!" interrupted Dad. "Have some faith in what you're doing, kid!"

Mum and I turned around bewildered. Dad hardly ever spoke until his meal was close to being polished off, and then only to request some more of whatever food was left.

He wasn't finished. "You can't start paying tithing and clearing those huge debts and then expect to do everything else at once, including dashing around with those pretty things who come to collect you for church. Incidentally, it must be years since you last went to church. It's good to see you going again."

"Yes, sweetheart," added Mum, "you have so much going on right now; so many changes."

"What changes are you referring to?" I wondered what else they knew about me that I'd never admitted.

"Gambling, for one!" cut in Dad. "Mum, pass the sweetcorn would you? Thanks. Mmm, yes, I don't notice you creeping in at all hours like you did when you first moved back. And your room doesn't smell like a brewery. This is good corn. Could I have some more butter?"

I laughed at his insight. "You're right about the gambling. I thought I'd suffer terrible withdrawal symptoms. But it doesn't bother me any more." Then a thought struck me. "But, hold on a second! 'Tithing', you said? How did you know I paid tithing?"

"Mmm, sorry? Say what? Ah, well," he looked across to Mum to rescue him.

"You left your building society pass book on the table one night, Jon," she explained. "We couldn't help noticing the strange phrase that you had written on it: 'The Windows of Heaven'.

"I'm sorry. We should have brought it up before. We're pleased as punch with some of the decisions you're making. Surprised, but proud."

"Look Mum, Dad. I feel embarrassed about paying tithing and then giving you hardly enough rent to cover my food and other expenses."

"Don't be." She looked at me shaking her head slightly. "What you're doing will have a far deeper effect than any money you could give us. Believe me. We've felt the effects in our life for a few years now."

"What?" I was stunned. "I didn't know you paid tithing!"

"Honey, there are a lot of things you've never noticed." She smiled, but there was pain in her eyes. "You were so self-absorbed, and our life has been quietly changing without you. But that doesn't mean we're not glad to have you home again though I could do with some help around the house!"

"Hey, I'm sorry. I never thought."

"Don't be," she said. "You might be a strapping thirty years old, but you're still lacking perspective in some ways. Life can be pretty confusing when you're young and have more talent than wisdom."

"Huh! You mean 'than sense', don't you?" I countered.

Then she laughed, and I could almost picture her as a young girl hiding her laughter behind her hand, her eyes betraying her mirth – and her beauty.

Upstairs, I sat on the edge of my bed replaying the conversation. They were right. A lot had changed in the last six months.

In spite of losing everything, I felt more confident. I felt, well, calmer I suppose you'd call it. I even began to consider the possibility that losing the business was not a near-death experience after all – even though the pain had been both real and deep.

Still in thought, I moved over to my PC and switched it on. Within minutes my new addiction, the Internet, had me back in its grasp.

I had made the decision to search for subjects and groups of people who had a burning need, a need that, perhaps, I could meet.

Using Google I went through the list that had tumbled out of a brainstorming session some weeks ago. Somehow, I had to find a subject that attracted the attention of millions of people. 'Debt', 'Millionaire', 'Property, Buy-To-Let', 'Career Development', 'Dating', 'Recruitment'. There was an infinite list to choose from.

But even if I found a subject that interested me, what solutions did I have to offer? More worrying was, even with the Internet, how would I ever attract the attention of one million people?

After two hours of hard work, which left my eyes aching and dry, I tumbled into bed exhausted and frustrated. I had to be careful. There was pressure on at work, and my new role put me in a high profile leadership position. I was now responsible for a whole division with a multi-million pound turnover.

Before my eyes closed, I managed to scribble a few lines in my journal about finally discovering my parents. Then the day felt complete.

LESSONS LEARNED

- Emotional maturity has little to do with age, and a lot to do with our ability to be less self-consumed;
- When I was five years old, I thought that my parents knew everything. At 15 I was convinced that they knew nothing. Now I'm 30 and they seemed to have become wise and shrewd!
- I never noticed how funny my dad was;
- I've discovered that my parents understood and paid tithing, long before I did.

PROGRESS TRACKER

- Nothing much that's new has happened in the last 18 days; not financially, anyway;
- I still have only paid £4,000 of my IVA so far. A mere £96,000 to go!
- Paying tithing into my building society account is so cool! I get a buzz just thinking about it;
- Thinking about the changes in my behaviour, it must have been three months since I last went clubbing. I miss my drinking buddies; but, in Naomi's friends, I've found an alternative source of fun. The bonus is, when I wake up, I don't have to worry about what I did the night before!

Chapter 9
Law Six : Residual Income Is King!

Saturday, 6th October

*A*utumn blazed as I drove through West Sussex for my meeting with Andrew. Nature's colours easily rivalled the fireworks that were already in the shops anticipating Guy Fawkes Night. Now and again, the countryside was punctuated by clusters of muddy men under the dark blue sky wallowing in their rugby or football kits.

Andrew had asked me to join him in the afternoon, which was a break from our routine. The rhythm of our meetings – always on the first Saturday of each month – had given a new structure to my life. It was an unspoken expectation that I would account for my progress and he would teach me the next principle. Then I would record whatever I learned in my journal while my thoughts were still fresh.

I kept the music down as I drove. Something – an elusive wisp of an idea – was irritating me like a splinter. I knew that it wouldn't take form while I was cocooned in the noise of Mercury FM. So I concentrated on the narrowing roads and left my subconscious to work on whatever was bothering me.

Entering East View's drive I noticed the borders and beds around the estate still spilling over with drifts of colour despite the end of summer. Always in awe of the size and beauty of this 'front garden', I announced my arrival with the ornate knocker that adorned the main door.

I was greeted, not by Andrew, but by the elegant figure of Louise, who wore a beautifully cut, russet coloured jacket over black trousers. Even she was autumnal today.

"You can put your shoes over there, Jonathan. We're in the family room. I'll join you in there in just a moment."

She was definitely the matriarch – brisk, efficient, and immaculate. It was only in those moments when the grandchildren called her name or Andrew put his arms around her waist that I would notice the softness in her face.

Registering the curious warmth of the wooden floor once more – the underfloor heating triggered by October's cool mornings – I strolled towards the long leather settee facing the open fireplace.

Falling back into the large cushions, I started doodling on my notepad. Fragments of ideas were forming and demanding my attention.

I tried to recall my conversation with Mum two weeks previously. What on earth was it she had said that now haunted me? Then I stopped, staring at the words that had taken shape as I scribbled.

That was it!

How could I have missed it?

Adrenalin pumping, I stood up and stepped towards the fireplace. Leaning forward, I rested one hand on the mantle, and with the other started slapping the wall again and again in my excitement.

"Jonathan, are you all right?" snapped an imperious voice behind me.

I whirled to meet the questioning stares of both of them: Andrew and Louise.

Incoherent, I stammered, "Yes. No. Fine. Really, I'm fine, Louise."

Andrew broke through my embarrassment, signalling me to resume my seat. Then they both relaxed with me; Louise into the padded alcove seat to my left and Andrew next to me.

"Jon, I've asked Louise to join us today. I think she can add perspective to what we're about to discuss."

"And," she said, handing me a small china plate, "with that added perspective, I knew you wouldn't say 'no' if I sweetened the lesson with some of these." Upon which she pointed to a larger plate rimmed with gold and stacked with…

"Chocolate fudge brownies!" I exclaimed. "and ice cold milk. Excellent! You should set up shop next to our office in London. You'd make a fortune!"

"I already have." She smiled sweetly.

"And that," said Andrew, "is why we're here today."

I popped a brownie between my teeth and tried to clamp it there while steadying pen and pad on my lap.

"We now come to the subject that you've been dying to discuss for the last eight weeks: the creation of streams of Residual Income." He said the last two words with some drama.

The sound rang sweetly in my ears.

"This type of income," he continued, "flows automatically even when you're not attending to it full time. It's income that repeats itself year after year, long after the initial effort of creating it. It's income that swells your bank account whether you're awake or asleep, working or on holiday.

In our view once you have gained control of your finances, this income is the key to Financial Freedom."

I was so mesmerised by what he was saying that the residue of crumbs that I would usually have polished off remained on my plate.

"Tell you what," he said, "why don't we take our discussion into my office for a while. I'd like to use the flipchart." Then he smiled. "Oh, and let's not forget the fudge brownies!"

As we walked through the dining room, I couldn't help recalling the scene of tears and prayers that had taken place there only weeks before.

Signalling for us to sit at his desk, Andrew turned to a fresh sheet on the chart.

"Now, where were we?" He began again. "Ah yes. Residual Income.

"Let's look at the impact it had on my business as an IFA, an Independent Financial Adviser. Then Louise will describe how she took the principle a stage further.

"So, Jon, the first thing I'd suggest you write is the subheading 'Linear Income'."

"Linear? What do you mean by that?" I asked.

He went on to explain how financial advisers had earned their income for many decades.

As an IFA he had earned large lumps of commission whenever he sold a policy. Alternatively, he had charged fees for complex work that might produce little or no commission.

When he made a sale, he was paid. When he worked an hour for a fee, he was paid for that hour. That's what he meant by 'linear' income: getting paid once for doing the job.

All that sounded pretty fair and logical to me. Fair, that is, until he described the sting in the tail.

The problem arose when his growing database of clients expected continuous service, particularly if they had bought a long-term investment or pension plan.

Sadly, the only way for most financial advisers to survive was to sell more products to new clients, not to service existing ones. More new sales produced new lumps of commission to fund the business. But it also produced new clients who expected long-term service. So the pressure to cope with both responsibilities simply spiralled.

This problem became known as 'The Servicing Debt'. The whole insurance industry had been designed to encourage selling, not servicing.

He concluded that it was a terrible and exhausting trap. It was a classic 'linear income' trap.

"Now, do you remember that seminar that we discussed in August?" he asked. "You remember, 'Wealth Strategies: A Better Way'?"

I nodded.

"Well, within that seminar there was the answer to my dilemma. What I heard that day was a different way of earning which opened our eyes to an array of other possibilities."

Andrew paused to draw breath and finish off his glass of milk. I used that as a chance for my scribbling to catch up with his passion — and to grab the last fudge brownie. "May I?" I asked just in time to show I had not forgotten my manners.

"Go on Prof. I'm with you," I said wiping crumbs from my mouth. This was what I was waiting to hear: the secret of lifelong residual income."

He took a handkerchief out of his pocket to dab his moustache and continued. "What I learned was that some insurance and investment companies had begun designing products differently. They were building in what they called 'Fund-Based Commission' sometimes known as 'Trail Commission'."

"What on earth is that?" I asked.

"Well," he continued, "what that meant was that you could choose to stop receiving the large up-front commissions that we had all become accustomed to. Instead, you could choose to receive a small annual fee based on the value of the client's fund. For example, if a client's pension fund was worth, say, £10,000, we would receive 0.5% of that."

At this Andrew scrawled a large '0.5%' on a fresh page, then looked at me, doubtless expecting some level of excited reaction. But I was puzzled and slumped back in my chair. "Sorry, I just don't see how you could get excited about half a percent. And anyway, where does the 0.5% come from?"

"Good question," he nodded. "Well, with some products the 0.5% came from the investment company sharing with us some of the annual management charges that it was taking anyway. With others we would inform the client that we were being paid that amount in addition to the normal annual management charges."

"What did they think about that?" I queried.

"That's the point!" he enthused, "they much preferred the Annual Fee approach compared to losing the large lumps that would otherwise be ripped out of their fund during the first year or so. And they loved the fact that we were being paid to provide a service, not to sell."

"Oh, I see." I said almost to myself.

"But, think, Jon, think!" he replied tapping his temple. "Don't you see the enormous possibilities for the future?"

I clearly didn't, so he continued. "I agree that, when you only have a few clients, with a few small policies, it's hardly worth thinking about.

But imagine this. Imagine for a moment that clients came to you in droves. Let's suppose that you gathered enough clients with enough investment and pension policies that the total value of their funds was – I don't know – let's say £5 million?" Saying this, he wrote that figure under the '0.5%' on the chart. "What then?" he asked.

I struggled through the figures working them out on my pad. "To my reckoning that would be a annual income to you of . . . £25,000," I said.

"No!" he retorted. "Not £25,000. Jon, it's £25,000 every-single-year, as long as the clients stay with you."

"Then what if the value of all their funds changed when stock markets rose and fell?" I asked.

"Great question," he replied, "that would mean our income changed with it." And he drew an undulating line representing the gradual climb of the UK stock market during the last decade.

"Oh, I see!" I exclaimed. "And if the value of the clients' funds gradually increased, then so would your income."

"Got it in one," he said triumphantly, stabbing his felt-tip at the graph he had drawn.

"But," I frowned and laid my pen down, "why would clients come to you in droves?"

"Wouldn't you?" he asked, "if I could show you a way of moving your pension funds or investing your cash into products where commissions and charges were much lower and the performance opportunities far greater?"

I nodded.

"And if I told you that this arrangement allowed me to give more attention to your affairs year after year into the future," he continued. "How do you think you'd feel?"

"Well, I'd guess, pretty enthusiastic."

"That's right, and they were. In the space of twelve months I had attracted many new clients, bringing with them about £6 million of new funds.

He wrote out the calculation. "That's £30,000 per annum, year after year."

But there was more. "Everything escalated in the second year. Once we explained what we were doing and why, clients were so impressed that the word spread back to the accountants and solicitors who had introduced them. They recommended more clients.

"By the end of year two, our clients' funds totalled £14 million, creating a Residual Income for our business of £70,000 per annum. Again, income that came year after year.

"And we had only just started!" He threw his arms up in delight.

I could hardly remain in my seat. "Wow! Now I'm beginning to see the point."

"By this time," cut in Louise, "Jessica had just met Daniel. Let me see. Corrin hadn't yet gone to university and was at school with Barnaby, whilst Naomi was still the baby of the family."

I glanced quickly at the photographs around the office. Most showed Andrew's love for Louise's raven-haired, high-cheeked beauty. But there were some equally breathtaking portraits of the children.

"With that consistency of income," Louise continued, "Andrew reviewed the purpose of his image-conscious business. Both office and staff had been designed to support the winning of new clients. With that need reduced he could afford to cut overheads, and work from home."

"Yes," continued Andrew, "that was a big turning point for us. I retained only one member of staff full time. Fortunately for us we had moved up the housing ladder to quite a large home where I built a decent office."

Then, as if by agreement, Andrew turned to Louise and handed her the black felt tip while they swapped places.

"What residual income achieved for Andrew," she began, "was a noticeably more relaxed business with no commuting and far less travelling to see clients. With his improved reputation and consistent income, he felt more relaxed about dealing with clients by phone or asking them to come and see him. The pressure was off. Paradoxically, people were even more attracted to doing business with him!"

"How does the saying go?" Louise smiled at Andrew, "if only we had known then what we know now?"

"But now comes the interesting part," she continued. "I woke up to the power of what was happening to Andrew and re-examined the small hairdressing and beautician business that I ran from the salon in our home."

"I had no idea you ran your own business!" I blurted.

"Well, you never asked." She raised her eyebrows, and I could feel myself blushing.

"I don't run that business any more, but it was very useful for us when the children were tiny and Andrew was struggling.

So, I hit upon the idea of trying to sell more products rather than selling my time by the hour or being dependent upon complex hairstyling requirements."

Putting her pen down, she walked behind us to a large dresser, converted into a bookshelf, and reached inside the bottom cupboard. Returning, she placed some attractive slim containers, dispensers and small tubes onto the green leather of the desk.

"We found a range of beauty products, much like the Avon range that has been popular for decades.

"Having displayed them carefully in the salon, they became so popular that clients recommended them to their friends. Within less than a year, nearly half my income originated from products, not services.

"Then I saw the potential of escalating the income by encouraging customers to market those products more actively to other people. That's when my business really took off!"

"Sort of like a distributor network?" I queried.

"That's exactly what it was: marketing through a network of distributors – or network marketing," she replied.

She caught my frown.

"Yes, I had always pooh-poohed that type of business as rather shady myself. I had even argued with Andrew when he introduced the idea earlier in our marriage."

As she spoke she walked back to the bookshelves and reached up to grab some books.

"But I did my homework. I spent months reading factual books on direct sales, product distribution methods as well as network marketing," saying which, she laid three of them in front of me. I noted one of the titles: 'Inside Network Marketing' by Leonard Clements.

"Finally, my clients changed my mind. They were delighted with what I recommended, and they were making some pocket money themselves by showing them to their friends. We simply focused on what we naturally loved chatting about and the business built itself."

She drew a diagram like a family tree to demonstrate the geometric growth of activity and income. Then she continued.

"The final injection of excitement came when I introduced health-related products from a distributor based in Utah in the USA. They included vitamins, minerals and a weight-loss range.

"The word-of-mouth advertising that came as a result saved us years of effort."

Andrew broke in to add his comments. "Within two years of me working from home, Louise had reduced her hairdressing activity and was running a busy and prosperous operation, creating about half as much revenue as my financial planning practice.

"And I was still home when my children needed me," she beamed. "It was astonishing!"

"My turn, honey?" cut in Andrew.

Louise chuckled and bowed. "The floor is yours." They swapped places again.

Andrew picked up the story. "Jessica was now married, had just moved into her own home, and our first granddaughter was on the way. This sparked another idea from Louise." Seated beside me, she grinned.

He turned to the chart and sketched the outline of a house. "With our confidence riding high, we decided to look at property, as our next income stream.

"We were complete novices, of course. But, as a financial planner, I had good mortgage broking, banking and legal contacts. I also knew a very bright young lady – Chrissie – who had built an extensive property portfolio. With that support around us, we remortgaged our home to provide us with an initial fund for deposits. Then we purchased three small properties on the South Coast and became landlords for the first time.

"During the second year we became more serious about doing things properly. We paid Chrissie to teach us a great deal about how to turn what was an interesting hobby into a serious business."

"Now," said Louise, "with the children almost self-sufficient, we have created a portfolio of over forty properties, some of them overseas. We're fortunate to be able to rent them to friends and families of church acquaintances. So we have run into very few problems over the years. That doesn't mean that creating and running the portfolio is casual work. But, with the help of some excellent property managers for the more complex properties, it's certainly not a full time task. We even turn property research into mini holidays."

Satisfied that he had presented a persuasive case, he pulled a chair from the side of the room and sat down, anticipating my questions.

"But Prof. Come on. How do you balance all three businesses with four adventurous children, four grandchildren who must want your attention and your weighty church responsibilities?" I asked, incredulous. "I just don't get it."

"I don't need to," he replied. "Five years after discovering the power of Residual Income, we sold the financial planning practice when the residual income alone was £200,000 per annum. That embedded value together with the quality client base was worth far more to the buyer than the normal list of clients that most advisers think they can sell."

Louise nodded. "It was that, together with the growth of my health and beauty business that allowed us to persuade the bank to come up with the funds when we spotted the dilapidated mansion. With their backing we've taken just three years to turn the rotting wreck that was East View into what you see today: a beautiful legacy for our family."

"Whew. You can say that again. It's magnificent!" I said getting up to look out of the tall study windows. One of them was open, the late afternoon sun having warmed the day surprisingly. I caught the musty smell of autumn leaves and spotted waves of starlings heading towards their winter shores.

"Well now, Jonathan," said Louise coming over to stand beside me, "have we persuaded you about the power of creating Residual Income?"

"I'm hooked, Louise; completely sold. My only problem is, well, how do I make this work for me? I think I've hit upon an idea. But it needs some research."

"And tell me", she enquired, "why were you beating our wall to death when we entered the room?"

"Aah! I responded with a grin, "we'll just have to leave the answer to that until next time."

Andrew threw his head back and roared. "Touché, Jonathan. Touché!"

We all turned as we heard a loud knock on the office door. As it opened we stopped in surprise, for the doorway was momentarily empty. Then, a pleasant, heart-shaped face appeared from the side. Dark brown eyes and a wide, mischievous grin greeted us.

Louise clapped her hands. "How wonderful! It's Chrissie! Come on, come in." With that, a tall, bespectacled brunette entered dressed in fashionable rural rainwear and followed by a jovial-looking fellow, slightly shorter than her and noticeable by his broad shoulders.

After a confusion of greetings, Andrew turned to me, his hand on my shoulder.

"Chrissie, let me introduce you to Apprentice Soul Millionaire, Jonathan Broom. Jonathan, meet Chrissie and Matthew Field."

Her stare unsettled me as she approached with a wry smile hovering on her lips.

"Well, well. Young Jonathan Broom. Fancy meeting you again." And she shook my hand slowly with a grip that lingered far too long.

I stood as if paralysed. I simply hadn't a clue who she was!

I learned a great deal that afternoon as we walked with Chrissie and Matthew. I had been warned to bring Wellingtons and was glad of the advice as we squelched through hidden puddles and sticky mud in the quick gathering of dusk.

I had been stunned by Chrissie's recognition of me a few hours earlier. For my part, I was convinced that we had never met. What was worse, she didn't seem in a hurry to refresh my memory.

There had been a few seconds of uncomfortable silence in that first encounter. But Louise had broken the spell, suggesting that we had been cooped up for far too long and needed some fresh air before sunset.

I walked beside Chrissie, hanging on to her every word and ignoring the hint of drizzle enveloping us. I soon learned that her speech matched the lightning speed of her mind. Listening left me exhausted, and it took Matthew to interject occasionally and explain things more slowly in his calm, deep voice.

Prompted by my questions, she spoke of her introduction to property only eight years previously when she had turned thirty. At an early stage she had built a team of advisers – her 'dream team' as she called them. She went on to discuss how you could buy property without a deposit, a practice she called 'no money down'. She had used this method sometimes to produce fast cash returns. She also talked about 'sourcing', in other words finding properties for other investors.

Before long my head was spinning, and I told her so.

Looking across at Matthew, she said, "Why don't we start Jonathan's education early next month. If he needs to have some serious cash in his bank by the end of next May, then we need to allow six months, in case of hiccups."

"Why such a long time?" I asked, trying to shake the rain from my hair.

"We need to spend time ensuring you understand the basics of property investment," replied Matthew. "Which means you'll have one or two books to digest – like *Renting Out Your Property for Dummies* and *How To Be A Property Millionaire* – plus CDs and other material."

"Then there's the Christmas silly season when little gets done for two weeks," added Chrissie. "With a fair wind we could achieve a profitable property transaction by, say, March. But if we need to do any major refurbishment, then we need to add eight weeks onto that timescale. I suggest that you meet us in November at our place, and we'll start the process. What d'you think Andrew?"

By now we had all pulled up our hoods to ward off the steady rain, and the temperature had dropped. Gravitating towards the driveway as the light faded, we started heading back to the main house.

"I think that fits our timetable nicely, Chrissie," said Andrew. "Incidentally, are you two staying the night? Jonathan will be here for the rest of the weekend, which would give you an opportunity to get stuck into his education."

"No, I'm sorry Andrew," she said, removing the mud from her boots with the century-old metal scrapers set into the side of the main steps. "We'd love to, but we need to get back to North London tonight. We have appointments to view some properties first thing in the morning. We need an early start."

With that enigmatic smile of hers, Chrissie bid me farewell. As she drove away I was already sifting through scenes from my life, desperately trying to recall where we might have met.

Feeling warmed and refreshed after a shower, I pattered down the wide staircase in my socks to be met by voices drifting from the kitchen. I recognised the clipped and rapid speech immediately. It was Louise and Jessica sounding unusually animated.

I stood in the hall feeling like an intruder as Louise spoke quickly about Barnaby, Naomi's brother and his recent letter from Germany. Louise's voice was husky as she read aloud some of the frightening experiences he was facing working for his church in Düsseldorf. 'Being chased by dogs and threatened by drunks on buses.'

I shook my head in amazement. Blimey! What on earth would possess a sane, good-looking young guy like that to set aside normal life and travel abroad simply to be abused every day? What on earth had got into him!

Later that evening the talk around the table flowed easily as we indulged in a game of Risk. Seemingly harmless, this board game has brought out some of the meaner and more ruthless qualities in players. But the room was full of much light humour and whispering. Having said that, it was quieter than usual.

"So, Jessica," I said, blowing on the dice before I rolled them. "Why aren't Danny and Nathan with us tonight?"

"We're being spoilt, that's why," she replied. "They have their orders to see to the children's bath and bedtime. Danny, bless him, is being particularly attentive 'cos I'm feeling a bit queasy today." And I caught her quick look towards Corrin.

"Come on Jonathan!" Louise broke in, "you're not sidetracking us any further. You owe us an explanation. Andrew was right. I thought you were going to knock our wall in, as we came into the lounge this afternoon. What got you so excited?"

The conversation lulled and expectant eyes turned towards me.

"I'll explain, really I will," I parried. "But first I have a question." This brought groans of exasperation.

I looked at Andrew, who nodded that he was ready to listen.

"I've come up with one or two ideas to create revenue. The problem is, I've never created a one-man business, particularly something that I'm likely to operate from home. I realise that you've explained residual income ideas that have worked for you, but my ideas seem quite different. So I'm not sure how to tell what will work and what won't."

"That's a question Louise and I have asked ourselves before each venture," responded Andrew. "You'll be glad to know that we've developed an answer."

"Do I need a notepad?" I asked.

"No, relax," he said. "I've some notes prepared on my PC. Remind me to print them off." Everybody eased back in their chairs as he moved into teaching mode.

"Over the last couple of years, we have constructed some guidelines – a formula, if you like – which helps us to measure any likely commercial opportunity.

"We've called the formula 'FREEDOM', which makes it easy to remember.

"The notes we've prepared will give you far more detail. But here's a brief summary:

"The 'F' in Freedom stands for 'Five' and for 'Free'.

"The question is: will this business venture or project allow you to break free from it within five years? If so, will it continue producing income for you, or will you be able to sell it for a substantial six or seven figure sum?"

"'F' in Freedom also stands for 'Force'," interrupted Louise. "Great force comes when you catch an idea like a surfer catches a wave. If you catch the wave too late, its power passes you by. So correct timing of a business idea increases its force."

"Yes, that's so important," agreed Andrew. "Now we come to:

"'R'. The 'R' in Freedom stands for 'Residual Income'.

"All of us here are now convinced that to start from zero at the beginning of each business year is to make life needlessly difficult. We're converted to the fact that, if you can create something that continues to pay income year after year – with or without your continued efforts, then that's a smart way of building financial independence and freedom.

"'E' in Freedom stands for 'Employee-Free'.

"Many an entrepreneur has discovered – often too late – that employees are not only their heaviest financial burden, but consume their time and energy.

"A couple of our close friends experienced this in their marketing business. They reduced their working hours, improved their profits and enjoyed a more fulfilling life when they finally let go of their employees. So, try to develop a business that is not heavily dependent on employees. That's likely to mean outsourcing work to other small businesses.

"The next 'E' in Freedom stands for 'Essential'.

"Your product or service might only apply to a certain segment of the population – a niche market. But make sure that what you offer targets a burning need, a colossal pain or a consuming desire. The more urgent or 'essential' the need feels to your target market, the greater your chance of success."

By now he was hunched on the edge of his seat as the passion for his subject gripped him. Then he caught a glance from Louise accompanied by a wide smile. Sitting back, he waved his hand towards her and she continued my education.

"I should think so," she said, her nose in the air.

"'D' in Freedom stands for 'Differentiate'," she said. "Make your business outstanding. From the outset the world must be able to spot what is so different about your offering to the market. You must excel or be unusual. You must provide superb quality that not only pleases but also astonishes your customers and alarms your competitors. Develop your brand around your difference, and you have the chance of long-term success.

"'D' in Freedom also stands for 'Desire'.

"The desire and passion for what you do will shine through and affect others. If you're just in business to make money, that won't carry you through the trials and disappointments you will surely face. But your desire and passion to touch others' lives with your business will influence those around you who can help you achieve your dreams.

"'O' in Freedom stands for 'Organised'.

"Your business must lend itself to being structured into a repeatable process. If it depends entirely upon your moods – your fitness to act, your available time – then it becomes very vulnerable to its weakest link – you! The processes should be clearly communicated in an Operations Manual and should be able to be repeated by somebody with far less skill than you. Otherwise, you don't have a business at all; you simply have a personality-driven, self-employed practice.

"'M' in Freedom stands for 'Multiply'.

"Can your service multiply itself by using Other People's Time (OPT), Other People's Energy (OPE) or Other People's Money (OPM)? For example, could you create an army of affiliates who would be happy to distribute your service or product to your market for a share of the revenue? Or does it rely so heavily upon your personal skill that you can only reach your market in ones or twos or, at the most, tens or twenties?

"This last factor, Jonathan, is a key to you reaching one million people!"

With the slightest signal of her eyebrows, she handed back to Andrew.

"Use this formula as a filter," he said. "This will help you to select ideas that have the best chance of helping you achieve the freedom you want, without wasting years of effort."

Just then Corrin leaned forward and took the dice from my open palm.

"Well, that's interesting, you two, but do I assume that I've won tonight's game? Or shall I make mincemeat of you all?" I laughed, partly taken aback by the challenge and partly by the fact that she could deliver it with a voice so soft and eyes so wide and disarming.

"I think we've lost Jon for tonight," chimed in Jessica. "And he still owes us an explanation about whatever got him so excited."

"Alright, I admit defeat," I said, putting my hands up in surrender. "The problem is that my thoughts are little more than a jumble. They're certainly not organised along 'Freedom Formula' lines. As for my excitement? Well, driving down here, I'd been fretting about a conversation I had with Mum this week. Something she had said haunted me, and I couldn't remember what it was. Then, waiting for you in the lounge, it came to me!

"I had been explaining to her how ideas were bubbling up inside of me, and if I didn't tell someone, or write them down, I'd explode. Then Mum had said, 'Like writing a book, you mean?'

"And I knew that was it!" I shuffled in my seat a little, plumped up the cushion behind me and cleared my throat. "You challenged me to create a way to touch one million lives. My question now is, what about a book? Don't books get sold to a million people? Then, if it starts to sell, surely earning royalties on a book is a classic way of getting this Residual Income?"

"Jon," exclaimed Corrin, "that's a wonderful idea! Come on you lot, admit it: wouldn't that be awesome?"

Andrew stopped in the middle of stacking away his plastic armies.

"Yes. Yes it is," he said slowly. "Certainly one of the options that I hoped Jonathan would discover. Now, tell me, budding genius. Have you considered what this book of yours might be all about? What would you write that could touch a million lives?"

My gaze dropped to the tablecloth.

"Aah. That's what hasn't come to me yet, I'm embarrassed to say. I don't think there is anything I know enough about that would attract a million people. My experience is just too normal and routine, I suppose."

Silence settled upon the room as I looked up to see Jessica's finger pointing towards me. In a tone of exasperation, she said, "For goodness sake, Jon. Don't you see? It's you."

"I'm sorry, Jessica. What's me?"

"It's you, Jonathan," she repeated. "Oh come on, don't be so daft! Don't you see what makes you different? It's you and your journal."

Now we were all looking at her as she calmly folded the Risk board, her smile spreading mischievously to her eyes.

"Don't you get it?" she continued. "The story is your story. And the storyline, well it's already laid out, day by day, in your journal. Think about it. All the lessons you've learned; all Dad's tips. But what would make it really unique is you. Your story. Your experience. That would give it the authenticity a good book requires."

"But who would be interested in my story?" I blurted incredulously.

"You are joking aren't you?" she retorted. "How many people have achieved what you have in such a short period of time?"

Louise took up Jessica's chiding. "Yes, Jon. How many people do you know who have been near the edge of bankruptcy, have started paying tithing when they owe £100,000, have agreed to repay that debt in twelve months? Come on!"

"How many people do you know who've been rapidly promoted whilst coping with all that pressure, having won some pretty major business accounts?" Louise looked around the room for assent. Everyone was nodding.

Now it was Andrew's turn. "Who else do you know who has determined to influence one million people without ever considering how? And all this whilst abandoning addictions and habits like gambling; then changing their friends and starting a new lifestyle?"

"And meanwhile, they've stopped seeing the person that they love," added Corrin, "for no other reason than because it felt the right thing to do even though they couldn't bear the thought. You're trying to tell me that isn't an extraordinary story?"

Now every face was turned to me.

"But, I don't know how to write a book!" I complained. "That's the problem!"

"You know how to write a journal, don't you?" said Andrew, frustration in his voice. "Look, I know at least one editor who can help you organise your thoughts. She'll make sure you write in a way that grabs the readers' attention and interest."

"But what about the cost of publishing? Then there's printing and selling it to the bookshops or whatever you do with it."

"Jonathan, Jonathan. Write your book," whispered Louise, her voice low but firm. "The rest will follow, you'll see."

I sat back folding my arms looking first towards the floor, then out towards the windows and the night sky.

Nobody moved.

"A book," I sighed. "Me?" I shook my head in disbelief and started to grin, in spite of myself.

A smatter of applause broke around me as Andrew quickly opened another bottle, topped up our glasses and proclaimed, "To Jonathan's book!"

"Jonathan's book!" echoed their voices, accompanied by my nervous laughter.

Then, more quietly he added, "And a story that's going to touch one million lives."

LESSONS LEARNED

- I now understand why Residual Income is King! Now I see why Time/Financial Freedom has more power than Wealth;
- Residual Income can free us from the Sell-Your-Time for Money trap;
- The Lamberts have persuaded me that I have the story and capacity to write an interesting book;
- Mum has greater insight than she realises!
- By focusing on the challenges and changes of my new life, I feel no need for the addictive excitement of gambling. I feel liberated!

PROGRESS TRACKER

- I haven't told Andrew that I've started a simple savings account. I'm not managing ten percent yet. But, I have to admit, the discipline feels good;
- 1st October was the fifth month of the IVA. I have paid £5,000 so far;
- This is my eighth month in my job;
- It's nearly five months since I said 'goodbye' to Naomi;
- Looking back, this was a day of great breakthroughs, and the start of some confusion. This first meeting with Chrissie Field has really unsettled me. Who is she, and why does she seem to know me so well?
- Next, I'm surrounded by Naomi's stunning girlfriends. But I don't look at them in the way I used to look at women just a few months ago. It sounds corny, but I see womanhood in a far different light nowadays;
- I wonder, how am I going to cope with writing my book, my job, and my education into property, which starts next month? I'll need to do some serious planning, and watch my allocation of time.

David J Scarlett

Chapter 10
Law Seven : Start to Live On Purpose

Saturday, 3rd November

I'd heard that leadership carries a heavy burden.

I don't mind admitting that this week I had felt it acutely.

An uncomfortable meeting with the UK sales director, Keith Martin, had forced me to explain why our competitors had beaten us in proposing for two new accounts. I had been a little surprised at his irritability and sarcasm. I had been even more concerned at his dismissal of the fact that we had recently expanded the level of recruitment revenue on two of our existing accounts.

In the face of his criticism, I felt well and truly deflated.

It had been the first time that I had known the bitterness of defeat since my promotion.

It was at 6:40 am on Saturday morning that I noticed my breath puffing out in frosty clouds for the first time since I had started running. I had raised my game from one mile to four in the space of four months and, by the time I staggered back to my parents' door, my lungs heaving, I felt more than heroic.

Elated after my run and looking ahead to a day of learning and discovery, I felt the dismay and weight of the week wash away as I showered.

I thought back to my last visit to East View. Andrew was right: I had come surprisingly far in a mere few months, and I still felt as if I stood on the edge of even greater adventure. Here I was, four months into paying tithing. Me, doing religious stuff like that! As I considered the concept, it seemed illogical even now.

I bounded downstairs and fell happily into the routine of helping to prepare breakfast for my parents and myself. I was getting quite used to helping out around the home these days. Humming as I moved between pan and grill, I quickly reviewed the financial impact of the last month's business successes, trying to set aside the failures. Hardly able to believe the figures, I recalculated. There was no mistake. By the end of November, I would be earning at the rate of £90,000 per annum!

For the next hour we enjoyed a relaxed breakfast together as I spilled out the thoughts that I hoped to turn into another chapter of my book.

Leaving Mum with a brief hug, I dashed up to the underground station and settled down to a long, noisy ride on the Northern Line heading for Woodside Park on the rim of North London. My companion was Thomas Hardy's classic novel *Far From The Madding Crowd*, from which I had started to draw descriptive inspiration for my book. I was discovering that authors learn to see wonder in each moment of everyday life.

Chrissie and Matthew's home was perched on the expensive edge of Finchley, comfortably set beside fields to the North and West. They had sympathetically refurbished and decorated their early Victorian home, which exuded warmth and character, muted colours and a faded softness. I felt at home the moment Chrissie greeted me in that hurried manner of hers.

The next four hours were crammed with the essence of all that they had learned in the early stages of their property business. I had no idea why this busy couple also felt inclined to help me, but I guessed that Andrew Lambert's influence had something to do with it.

"Let's take you through a typical buy and sell cycle," she said, "so that you can understand what we're trying to achieve when we do it for real."

Then she explained each step in the process creating a huge spreadsheet on graph paper spread over their dining table.

"It's early November now, so we'd need to have spotted an ideal property for you soon, and have made an offer before Christmas," she began.

"That means that during January, you should be exchanging contracts . . ."

"Then before the end of January we can start the work on any major refurbishment," interrupted Matthew. "Let's assume that the work will take about six weeks. That takes us to the last week in February."

"At that point," continued Chrissie, "the house, completely transformed with new kitchen, bathroom and frontage, will be back on the market. So we – I mean you – would expect an offer, plus exchange and completion, just before Easter."

Each step in the process had been carefully listed on the spreadsheet, and, thankfully, they took great pains to translate all of the property jargon for me.

Matthew concluded with a flourish. "By 1st April, the money should be earning interest in your account. Voila!"

"That's excellent!" I enthused. "Just in time for my birthday on the 10th April. What a great present!"

"I know you have commitments for this afternoon," said Chrissie. "So why don't you have a look around our house and see Matthew's talents at their best. He'll be practising his other talent in the kitchen, which is creating the best Indian meal this side of East London."

As we made our way upstairs, Chrissie responded to a question that had kept me intrigued for weeks: the possibility of buying property without having to find a ten or fifteen percent deposit.

"People say it can't be done in the UK. But that's nonsense," she said, opening a door to display a newly finished nursery. As she pulled the door closed, she moved her hand across her swelling waist and smiled.

"The most enjoyable deal," she went on, "was when our credit card company paid a deposit cheque straight into the vendor's solicitor's account. Within hours we transferred the credit balance onto another card that offered zero percent interest for six months. Of course, within that time we had refurbished the property and sold it for a tidy profit, allowing us to clear our credit card.

"There you go: no money down of our own. Brilliant! But it's not a tactic I'd recommend others depending upon. And like many 'No Money Down' approaches, it increases your risk. But it shows what can be done when you're pushed to think outside the box."

She was right. Matthew served an amazing meal, and I headed back to South London wreathed in the aroma of Indian spices and with a briefcase crammed with notes, books, CDs and project lists galore.

However, before I left she gripped my hand and fixed my eyes with that same disarming stare that I recalled from our first meeting. "How interesting that we should work together like this."

Then she cut off my queries with a brief, though not unkind, farewell, and I was sent on my way.

Back in South London that afternoon, I scraped the grime from my windscreen and headed off through Mitcham and Wallington on my way towards East View.

As I spied the mansion's many chimneys, I couldn't help marvelling at the thin blanket of mist that still hung inches above the top of the grass. Touched by the weak afternoon sun, it endowed the fields with a whisper of the winter to come.

Opening the boot of my car to find the bag I had crammed with warm clothes, notepad and diary, I heard steps on the gravel behind me.

Turning, I was met by Corrin's radiant smile. With one arm she held little Joshua, whilst her other was outstretched towards me.

Momentarily blinded by the low, mid-afternoon sun, I only vaguely saw what she held in her hand.

"It's for you Jon. It arrived this morning." Then my fingers grasped an envelope.

By the time I had gathered my thoughts and lifted my eyes from seeking clues from postmark and writing, she was walking quickly back to her own garden gate.

"Thank you," was all I could blurt out as she threw a smile back to me over her shoulder.

I leaned against the car boot, my hands trembling. There was only one person who would write to me at East View. But what urgency had caused her to break our agreement?

I squinted again at the postmark. "Düsseldorf? That's ridiculous! Who could possibly be writing to me from Düsseldorf?" Yet there was my name, unmistakeable, 'Care Of East View Mansion'.

Slowly I unfolded the contents.

Dear Jonathan,

No doubt this comes as a mystery and surprise to you. We've never met, yet I feel I know so much about you from my baby sister and my parents.

I flipped over the page and glanced at the signature. It was from Barnaby. He went on to describe some of his experiences in Germany. That was interesting, but it was the final words that really struck home.

If you had known me even a year ago, you'd be gob-smacked at what I'm doing now. I remember fracturing my ankle trying to escape from the house at night to join my friends in the forest. Don't ask! Then there were the fire extinguisher fights that I used to start at college. And my sisters will tell you how they used to watch out for me, when I staggered home roaring drunk, although I'm sure Dad knew what was going on.

But you know something? I changed. I grew up. And . . . forgive me . . . but it sounds as if you have too. So welcome to the club!

If even half of your experiences that Mum and Dad write about are true, then I will be the first to purchase your book and feel privileged to do so.

I realise that I'm no more than a name to you, but may I offer this word of encouragement? In the darkest moments, when everything seems impossible, promise me that you'll never give up on the book. Someone out there needs to read it!

Until mid-July next year,
With kind regards
Barnaby Lambert

I read it through again, softly chewing my lip as I considered why he had written to me. What I clung to was the fact that Naomi and her parents had written to him about me. More than that, it would seem she'd written with some affection and praise.

Whatever Barnaby's purpose, his letter had lifted me and given me hope.

Suddenly, I was jolted out of my thoughts by the sound of my name.

"You can wait out there all day, but – if it's okay with you – there's work to be done."

It was Andrew, hands on hips, booted and comical with a woollen hat crammed over his head and flanked by both Nathan and Daniel.

"What's the order of the day, you guys?" I asked, wondering what I had let myself in for.

"A few solid hours of wiring in Daniel's house."

"Come on Prof! What do I know about wiring a house?"

"We're about to find out my good man!"

I groaned audibly, picked up my change of clothes and, grinning despite myself, headed after Nathan and Andrew with Daniel thumping my back in greeting.

There was no respite. The work was exacting, grimy, sweaty and went on until the afternoon sun had set. Whilst I had been little more than a 'gofer' I staggered out of Daniel and Jessica's home with a sense of achievement as great as any felt whilst jogging four miles.

I had agreed to meet later with Andrew in his study and knocking gently on the warm oak panelling, I entered his sanctuary.

"Come in, Jonathan. We don't have a great deal of time before we drive off but enough to dig into the next of the Ten Laws."

I slipped into the padded high-back chair on the window side of his desk and laid my notepad and Day Planner expectantly in front of me.

"You're ready for **Law Number Seven**. I'll give you the title of the law in just a moment."

And with that he launched into the lesson.

"Being successful is one thing," he began, "but being effective and happy; now that's a different matter all together."

No doubt he could hear my mind crunching away trying to work out the difference between the two states as I listened intently.

"I've observed those around me who have done two things superbly well," he said. "Firstly, those who have excelled in their chosen field of work, secondly, those that have combined this with joyous and fulfilling lives. In all cases, I find that this has not come about by accident. Such lives have developed by design.

"That's the first note I'd like you to make."

"So what you're saying is that they weren't just lucky?"

"Oh no! I'm not suggesting that," he said, and waved the thought away. "Into each life may come many wonderful coincidences and life-enhancing accidents where time and events seem to harmonise – synchronicity if you like. The point is that some lives are so crammed with hectic activity and material pleasures that fortune floats by unnoticed, or gets smothered before it can blossom."

I was waiting for the 'but' in his next sentence.

"Have you ever asked yourself why some people seem to be continually growing, constantly excelling, comfortably achieving, and yet – how shall I put it – they carry with them an aura of peace and security?"

Before I could answer, distant crackles and tiny explosions echoing across the darkening sky distracted me.

"Haven't you ever been in the presence of someone like that, someone to whom you are inexplicably drawn?"

"Well, yes. I think I understand what you mean." The fact is I knew only too well what he meant. To me Andrew was just such a person.

"Yet," he continued, "they have the same 24 hours to live in that we do. So, tell me, are their IQs multiples of yours? Of course not! That's daft!" he scoffed. "Do they work five or ten times as hard or as long? I sincerely doubt it!

"So what is their secret?" he posed rhetorically. "Choice, Jonathan," he proclaimed triumphantly. "They choose to work on those things that will have the greatest impact on their lives. They know how to leverage the best use of every hour."

The light from his table lamp was enhanced by the almost noiseless pulses of light from the sky behind me.

He held me spellbound. "They know what comes first in their life, and they make sure that what matters most gets done first, each week, each day. That is why they are so successful, effective and happy. They live on purpose, not by accident."

Then he pointed to my notepad.

"And that is the title of Law Number Seven: Start Living On Purpose."

I carefully underlined the heading.

"In my view," he continued, "the wise and effective use of our time is such a profound human skill that I wonder why it's not taught as a foundation of our education system.

"Just think what would happen if you could achieve in one year what would normally take others five years."

"So," I said, posing the obvious question, "how do they know what matters most each day? I mean, I make 'To Do' lists every day at the office. But sometimes I wonder why I bother, when I crawl home frazzled with the tiniest dent in my list. Then, by 10 am the next morning my list is larger than it was the day before!" I could feel the frustration that was so familiar to me just by describing the process.

"Ah, yes. 'To Do' lists," he sighed. "Why don't we try ditching those for the sake of this discussion?"

"If you can show me a better way, you have my attention," I said.

"Eagles. That's the thing," he said.

"Of course it is. Eagles, yes." I said without having the faintest idea what he was on about.

"You may well smile, young Jonathan, but Eagles, is where you should be directing your energy each day."

Then he drew a large square on a fresh page dividing that square into four equal quarters. Then numbering each quarter from one to four, he started to scribble as he spoke.

"What 'To Do' lists achieve is merely to prioritise what you feel is urgent."

Then he wrote the word 'Rooster' in the square labelled '1'.

"The first square, or 'Sector 1', is the Sector of The Rooster. I've used the names of birds because they help me to remember the principles.

"The Rooster represents those things that crow at you annoyingly. They are projects and actions that feel insistent and noisy, demanding your attention. They won't be silenced until you deal with them. It's important that you wake up to them because the day and opportunity might pass by without you. They press upon you. They're usually deadline driven tasks or problems, sometimes crises."

"But," I puzzled, "Surely those things need to be dealt with, otherwise our lives, particularly our businesses, would suffer?"

"Absolutely," he nodded. "The problem is that we become so addicted to the relief of silencing The Rooster that we become trapped by the habit. Our big kick – our adrenaline buzz – then comes from thriving in this area. What we fail to notice is that constantly living on a high means that more important things in our lives get sidelined until they collapse or die."

"Which 'more important things'?" I asked. "You've just suggested that Sector 1 is not only full of stuff that needs to be dealt with promptly but that could be critical."

"Good question," he said, slapping the desk. "But the problem is that The Rooster crows every day. So, whatever you do, the noise of this sector will return to annoy you. The answer to purposeful living lies in the power of Sector 2: The Eagle." Then he started writing in the second square.

"The Eagle soars above the insistent urgency of The Rooster. The Eagle doesn't flap. In fact it sometimes glides effortlessly. But to climb to the Eagle's height takes strength, discipline and courage. If your life is all about reacting to the crowing of The Rooster, you might never have time to even notice The Eagle's existence. But high above the scurry and panic, The Eagle can see further and more clearly in a moment, things that a Rooster might never see. Spending time in Sector 2 with The Eagle, we develop those activities which create the greatest long-term results in our lives."

"Such as . . ?" I interrupted.

He challenged my question with another. "Would you say that building relationships or networking with business leaders was an urgent action every day – particularly relationships outside of business? How often do you write that as the 'A1' priority on your 'To Do' list?"

I began to see his point and shrugged.

"Then there's the time needed to work out your own mission and three-year vision as we discussed before.

"And how about a physical routine to keep fit and flexible, slowing our physical deterioration? That seldom seems urgent until we have to rush to Doctor Feelgood, hoping he'll patch up our misuse of our bodies."

He paused as I thought about the implications. Continuing, he said, "as we get busier and our clients multiply, planning and preparation become luxuries, don't they? We have so much to do and feel the need to act faster. But planning requires you to do the opposite. So it seldom feels urgent."

"Yes, I think I see what you're saying," I said. "Sounds to me like flying with The Eagle, as you put it, is where the important stuff – the Big Picture – is worked out. Is that it?"

"That's it exactly!" he exclaimed, his eyes flashing in the lamplight. "We have so much to do every minute of every day. Yet there is so little time available, it seems. So we need to go more slowly and discover that, like magic, this actually *creates* time."

Then he stood up and walked across his office. Following his movements, I noticed that the night sky was momentarily brightened every few seconds

He smiled at the sights outside, and went on. "Flying with The Eagle in Sector 2, we can prevent problems arising. For example, we can develop our skills and knowledge; we can spend time honestly listening when our child needs us to be completely, mentally present.

"All of these activities – the planning, the thinking, the exercising, the spiritual development – all of these are classic Sector 2 activities; yet they're too easy to push aside for a million things that feel more urgent.

"I'd say The Eagle is where the quality of our life is formed."

Thinking out loud, I murmured, "So, journal-keeping is a typical Eagle activity. But where does writing my book fit in? I have a deadline, but it is also very important to me. Which Sector should that be in?"

Turning back from the window he replied, "You're going to need to work that question through yourself, Jonathan. But don't be dismayed. By the end of this evening, you'll have all the clues you need to help you decide."

Just then we heard a hubbub coming from the hall.

"Sounds as if the others are ready to set off," he said, opening the office door. "We'll have to continue this in the car on the way. Hey! It looks chilly tonight. I hope you're prepared to wrap up warm."

"Me? I was raised a country lad on Hertfordshire farmland. This is nothing compared to the chill we felt back then on Guy Fawkes' nights."

Scarved, gloved and booted, we rode alone in his car, the rest of the family ahead of us in convoy.

I was still determined to take notes, using the reading light in his glove compartment.

"So, where were we?" he said to himself. "Ah yes. Let's move on to Sector 3."

"Now, this is where many lives and businesses lose their way."

I carefully labelled the third Sector and continued scribbling as he spoke.

"Sector 3 is The Chicken.

"Now, The Chicken is deceptive. It looks much like The Rooster. But rushing around in this Sector, our lives become crammed with those things that feel urgent but are seldom important. If we try to live our lives driven by The Rooster in sector 1, this is where we end up: headless and panicking in The Chicken.

"Interruptions and lots of noise are at the heart of The Chicken's life. Email is a classic Chicken time-consumer. Because they have been sent with such speed, they take on the guise of being urgent. But with email and many phone calls too, you can be governed by other people's musings, passing fancies and casual questions. You find yourself clucking around, trying to cram what is important to you around other people's jokes, newsletters, latest offers and seemingly critical seminars."

I nodded thinking of the barrage of emails that bore down upon me every time I switched on my home PC.

"It's all very enticing," he continued, "and it can stop us living with purpose. Telephone calls are similar, particularly if we leave our mobiles on. Everybody and their grandmother intrude to carve our lives into thin salami slices, leaving pitifully infrequent moments of quiet sanity. No wonder we can feel as if we're falling apart!"

"Well, that covers everything, doesn't it?" I said, slightly confused. "But what feathered friend can be left for Sector 4?"

"Well, Sector 4, that's The Magpie," he answered, smiling at my obvious confusion. "Let me explain why."

Our concentration was broken as we gasped at an enormous explosion of green stars low in the sky before us.

"The Magpie has developed the reputation of being a thief, lining its nest with its ill-gotten gains. Sector 4 is definitely a thief. Here, the precious stuff of life is frittered away," he continued slowly and deliberately. "Time-wasting and escaping from reality fall into this Sector."

"How do you mean, 'escaping'?" I asked.

"The most obvious example of escapism, and, in my view, the greatest time-waster of all must be television.

"What else regurgitates so much trivia, so much that is meaningless mental and emotional fast food? I once heard it likened to 'chewing gum for the mind'. It keeps your brain busy whilst providing minimal nourishment. And that only describes the best of what's on offer!" I could hear his breathing quicken.

I smiled. "You sound pretty passionate about this."

"I am," he retorted. "Whilst it's a miraculous tool, it has the hypnotic power to stop people living, and cause them to sit, merely observing life. It's a classic Magpie, weekly stealing hours of life from hundreds of millions of people."

"I hadn't thought of it like that," I said. "But coming back to managing myself in the office: I agree that it's easy to get caught up in stuff that happens to cross my desk. The most enticing are those things that seem to gain me popularity."

I could see his brow crease in surprise. "That's a keen insight. Popularity tends to be a great temptation where time and energy are concerned."

I heard the crunch of gravel as we swung off the road into the Lingfield racecourse car park.

"So, Jonathan, have you grasped the point about choosing carefully which bird you want to flock with?"

"Phew!" I puffed, undoing my seatbelt. "It's a lot to take in. Is that it? Is Lesson Number 7 complete?"

"Not quite," he chuckled. "I want to make sure that you have the best tools at your disposal for the next few months; there's time for one more rule."

"Okay. Bring it on. But I'm warning you, I'm not sure how much more my brain can handle."

We were still sitting in the warmth of the car, me with pen in hand, while the rest of the family bustled over to the rails, the children jumping in anticipation of the ritual of lighting the huge bonfire.

"There's a second principle and practice that goes against 'To Do' lists. It's another part of the **Seventh Law**; it's called '**Looking Through The Lens of The Week**'."

He looked at me, smiled and continued.

"Take your Day Planner or diary and open it to the month overview," he said, nodding at me to do just that.

"Now, look ahead at the next week. Right, imagine for a moment that there were no meetings scheduled yet. Imagine the week was a blank page. So, what you do now is to take a blank sheet of A4 lined notepaper and list the days of that week down the left hand column."

I struggled to balance and shuffle pad and planner on my lap.

"That's it," he said, when I was settled. "Now, take up to three Eagle projects – they're important, but don't crow at you like Roosters, remember – and schedule in some time for those during that week."

"Okay." I mumbled. "Let's see. I reckon running in the mornings and writing my journal at night fit in there."

"Yes. Now, what about projects that have an even less immediate payback?" he challenged.

"Oh I see. Well, I was thinking of setting a schedule of training sessions for Steve, my immediate assistant. I aim to teach him things that he doesn't have to know immediately so that he can take on more responsibility."

"That's more like it. And you need to define a start and finish time for each one.

"Wonderful. Now take your first three most urgent and important tasks – Rooster activities – and schedule them around your Sector 2, Eagle projects."

I could see the week taking shape in front of me. I had to produce a proposal for a prospective client by the next Friday. I also had to report back to my largest client about the progress of recruiting six technical consultants for his telecommunications project. This meant first meeting with the support team responsible for searching our database for candidates.

And I had to start writing the next chapter of my book!

He continued. "I can imagine that you already had some tasks scheduled for that week. So ask yourself whether what was previously scheduled is more or less important than the Rooster or Eagle projects that you've just entered. If less, then move them."

Within a few seconds, my week was restructured.

"Can you see," he asked, "how matters that have the greatest long term impact on your life become an integral part of each week?"

I closed my pad and planner and shifted around to look at him. "So let me get this right. The essence of the 'Looking Through the Lens' rule is to '**Plan by the week, not by the day**'."

"That's it Jonathan. That's the way to make sure that Sector 2, Eagle activities don't stay stuck on your wish list."

I looked away from him and tried to focus on the rising noises and flashes of colour outside.

"Ironic, isn't it?" I laughed, sourly. "The most important thing – person – in my life doesn't get a place in my diary."

"That's why we keep journals," he replied softly.

Together we heard the eruption of screams and whistles and turned to see a colossal bonfire burst into flames, accompanied by shattering explosions and cascades of multiplying rockets.

"Well this is a huge public display," he said. "So we'll need Louise's tomato soup, baked potatoes and hot dogs to keep us going."

Our boots slipped deep into the churned mud as we followed the family from the packed car park towards the fenced field, where the roar of the bonfire greeted us. Guy Fawkes' effigy blazed to the mixed hoots and cries of the crowd.

Following the lead of open-mouthed children, we roared and cheered at the profusion of noise, lights and colours until our throats were sore.

The evening drew to a close as the 1812 overture cannoned into the night from the surrounding speakers. I stared through the swirling air, now wreathed and pungent with gunpowder, and I wondered.

Perhaps, somewhere near another bonfire stood Naomi, her face tilted to the cloudless heavens. I romanticised that if she were gazing at the same dancing stars, then the sky would have to be our only rendezvous.

And I smiled wistfully.

LESSONS LEARNED

- There are four sectors where we live out our lives:
- Roosters: those projects which demand our attention and are likely to be pretty important
- Eagles: those projects which have the deepest long term impact on our lives but seldom seem urgent
- Chickens: projects which seem urgent at the time but looking back have very little importance or benefit to our happiness
- Magpies: activities where our lives are wasted away;
- Learning from Andrew this weekend has been like stepping out of a fog into bright sunlight. That's how it feels when I think about planning my life 'On Purpose'. I can't wait to get back to work to try these ideas out;
- As each month progresses, I understand why they call Andrew 'The Professor'!
- I've learned again how important it is to prioritise time with your family. Andrew relishes experiences where they can laugh and play together. I want to remember that, for when I become a dad.

PROGRESS TRACKER

- Running four miles every other day; I'm fitter than I have been for years;
- This is the sixth month of paying the IVA. I've paid back £6,000;
- This is the fourth month of me paying tithing into my building society account;
- This is my second month of paying into a savings account;
- This is my ninth month in this job;
- I'm earning pro rata £90k pa;
- I feel much more confident now about entering the property market even though I have little spare cash for making a deposit – a point which I've been too embarrassed to mention;
- The mystery of my connection with Chrissie continues to grow;
- It's almost six months since I spoke to Naomi. I wonder what the future holds? I wonder if we'll ever meet again?

David J Scarlett

Chapter 11
Clinching The Property Deal

Saturday, 8th December

I huddled into a sheltered corner of the King's Cross Thameslink platform, recalling the telephone conversation just 24 hours before.

Chrissie had answered her mobile after just two rings.

"Oh, hi Jonathan. Thanks for returning my call." She sounded breathless.

"What can I do for you?" I asked. She wanted me to go to Hertfordshire the very next day, to Elstree.

"Meet me at eleven outside the station," she said.

She had been quite firm. I had to be there the next day, Saturday. There was a decision to be made, and I was needed urgently. It all sounded rather cloak and dagger.

Fortunately, my train was on time and I found a seat easily. I took this as a good omen despite the terrible weather. Sipping at my plastic cup of mediocre coffee, I settled back in my seat and watched the heavy grey clouds moving to blot out the clear winter sky. Small bullets of sleet began to strike and slither across the windows as we rattled onward.

Gripping my Day Planner, I thought how odd it was to be visiting the town where I had been to school. I hadn't returned to the area for 17 years. I felt strange, as if the train was taking me back in time, back to the time when my life was ruled by tradition, discipline and towering teachers.

I recognised Chrissie's wide grin as I stepped into the cold bleakness. There she was, leaning against her car with Matthew waving as he caught sight of me.

She started talking animatedly as soon as we pulled onto the High Street.

"I know I didn't tell you much on the phone. But I wanted you to see this property before we went into any detail. Time is short because the agents will only hold it until Monday, when other offers are considered."

"Wow! There's that much competition?" I exclaimed.

"Yep, although it's not surprising," she said. "The owner was in his eighties and died recently, leaving the house in a bit of a state, poor fellow. His children live hours away, around the Manchester area as well as overseas. They seem to be struggling with all of the probate problems. We're assuming that this property is just a nuisance to them, and the asking price is unusually low. Ah, here we are."

We had pulled into a quiet cul-de-sac lined with spacious, almost identical houses, which looked as if they dated back to before the last War. The front gardens and lawns were neat and well preserved. Most of the properties had reasonably new windows and front doors. All of that only served to expose the ugliness of the house now facing us as we clambered out of the car.

The windowpanes were caked in dirt. The paint on both the windows and doors was not only peeling and flaking, but black patches showed that they were probably rotting.

I turned to look at Matthew as he ran his keen eye across the frontage.

"Those windows'll have to go. That's sad; we'll never recover that cost when we sell. Ah! Here comes the agent now."

Within twenty minutes we had been through every grubby room, and Matthew had pointed out the main areas where the greatest work was needed. I watched as Chrissie's keen eye picked out points that she had missed in her earlier inspection.

Stepping gratefully out of the gloom, we stood together, our backs against the moss-covered brick wall.

Turning to Matthew, Chrissie voiced our question, "Matt?"

"Yeah. It's good," he replied slowly. "We can make large margins on the kitchen and bathroom and on the purchase price. The vendors are eager and the agent glad to have it refurbished. He has two other properties in the crescent that would be easier to sell without this eyesore."

"Let's do it," snapped Chrissie. "Jonathan, why don't we talk about money and see if you want a part of the action?"

Chrissie had arranged with a close friend that we use one of the meeting rooms in a nearby office centre – at no cost. I was to learn that was typical of her cheekiness.

Soon we were relaxing over several plates of sandwiches prepared by the office centre staff who were expecting us.

"Jonathan, Matt and I are excited by the possibilities in that property. Matt reckons we can turn the work around in eight weeks. Even before we finish the work, we can invite buyers to start viewing." She paused to top up our coffee.

"You mentioned that you hoped to raise £20,000 from property by the end of May as part of your plan. Is that right?" she asked, looking at me over the rim of her glass. Then, before I could respond she added, "Let's work out if this property could create that amount of net profit for you, after we've taken our share. If it can, that'll be at least £40k between us. Not bad for a few weeks' work, eh?"

Listening to her, I was hovering somewhere between excitement and panic. "Well, I won't be penalised if I don't get that amount. But I've accepted the challenge, and I'm determined to beat it."

"In our last conversation you mentioned that you only had £1,000 cash to spare?" quizzed Matthew.

"Yes. I'm committed to setting aside a tithe from my gross income. Now that I've started that, I certainly don't wish to stop. It's become a matter of integrity. The rest goes on the IVA – the voluntary arrangement to repay my debt. Meanwhile, I'm managing to live pretty frugally and save a little."

"Hmm," Matthew continued. "We need to put down a deposit of £16,500 between us. Now, our proposal is that we split the profits

70/30 since Chrissie and I are putting in all the time, labour, materials and expertise."

"That seems fair," I said.

"In which case," continued Matthew, "that's a deposit of about £5,000 needed from you. Chrissie has a sense – an intuition, if you will – that we should go in with you. For some reason she is dead keen to get you going on this property business, and I've learned that there is no point arguing with my wife."

I laughed. I knew just what he meant.

"But we need to make an offer by Monday lunchtime. That means you stumping up the money by then." He waited for my answer.

"Look," I responded. "I don't want to leave you hanging on promises and whims. Whilst my income is increasing steeply, I probably can't raise more than £3,000 in total by the end of this month, if I wish to continue with my tithing commitment.

Matthew looked at Chrissie, who was busy staring at the table and playing with a vol-au-vent on her plate. She looked worried as she lost herself in thought.

Eventually, she raised her head slowly and looked at me. "Look, there's every reason why I shouldn't go along with you," she said, somewhat harshly.

I was bemused. One minute she was bending over backwards for me and the next she seemed against me. This was the first time she'd been reticent. She didn't seem to be referring to my lack of cash. It was something else. But what?

"And yet," she continued, looking hard at Matthew, her voice mellowing. "I say we cover Jonathan's cost and deduct the balance by the time we close."

A few seconds elapsed as they looked at each other.

"I'm comfortable with that," seconded Matthew finally.

"Thanks, both of you," I breathed, hardly realising how tense I had become in the last minute. "But tell me, exactly how much profit do you hope to make out of this? You said £40K. Did you pull that figure out of the air?"

"Let's see . . ." said Chrissie, who became lost to us for a number of seconds whilst scribbling figures on her pad. "Yes, here we go. Purchase price £166,000 plus all fees and stamp duty, which brings the purchase cost to around £172,000. We reckon that we could eventually sell for about £260,000. That's nearly £90,000 profit. From that, take the cost of improvements, plus all running costs, including mortgage interest during those months. That'll probably come to between £40,000 and £45,000. I make the eventual profit a cool £45,000 profit to share between us – £13,500 for you, £31,500 for us."

"Well, it's not the £20,000 I was dreaming of. But with no deposit and someone else doing all the work, I couldn't ask for more than that. If we can do it in twelve to fourteen weeks," I thought out loud, "that's not far short of £3,500 profit per week between us. Pretty good returns, I'd say."

"Want to come into the property business, Jonathan?" she laughed.

"Let me get over the next few months, and I might take you up on that," I answered.

They drove me back to the station with Chrissie dominating the conversation in her ebullient way.

Pulling into the station forecourt, Chrissie opened her door to step out and promptly sat back in her seat. Twisting around, she looked at me, concern on her face. "Jonathan Broom. I've been unfair to you, and it's time to clear up your confusion."

"About you seeming to recognise me, you mean?" I asked, feeling strangely vulnerable.

"Yes. The fact is I've seen you numerous times. I even remember being subjected to your photo for months on end. But it's possible that you never caught more than the merest glance of me."

I was already starting to feel flustered. But she pressed on.

"If I were to tell you that my maiden name was Stewart, what would that do for you?"

The name was horribly familiar, and yet I struggled to recall why, until the memory hit me. I felt myself change from flushed embarrassment to pale-faced horror as my stomach lurched.

"You remember her, don't you?" She wasn't smiling. "Melissa Stewart was my little sister. And you . . . you hurt her badly, Jonathan Broom!"

A strangled murmur crawled from my throat. "I'm so sorry," was the only feeble response I could muster.

"So am I," she replied. "For crying out loud, she was a child, Jonathan, barely seventeen-years-old. Your behaviour was nothing less than callous. You ought to be strung up!"

"I was scared of being tied down. I was twenty-five-years-old and scared," I pleaded.

Now there was sharpness in her voice. "And you don't think she was scared when you packed her off home when the thrill of trying to run away with her had worn thin?"

Desperate for something to say, I asked, "How is she now?"

"Oh, don't you worry yourself; she's fine. You already know her pregnancy was a false alarm. She's only recently left university and is at the start of a promising career. In fact she's madly in love and has just got engaged."

I felt horribly sick, sad and more than a little confused.

"Chrissie, I'm so sorry," I breathed again. "But, if you knew who I was, why on earth did you agree to help me? I don't understand."

"No, you don't, do you?" she smiled weakly. For a long while she said nothing and looked clear through me, hardly registering my existence.

Then she continued. "I suppose Andrew has that effect on people. He's a persuasive fellow, Jon, and I've grown to trust his judgement. I must admit that I'm impressed by what has happened to you recently. With Andrew's influence this is my way of saying that I forgive you."

"I'm not sure what else to say," I mumbled again. "But I beg you not to tell Andrew about this."

"What do you take me for?" she said. "Now that you know, let's leave the past behind us, shall we?"

"Thank you," was the best response I could manage.

LESSONS LEARNED

- The Law of The Harvest rules consistently. What we sow, that shall we reap. Truly, the corny sayings, such as 'What goes around comes around' have their source in experience;
- Our behaviour catches up with us: whether internally or externally; sooner or later, we will be called upon to face the results of our actions. Who could possibly have predicted that my life would cross with Chrissie's like this?
- Getting into the property market is not as easy as the wealth gurus on the internet would have us believe;
- Having said that, property continues to be a great investment – as long as you know your stuff and understand the risks.

PROGRESS TRACKER

- Now that I've solved the mystery of Chrissie's knowledge of me, I almost wish I hadn't. This was a hard lesson;
- I'm involved in my first property investment deal, which means that for the first time, I can see the possibility of paying back £100k in 12 months;
- I'm now in the seventh month of paying the IVA. I've paid back £7,000;
- I can hardly believe that I've been paying into my tithing account for five months;
- This is my third month of paying into a savings account;
- This is my tenth month in this job;
- I'm earning pro rata £90k pa;
- It's been almost seven long months since I last spoke to Naomi.

Chapter 12
Discovering The Spirit of Christmas

Saturday, 15th December

Whatever your feelings may be about working in London, there is a magic that pervades this historic city on a December evening. Long before the crowds leave for their damp journey home, the sleeted pavements reflect the lights of a city slipping early into the dark of winter's night. The air is still and expectant, and the streets and buildings reflect the mood of this strangely addictive month.

I was determined not to let the Silly Season affect my business performance and had booked as many appointments as I could with strategic clients.

It was precisely because others around me were increasing their social activity that I pushed my team to improve their business performance. We effectively had two weeks, instead of four, to produce revenue.

Our sense of excitement and energy was maintained by some good news received in the last week in November. The contract we thought we had lost was surprisingly awarded to us. News on the grapevine suggested that our competitor had clinched the deal on the basis of a single relationship with one of their managers. However, the individual in question had just announced her resignation, which left the client high and dry.

Our team was the natural successor, and the deal was signed on the first Monday in December.

We had already completed two months of the Winter Revenue Sales Competition. I was one of half a dozen people in the frame for a one-week holiday in New York, and I was determined to finish the first half of the competition period in a strong position.

I hoped that 'somebody up there' was watching over me!

Heading home in the stuffy Northern Line underground carriage, my normal escape into a fast-paced novel had given way to musings and scribblings. I was surprised at how quickly my book was beginning to emerge from a jumble of thoughts and memories.

During the evenings, having banished the enticing Magpie activity of television, I sat at my home PC, writing instead. And as I wrote, the unfolding story gave me the energy to carry on. I surprised myself by how little I missed staring at TV all evening and soon realised it had drained me of energy rather than relaxed me.

Closing my journal for the night, I considered how in two days I would be travelling to East View for the last time this year. I could hardly believe that I had learned so much, and come so far.

Before drifting off I thought about the request from Mum earlier in the week.

She had asked me to help them out on Christmas Day, serving Christmas dinners at a shelter for the homeless. A sense of pride, mingled with discomfort, welled inside me as I pictured myself working alongside them.

On the other hand it seemed a reasonable way to spend a day that, for me, had lost much of its magic.

I indulged in a smile as I recalled the tickets for London's Albert Hall tucked inside my wallet. Mum, in particular, would revel in the famous Christmas Carol Concert that was my surprise for them this year.

For some reason Andrew had changed our monthly meeting to the third Saturday of the month. Mysteriously, he had asked me to arrive at lunchtime and stay overnight. It was strange to think that Naomi would be coming home for Christmas the following week, and yet I'd be as far from her as ever.

The wind that gusted on the open dual carriageways south of Croydon threatened to push me from lane to lane. That, together with the unshifting gloom of the day and a slow horse-trailer, combined to demand my full attention.

Lunch with Andrew, Louise, Daniel and Jessica was a lively affair, largely because of Bryony, wildly energetic and the oldest of the granddaughters.

"Come on, everyone," I ventured, "What's the secret about this evening?"

Jessica's eyes widened in merriment whilst everybody smiled knowingly.

"Tonight, Jon," she began, "you help us to bring the house to life!"

"Hmm, sounds interesting. Do I get to know more or am I to be left in blissful ignorance?"

"Mate, 'blissful' won't be the word you'll use by the time we've finished," chuckled Daniel.

I shook my head. I couldn't wait to see what secret custom I was being roped into.

We worked outside for the rest of the afternoon and long into the evening. Although the wind had weakened, it was still enough to make our efforts a struggle.

We clambered up and down ladders and squeezed into trees stringing up miles of miniature lights. Mercifully, a brief squall of cold rain passed quickly but left slippery branches, which led to a few skinned knees.

The results were worth every aching limb.

At precisely 7:30 pm the lights were switched on to a chorus of cheering and laughter with whistling from Daniel.

Around the mansion trees were ablaze and laden with a haze of the tiniest lights. Their magical effect on both house and grounds was accentuated by their reflections in the vast array of windows causing the air to shimmer.

Next, half-remembered tunes rose from beneath the eaves, which had been cleverly rigged with speakers.

For a few minutes everyone stopped what they were doing and stood quite still to marvel at our creation. Even the children knew not to break the spell.

East View was alive. And so was I, in spite of the fact that Naomi was missing.

I turned to Andrew in a whisper. "I know you've asked me here to learn another principle. But I was wondering, am I supposed to take notes, 'cos I can see a metaphor coming?"

Looking at me, he smiled and paused before replying, "All I ask is that you share your thoughts with me by the end of the evening."

Doing so later was to prove difficult.

From kitchen and dining room, through lounge and reading room, hilarity and conversation filled the house. In addition to several relatives, numerous friends appeared to add to the mood and the bustle. With each greeting I couldn't help but feel flattered by the warm manner in which Andrew and Louise introduced me.

Uttering feeble protests, I was carried along joining in silly games that I thought I had left behind in primary school. Over here, fully grown men giggled helplessly, barging each other out of the last Musical Chair. Over there, charades collapsed into chaos as competition gave way to over-acting. In this room children ventured to learn the 'Jurassic' art of Squeak Piggy Squeak, whilst through that room I was embarrassed beyond reason as the centre of attention in Blind Man's Buff.

As the hours slipped by, I felt increasingly less like an observer. The evening, steeped with English tradition, progressed from stage to stage without sign or instruction. Everyone seemed to understand the rhythm of events instinctively, and if I became confused, a hand would drag me into the thick of the action.

Later I found myself inveigled into singing carols. As we gravitated towards the piano in the reading room, even I recognised the sound of basses and tenors joining with sopranos and, what I believe you'd call, altos each slipping into their parts as if carefully practised. Standing by Andrew, I found myself holding a booklet of words and music, which had mysteriously fallen into my hands.

With a newly decked Christmas tree behind us and old English classics in amongst the better-known carols, I felt as if we had been teleported into a Dickensian scene.

Later, I stood with the family at their open front door, bidding goodnight to their other visitors before following Andrew into the quiet of the reading room.

"Well?" was all he needed to say.

"I must have been all of ten years old tonight." I was struggling. "But something else happened, and I simply don't have the words to explain. It was about much more than the lights and the games and the singing."

Andrew studied the flickering fire before turning to me. His countenance seemed to match the mood of the evening.

"Those things that touch our lives most deeply can seldom be described easily with words," he said.

"There is a special Spirit during this season that falls upon us like a warm cloak, if we allow it," he continued carefully.

"It lies neither in spending money, nor in partying. It's not found in the oblivion of drinking, nor in the coarseness of throwing aside caution and doing things we invariably regret the next morning. The magic lies mostly in simplicity, in becoming quiet inside as we welcome its mystery and allow ourselves to be touched by its tenderness."

I was mesmerised by his words as his face and greying hair were caught by the glow of the fire. I eased myself into the comfort of the elegant cream settee.

"As we grow up we tend to 'put away childish things' as Paul wrote in the Bible."

He stooped over to alter the setting of the flame effect on the fire. Then he continued.

"But what Paul was talking about was being emotionally and spiritually *childish* – that is never getting past that adolescent state of spiritual rebellion and intellectual arrogance. We should never confuse that with being *childlike*: that is, setting aside our adult pride and being willing to listen to that whispering which says, 'something quite wonderful – something outside of my understanding – is happening here, and I need to be open to its influence'.

"Does that make any sense?"

I spoke quietly in response. "Yes. Yes, I believe it does."

"This is my reality," he went on. "It's at times like this, with my family and close friends, that I remember why I am here. This evening symbolises the whole point of everything I do. Sensing this kind of magic, or spirit, shows me that I am getting things right in my life, and then I'm close to heaven on earth. When my heart is touched by such simple pleasures, then I agree with Dickens, 'these are the very best of times'."

"But surely you feel sad that Barnaby and Naomi aren't here this year?" I asked.

"Yes, I do," he answered with difficulty. "Barnaby will start missing home terribly right now. For Naomi this is the first time that she's missed the 'lighting of the trees'. But we discussed it with her, and she wanted you to have this experience."

"Oh, for crying out loud! Why did she do that? I'm so sorry." I felt terrible that I had kept her away while I was enjoying myself.

"I'm surprised you need to ask. And don't be sorry; it was her idea," came his reply. "Don't worry. We'll be having a special family gathering just for her next Monday evening.

"Tonight, I wanted you to sense this spirit for yourself. You know, this could well be the most important lesson you learn this year."

"I'm glad that I was here tonight," I said, looking at him square in the eyes.

"Me too, Jonathan," he nodded. "Me too."

LESSONS LEARNED

- The deepest, sweetest rewards are not to be found in living to excess, nor in the achievement of accolades and wealth. Rather, they result from investing deeply in our relationships;
- Even in the midst of enjoying 'good times', we gain more by being still inside. There is so little time and so much to do; we need at times to go more slowly;
- Often, we are stuck forever in the throes of a teenage spiritual rebellion. We reject the time-tested wisdom of generations before us, without replacing that with coherent answers to life's biggest questions. We confuse this childishness with the emotional maturity of being childlike.

PROGRESS TRACKER

- I'm managing to be both disciplined and consistent with my money;
- At work, I feel highly respected, and I'm enjoying unquestionable success;
- This is the seventh month of paying the IVA. I've paid back £7,000;
- I've been paying into my tithing account for five months;
- This is my third month of paying into a savings account, and I've already saved £1,200;
- This is my tenth month in this job;
- I'm earning pro rata £90k pa;
- It's been exactly seven months since I last spoke to Naomi. Despite my considerable successes and progress, the emptiness inside has been slow in filling.

Chapter 13
Enjoy The Ride

Friday, 21st December

I smiled as the tinny blare of Christmas carols echoed from one of the small roads across the High Street. I recognised the sound – it was the Rotary Club car, probably towing Santa's sleigh back to the North Pole after handing out sweets to the local kids.

In spite of the icy drizzle, I felt my spirits lifted as the music evoked sharp, sweet memories of childhood. I was heading home from the office, late again but anticipating a token half day in the office the following Monday before a welcome Christmas break.

Neither did the chill and mist seem to dampen the spirits of some of the passers-by, many of whom were already laughing a little too loudly, walking a little too deliberately and cheering at each other across the High Street.

The Christmas season was pouring in and out of pubs before the night had hardly begun.

I noted how very different this was to the world I had glimpsed at East View only six days previously. I pulled my attention back to the present with some sadness.

I remember smiling at the group of youths who were grinning and waving as we approached each other.

I remember nodding in response to their bellowed Christmas greetings.

I remember mumbling "excuse me" as they started to separate to let me through.

I remember my confusion at the blinding flash and the noise exploding from inside my head.

I remember noticing little things, like how cold and terribly hard the concrete was on my face in the winter; or how strange the shops looked, viewed sideways.

I remember wondering why my body and head were in a chaos of pain as voices screamed furiously around me and legs and arms blurred in turmoil.

I remember making feeble attempts to lash out at whatever I could see.

But I remember very little after that.

The voices were muffled. There were no words, just sounds. But there were shapes, dark and hazy. I think I recognised one shadow, and I think I was glad. Somewhere, from a distance, I heard a low cry, a moan, a sob. Then it was dark again, and I heard nothing for a while.

Something was wet on my face, my mouth, my eye. My fingers gripped a hand. A voice spoke softly and kindly.

"Welcome back." It was a woman's voice. A voice I knew. "You had us worried, Jon."

I heard myself trying to talk. But the face I saw swimming before me was a young face, a lovely face. I tried hard to think where that face fitted into my life. But concentrating was a struggle.

"You certainly kept me on my toes, Mister Broom," the Lovely Face said.

I could feel my hand being squeezed. "But you're back now," said the voice-that-I-knew.

I tried to tell the face and the voices that I was tired…so very tired. But they slipped away again.

When I finally awoke, something was being pushed between my teeth.

"No, don't bite the straw!" said Lovely Face, leaning over me. "Try sucking through it. You need to drink."

I tried to turn my head, looking for the other voice. But the pain that shot through my head and back took my breath away.

"Jon, you're doing fine. But don't try to move just yet." Mum's voice! She hovered into view just over the shoulder of Lovely Face, who was busy doing something to my wet head.

I tried to talk again although my lips wouldn't work. I grunted out some noises, which sounded broadly like, "Where am I?"

As Mum sat down beside my bed, I heard a door close and assumed that Lovely Face was leaving. Soon the room was quiet, and I felt my hand being held again.

I could do little more than listen as she spoke. "You've been unconscious for two days. You're in St George's Hospital now. You were almost home. One of the neighbours saw what happened and had the police fetch us. So, we were able to go with you in the ambulance. I've been sleeping here; the hospital has been so good."

She explained how people in the street had witnessed the attack in the gloomy winter night and had run to help. But it was over in seconds. Apparently, my wallet had been taken, together with my mobile phone.

I tried to turn my head again and noticed for the first time that my right eye was covered. I let go of Mum's hand and tried to touch my face. I could feel wrapping – bandages – and pain shot through my eye and the side of my head.

"What's happened to me?" I mumbled slowly, feeling fear rising like bile inside my stomach.

"The doctors say you're doing fine," she replied, her face looking strained.

I could feel my lips heavy and swollen.

"Need to know, Mum," I croaked dryly.

"They say that it will take a little while for your eye to heal. It was cut pretty badly, Jon."

"Will it work?" I was struggling to put the words in order. "Will I, uh, see again?"

She looked at me. There was silence between us. A tear slipped down her face. "I'm not sure." Her hand tightened on mine. "But there's every hope."

"I see," was all I managed, looking away from her and concentrating hard on the ceiling.

For a long while we were both silent. I was finding it difficult to hold onto a single thought. I rolled my head to the side and tried to look at her again. It was then that I noticed the tinsel hovering incongruously over her.

"Christmas?" I asked, my throat burning as I spoke.

She smiled. "In two days' time." Her features collapsed into sadness again.

"Merry Christmas," I groaned. I was surprised to hear my bitterness.

"Oh, Jon," she whispered. "You'll be home soon enough. And we'll be here Christmas Day. We'll be here every day until you're out."

"Like to sleep now," I whispered.

"Of course you would," she responded and continued holding my hand as I closed my eyes.

The daylight hours crawled by as doctors came to prod and murmur. Bandages were carefully removed and replaced and small, burning lights were shone into both of my eyes. I shouted involuntarily when liquid was dropped onto my right eye, the burning sending my head and shoulders into spasms until I collapsed in exhaustion. I grew accustomed to the companionship of the monitor blinking beside my bed.

The Christmas crescendo was rising as I heard familiar – sometimes laughable – music coming from different points along the corridor. The memory of that wonderful singing at East View returned to mock me, and I was gripped by a sense of helplessness I hadn't felt for some time.

It was whilst touching my bandages and considering the worst possible outcomes of my injuries that I sensed a body beside my bed. Strange, I wasn't expecting Mum yet. Carefully, I turned my head to the right to see Nathan smiling down at me.

But it wasn't Nathan who spoke. The voice came from the other side of the room. "Hi Jon. Merry Christmas. How're you feeling, mate?" Nathan looked away from me and across my bed. I rolled my head to the left.

It was Daniel! I could feel myself beginning to grin, and my lips splitting as I tried to control my mouth. "What're you doing here?" I croaked.

"It's Monday – Christmas Eve – and what better way to avoid the last minute panic at home than to jump in the car, drive up to London and visit ol' friends?" He rubbed his hands together and chuckled. "But, look at you!" he went on without the slightest hint of sympathy. "Looks like you've done three rounds with a rhino!"

"Daniel!" said Nathan. "Take it easy on the poor guy!"

"Sorry, Jon," responded Daniel. "But, tell us, buddy; how d'you feel?"

I looked away from him and rolled onto my back. "I'll know better when I find out whether I'll get my eye back," I said, sounding a little grim.

There was tension as we lapsed into silence, and Nathan coughed. "I guess you're worried about getting back to work," he said, filling the void.

"Yeah, I guess," was my lethargic reply.

"What else, then?" asked Nathan.

I was silent again. The crack at the edge of the ceiling formed an almost perfect outline of a woman's face. I felt a warm tear slide down the left side of my face and into my ear.

"It's Naomi, isn't it?" said Daniel quietly.

"Yes," I answered, my mouth only half in control and my jaw aching. "The Beautiful Naomi. And me blind in one eye," I stopped for a few breaths. "And scars all over my face." I could hear the anger in my voice.

"Have they told you how bad the damage is?" asked Nathan too quickly.

"Uh-huh," I spoke slowly, stumbling on the words. "Doctor Prod-It showed me this morning." I stopped to rest my mouth. "When they took off the bandage I couldn't see a thing… with my right eye." I paused again, to try to lick my lips. "And the right side of my face," my hand went involuntarily to my bandages, "looks like someone has…slashed it…with a bottle."

I heard something scrape on the floor and turned slightly to see Daniel pulling a chair close to the bed. "You wanna know something?" he began.

I attempted to nod my head, then waited.

"I know it will heal, Jon," he said earnestly.

"How d'you know?" I croaked back.

"I don't know how I know," he said, shrugging. "I just know."

"Right," was my sarcastic reply.

Daniel folded his arms and smiled wryly.

"What are the chances of going back to work soon?" asked Nathan.

I didn't even turn to face him. "Nothing wrong with my legs. Apart from some lumps and bruises," I said. "Hurts to breathe though."

Nathan walked over to the window behind Daniel and fiddled with the blinds. "Your mum said that your ribs took a pretty good kicking," he said, "but nothing broken, I hear."

"Lucky, me," I said, with a sigh.

There was embarrassed silence again.

I was about to speak, feeling guilty about my reaction, when Nurse Lovely Face bustled in, all smiles and energy. She shot her disarming smile at me.

I grabbed the moment. "Guys, meet Nurse Lovely…" I began.

"Bryant," she interrupted.

"Is that it?" grinned Daniel. "No first name, Nurse?"

She tried to look stern, planting her hands on her hips. "Rosalind. Rosie."

"Well, Nurse Rosie," Nathan joined in, "thanks for looking after our Jonathan. Seems to me you're spoiling him rotten."

She waved her hand dismissively. Then, looking at me, head slightly to one side, she said, "I'll be off duty soon, so I'll say goodbye for now. You're making brilliant progress already. Healing really nicely. Must be that Miracle Man, I'd say."

"Miracle Man?" I was confused.

She produced a thermometer and shook it. Dutifully easing my mouth to let her take my temperature, I felt her take my arm and place her fingers on my pulse.

"Your mother came early this morning with a friend while you were still sleeping – sedated." She moved to the foot of my bed and started scribbling on a clipboard. "He put his hands on your head and said a prayer or something."

She stood beside Nathan. "Only took a few seconds. But it was very moving. I've not seen that done before. A 'blessing', he called it I think. Nice looking fellow he was," she raised her eyebrows in recollection, "with a short beard."

Then, she nodded at us, tucked a loose strand of fine, blonde hair behind her ear, reminded me that she'd be back to give me my tetanus injection and briskly strode out again.

"Ouch!" said Daniel. "Rather you than me with that injection. And a Merry Christmas to you, Nurse Rosie."

"The Prof," I said quietly.

"Of course," said Nathan. "That's typical of him: quietly turning up to give you a blessing of healing."

"I wish I had been awake," I moaned. "Good ol' Prof." I said the last word with some difficulty. "Got his life together. He's so, uh, content with…everything."

"And you're not," Nathan completed my thoughts.

"What do you think?" I snapped. "Things were going my way. There was hope." I touched my lip as it split again in my anger. I paused. "Maybe Naomi. And the debt."

"Then what?" queried Nathan, pulling up a chair to join Daniel.

"Then, I'd be happy, I guess." I sighed again.

"Oh, right. I see," said Nathan leaning back and crossing his legs. "You'd be happy when your three challenges were complete, you mean?"

"Well, yes." I couldn't see where the conversation was leading. "That's the whole point, isn't it?"

Daniel joined in. "Oh, I get where Nathan is going. You'd be happy 'when'."

"What are you lot talking about?" I was getting irritated quite apart from being frustrated by having to slur my words.

Daniel continued. "Something The Prof taught us a long time ago. People think they'll be happy 'when', like when some great thing happens for them."

"What's wrong with that?" I rasped, my throat dry again. Nathan went back to my bedside table and brought me the plastic cup with an angled straw. I was grateful.

"Well, his view is that's not what being happy is about," said Daniel. "He says you've gotta make friends with mortality, Jon."

"What on earth does that mean?" I said as I spat out the straw.

"Well," Nathan stepped in, "it's like M. Scott Peck said in his book *The Road Less Travelled*. The first sentence states: "Life is difficult."

"That's right," said Daniel. "The Prof taught us to recognise that life is tough. 'Get that straight in your head', he says, 'and you won't be shocked when the going gets rough' That's the first point."

Nathan took over. "Secondly, if we expect to be happy only when a special event or possession arrives, we're going to be seriously disappointed."

"If you're trying, er, to cheer me up, you're doing a lousy job." I reached across to put my cup down on the locker.

"Sorry mate," said Daniel sheepishly.

But Nathan pressed on getting off his chair and sitting himself on the edge of my bed. "I don't pretend to know how much pain you're in. But I guess this looks like a pretty scary time for you, right?"

I grunted in agreement.

He squinted at the bedspread as if he was trying hard to remember something, then continued. "Being truly happy isn't an event." He looked up again, his eyes alight. "It's how you are. It's a state of being. To understand what I mean, you start by thinking about the times when you were most happy."

He paused, willing me to search my memory before continuing. "I can tell you, of the times when I've been most happy, I'd say the best times were when I was looking out for others, not myself."

"Like your mission for the Church?" queried Daniel.

"Particularly that time," Nathan responded, nodding firmly at Daniel.

"Look, Jon," Daniel took over, "this might seem a lousy time to talk to you like this. But now we're on the subject…I've learned, it's not about looks or being popular or cool, really it isn't. Even though I know you're worried about how Naomi will feel about your eye and your face and everything."

"Wouldn't you be?" I shot back.

"A little," he nodded, "but how worried would depend upon what it was we found attractive about each other."

"The point is," interjected Nathan getting up from the bed and rubbing the back of his leg, "if you're building your happiness upon 'when this happens' or 'when she does that', you're going to be disappointed. That's handing control of your emotions to things outside of you. And it will always leave you feeling empty and cheated."

"Yeah, Jon," Daniel joined in again, "quoting The Prof. 'Our greatest joy often depends on how we respond to the most difficult times. It's about the quality of your character, not the quantity of what you receive.' I reckon these past few months have shown me, you're quite a character."

"Whoa! Get You!" I croaked. "Daniel the Philosopher."

"Hah!" he said triumphantly and rose from his seat. His voice softened uncharacteristically. "Right now, this might sound callous, but I'm convinced you're going to get better. So, it seems to me, this could be one of those times when you learn about 'enjoying the ride'."

He stuck out his large hand, and I eased my arm forward to grasp his. "Sorry, mate. We've gotta go. There's over-excited kids to put to bed and a long, long day ahead of us tomorrow."

Nathan stood still, crossing his arms and looking at me. "Think about it, Jon," he said. He opened the door, then turned back again. "Oh, and Jon," he was smiling.

"What now?" I immediately regretted the sigh of annoyance in my voice.

"I've seen Daniel when he's this certain before. If he knows that you're going to be all right, then I believe him. So I'm going to wish you a Peaceful Christmas."

I nodded with difficulty. "Thanks," I said, wishing they would stay longer. "Merry Christmas to you." Then, with some attempt at 'high fives' between us, they were gone.

My eyes drifted to the ceiling before I fell asleep. The optimism that was present when they were in the room quickly evaporated.

With only one functioning eye, I had to face the fact that life might never be the same. More painfully, I might as well give up hope of ever getting back together with Naomi.

With her gone my striving over the last few months began to seem so pointless.

LESSONS LEARNED

- Life is difficult. If we start with that assumption, then disappointments, even disasters, won't surprise us;
- If we're waiting for an event, the achievement of some goal, the acquisition of a desired item to bring us happiness, then we are setting ourselves up for disappointment. 'When I get this, I'll be happy' is a sure route to emptiness in life;
- The trick in life – or so says The Prof – is to embrace the roughness of mortality, and enjoy the ride. That would be a good trick to master!

PROGRESS TRACKER

- What has happened might stop my success at work in its tracks;
- I'm not sure what chance I now have in winning the sales competition;
- Having only paid £7,000 of my IVA, I would say that my injuries have put paid to my fulfilling my Three Challenges;
- Frankly, the one thing that has kept me going during these last seven months has been the hope of seeing Naomi again. Right now, the possibility seems less than remote.

Chapter 14
A Lifelong Stream of Profitable Clients

Saturday, 12th January

"*M*ind that barbed wire, fellas!"

One by one, the four of us gingerly negotiated the snow-soaked stile whilst the others held the barbs at bay. Only Andrew slipped but retained his dignity with his face inches above a frozen black puddle.

I was particularly sensitive to the barbs being near my face, so was even more careful than the rest.

My gaze swept the undulating fields, sprinkled lightly with snow. The air was clear, and our cold breath formed a hovering mist before us. The most obvious landmarks were a converted oast-house to the east and a pair of pointed church steeples stark against the bright fields to the south and west.

I had joined Daniel, Nathan and Andrew on their 'annual boys' walk', their way of burning off the excesses of Christmas and Boxing Day. This year they had asked me to join them and delayed the tradition until Naomi was back at university.

"'Ere, 'ave you taken a compass bearing, Red Leader, or are you going on instinct?" asked Daniel, only half smiling.

"You doubt me?" responded Nathan petulantly. "With that lunch waiting for us, you don't think I'd let us be late, do you?"

"No, guess that figures," Daniel conceded, taking the sting out of the conversation. "We'll let your stomach guide us."

Turning to me, Andrew deftly changed the subject. "So, Jonathan, how is that eye of yours?"

I gently ran my finger across the scar starting on my forehead. "It's strange. I miss my eye patch. I thought it looked pretty daring at work. Apart from that I still occasionally get blurred vision on that side, but it's the scar that's so ugly. It's such a horrible red mark down my face."

His face was serious, and I continued. "Having said that, I suppose I should consider myself lucky. I can see. The consultant is a bit surprised by how quickly it's healing. But it's still a real shock when I look in the mirror."

"Hmmm," was all he said, his stare making me feel uncomfortable.

"I hear you got some pretty good TLC during Christmas Day." chipped in Daniel.

Now I was smiling. "Yes, I was miserable and worried to start with, I have to say. But I was fussed over by our favourite nurse," Daniel hooted at that, only partially intent on checking Nathan's map. "Plus mollycoddling from Mum," I continued.

"From what your nurse suggested," Andrew said, "it could have been much worse."

"Yeah, she's right," I admitted. "In fact, I was back in the office by 3rd January, which surprised everyone. I can tell you, I felt pretty weird . . ."

Nathan interrupted my response. "Before you two get carried away with post mortems, I've been looking at the map. We've just over a mile to go. A roaring fire and Kentish comforts are only twenty minutes away by my reckoning."

Another twenty minutes! I was already exhausted. Before landing in hospital I had built up my running to a regular twenty miles per week. But much of that had been lost as I recuperated and overate during Christmas. Realising this made me even more annoyed that Andrew had hardly broken sweat.

As we trudged and stumbled over a stretch of iron-hard ruts in a field, Andrew eventually broke the silence. "Oh, I almost forgot to ask you how things are progressing with Chrissie Field?"

"Oh no! I can't believe I haven't told you," I said, breathing hard. "We're exchanging contracts on the Borehamwood property next Wednesday or Thursday. But that's the least important piece of news."

I never did finish my train of thought. Daniel's loud cheer announced the sighting of the car park where we had started our walk three hours earlier. As we entered the remodelled farmhouse and burst into the warmth, I noted for the first time how parched my throat had become and headed gratefully towards the welcoming bar.

"Now, Jon, what about this book of yours, mate?" grinned Daniel, slamming his half-empty glass on the table and wiping his sleeve across his face.

"It's strange you should raise that, Daniel. Although I've already written the complete outline of the story and mind-mapped every chapter, I'm beginning to struggle with the detail."

"Oh, 'mind-mapped'. Get you!" crowed Daniel.

"Cut it out, Daniel" said Andrew. Then looking at me, he queried, "Writer's block, Jonathan?"

"Not quite," I answered. "What I'm more worried about is style. Bluntly, I wonder if I'll be the only one not bored by the whole thing."

"Hmmm. What do you think, Prof?" Daniel asked, examining the menu closely.

"Many writing skills are teachable," Andrew confirmed. "If you can create a story which grabs the imagination, we can make sure that Diane Turner, my editor, is available to help turn it into a riveting read."

"That would be amazing! Could you, really?" Relief flooded over me. "Would I be able to talk to her next week? Maybe I'm just reacting to the misery of the winter, but I need someone to give me a boost."

"I'm sure I can organise that. Let me make a call this week and come back to you," he said, reaching for his tiny notebook to scribble a reminder. "But first, I wonder if you'd like me to share some of the secrets we've used in writing and marketing our own books?"

"What! You never told me that you wrote!"

"You never asked!" he said. "But seriously, you're not the only one here with a good story, you know."

"No, I recognise that, but . . . "

"And, surely," he continued, sidestepping my doubt, "if I'm passionate about the principle of Residual Income, shouldn't one of my income streams be royalties of some sort?"

"Well, I suppose it's obvious," I grunted as I struggled to take off my padded jacket.

"Besides which," he said, "look at the credibility that publishing a book brings. It's no accident that the word 'author' and 'authority' have the same etymological route." This brought a hoot from Daniel. "When your name is on the front cover, I can assure you, peoples' perception raises you to the level of expert."

"Really? I'd not thought about that," I said.

"Meanwhile," he continued, "it may help if I tell you how I keep my thoughts flowing when I'm writing."

My attention wandered momentarily as I joined Daniel in studying the menu.

"Sorry, Prof. Go ahead please, I'm listening."

He grunted as I gave him my attention. "Mind-mapping each chapter," he said, "is exactly the way I kick off my projects too. But, once I can see the pattern of ideas forming into groups of related topics – like this," he started to draw an imaginary mind map, with it's connecting circles and lines, "I take a clean page and convert each group, or family, into a list of topics – like this." I could see the process unfolding as he wrote.

"I then place them in the order in which I'll eventually write them – like this. As I continue, I use this same 'pattern' – or 'formula' if you like – to create chapter after chapter. I guess what I create is like an extra large list of contents. This means that when the list is complete, I've already planned not just the chapter headings, but the outline of many of the key paragraphs. So all I have to do is to sit down and work on however many topics, words or pages I can cope with at a sitting. The book almost writes itself."

Laying his pen down, he paused. "Does that make sense?"

"Guess so," I nodded furiously, trying to copy his sketches into my notebook.

"Now, you remember I just mentioned Diane, who does all of my editing," he continued. "Not only can she help you with everything from the concepts to the detail of grammar. She could even go as far as to ghost write the book for you. However, she'll want you to do some of the work!"

"Perhaps she'll let me discuss the different options with her?" I suggested.

"Quite right," he said. "However, I know that the first thing she'll want from you is a list of contents, followed by an introduction and a couple of sample chapters. It's better that you get an expert opinion before you spend time writing badly, wouldn't you agree?"

Andrew's gaze drifted away from us for a few seconds. Nathan held his hand up to stop either of us from talking further. We watched and waited.

When Andrew's attention returned, he spoke more quickly and quietly. "And another thing. Jonathan, before you've finished, I think it's worth taking your project to some marketing and Internet experts." He was leaning forward. "I'm convinced that they can help you transform what you've written. I think you're on the edge of something big: a whole list of activities that could help you to create streams of clients and income for the rest of your life."

"I'm not sure what you mean," I said. "But you've got my interest." We all looked up to give our attention to the waitress hovering to take our order for four very large, very English, lunches.

"Let's assume for a moment that your book has the potential to sell a few thousand copies," he continued. "The first question is, do we need to involve publishers and printers straight away, or can we market it with minimal cost – for pennies rather than pounds?"

"How would we do that?" I asked.

"The Internet seems a great place to start. We could get a designer to create a version that could be bought from your website, you know, an electronic book, or an eBook as it's often called. There are no printing or publishing costs there, so you'll minimise all your risk. You just pay for some design. Then you can create what's called a 'PDF file', which is even cheaper and which people can easily download to their PCs and then print off."

"That would be superb," I enthused. "Right now, with the IVA taking £1,000 per month from my net income – not to mention my tithing and my regular savings – I might be earning a handsome income, but tax is high and things are still tight."

"That's alright," he said. "We can test out the market's response to what you've written whilst keeping costs down. Once you know that you're on to something worthwhile, you can move to the next step."

"Which is?" asked Daniel. I was surprised that Daniel did not know about everything his father was involved in.

"Print On Demand," replied Andrew. "If your eBook attracts enough attention, you're likely to gain opportunities to speak at seminars, networking sessions, Chambers of Commerce meetings, that sort of thing. You can print a few books – as you need them – for each event, and sell them at the back of the room when people are still buzzing about your story. You should be able to print them for 25% of the retail price, which means you make 75% profit."

"What? 75%? My story? Do you honestly think people will be interested in listening to a talk about me, then buying my book too?"

"Come on, Jon!" interrupted Daniel. "You started the book, 'cos you realised that people could be interested in reading your story. Why shouldn't they want to listen to it as well?" His outstretched arms and surprised face confirmed his amazement. He may not have possessed Andrew's writing and marketing savvy, but he clearly knew how to milk an idea.

"Daniel's right," said Nathan, tapping his glass with his knife for emphasis. "You're going to find out that people love a tale where someone picks themselves up from disaster, then creates a roaring success. And that's what you'll be giving them."

"Huh, I'm not sure 'roaring' is the expression I'd use."

"Now you're being modest," said Nathan. "Believe me. People will want to hear your story." He paused. "And did you realise that speakers can easily earn over a grand for one forty-five-minute keynote speech. Some earn ten times that, maybe more."

"But Andrew," I said, shifting attention from myself, "you suggested creating – what was it – 'a lifelong stream of clients and income' or something like that. I'm not sure I follow how you'd do that from one little electronic book."

"That's the point. You don't," pounced Andrew, his eyes gleaming. "You repackage it over and over again and present parts of it in different formats. Not everybody will find it convenient or relevant to read your whole book. So why not use other media and methods, such as . . . "

"Podcasts and CDs?" I ventured, suddenly grasping the possibilities.

"Workshops and seminars," added Daniel.

"How about 'Hot Tips' booklets and free reports that you can download from a website?" added Nathan.

"Come on! Let's think more audaciously than that," burst in Andrew. "What about DVDs, videos and CDs packaged with workbooks and correspondence courses?"

"Whoa! Hold on Prof! Videos and courses?" I exclaimed. "This is getting out of hand."

"Why not?" exclaimed Daniel. "With a fit-looking guy like you in front of the cameras, customers'll be eating out of your hand."

And the laughter broke the intensity of the moment just as our lunch arrived. The sight and aroma of our plates piled high with steak and kidney pie changed the subject instantly.

Eventually, I started thinking out loud. "What worries me is how I go about writing in a way that allows for all those different media we were talking about.

"Don't worry," said Andrew, "you'll initially be guided by Diane, that editor I mentioned. But I can see that when we start to involve other experts, they might need to alter the material to make it suitable for all those different ways of delivering your ideas. I'm convinced we can develop a complete marketing strategy to produce some really big returns."

Before giving way to the temptation of the suet piecrust, I voiced another niggling thought. "I don't want to seem stupid here, but – apart from the publishing, printing and marketing costs – is there any reason why you are talking about doing this ourselves rather than going to a mainstream publisher? I was thinking about Pearson's or someone like that. That's kind of what I thought would happen."

"Good question." Andrew paused to enjoy his first forkful before continuing. "Firstly, a mainstream publisher is unlikely to take you on as an unknown. They want to be pretty sure they can sell thousands of copies, get it translated into foreign languages and make a killing.

"What's more, although you'll get an advance on royalties, those royalties are only likely to amount to between 7% and 10% of net receipts. That's not 7% of the retail price. Oh no! That's 7% of what's left after people like Amazon.com have taken more than 50% commission and bookshops about 35%. What's more, it can take more than a year to get on the bookshelves, so you are not going to be making any money for ages."

"I see," I said, my mind boggling with all those figures. "So, in a nutshell, traditional publishing can be slow and may not make that much money for me anyway?"

"That's about it," Andrew continued. "However, once you have made a name for yourself, the mainstream publishers will be beating a path to your door. Then you're in with a chance of a big advance, a great publicity campaign and some decent sales. Now, let's enjoy our lunch, shall we?"

We all nodded in agreement and settled to the task on our plates with Daniel ordering another round of drinks. But, it was mere minutes before Andrew set his knife and fork down and began again.

"Look, I'd like to get back to the subject of writing a book that will attract that lifelong stream of clients." Then he mumbled to himself, "Hmm, I like that phrase."

"I'm up for that, Prof. So, I guess I need to make some more notes?"

He shook his head. "I've recorded these steps already. In fact, I have a CD, a tips book and an eBook on the subject," he chuckled. "I'll send a copy of the notes in the week."

"Thanks," I replied, relaxing. The man was unstoppable!

"Before you get stuck into writing, you need to be clear about who you're writing for. The question is this: Who is your target market? Once you've decided that, make sure your book gives them exactly what they want." And his voice punctuated the final words.

"Okay. I have a story to tell, about rising from disaster to success," I hesitated. "But I'm not sure who the target market would be."

"To be clear about that, you need to recognise that there are five characteristics that your market must have. We call them **The Five Rules of Publishing Success**."

We reluctantly lifted our concentration from our plates as he shifted the small salt cellar to stand in front of him.

"Go on," I prompted.

"**Rule number one**:" he continued. "*They must have a painful problem or burning desire*."

"So in my case, that could be overcoming a financial disaster?" I asked.

"Or any type of disaster," suggested Nathan. "Or, getting off a financial treadmill to create a more prosperous life?"

"That's the sort of thing," Andrew continued, moving the pepper pot to stand beside the salt.

"**Rule number two:** *they need to be conscious of their problem or desire*.

"In your case most of the people you're likely to attract will be painfully aware of their problem and their desire to get out of it."

Standing up, he leaned over to an empty table and grabbed a sugar bowl. He set this down beside the salt and pepper.

"**Rule number three:** *you need to be able to access your market easily*.

"Who can help you talk to your prospective clients? Who has access or regular contact with them? We'll discuss that in more detail later."

Nathan shifted a jar of mustard to join the line.

"Thanks Nathan." Andrew continued: "**Rule number four:** *they must have available funds to deal with their problem or desire*.

"So in your case, if they are in the middle of a financial disaster, number four might rule them out altogether."

"Ah, but if they are simply ground down by never having anything to spare, in spite of a good income, they might choose to find the money?" I offered.

"Exactly!" he said.

"And finally, **Rule number five:** *they have a history of spending money to solve the problem, or fulfil their desire.*

"That's more difficult to identify and will probably define the type of people you talk to first." Taking Nathan's lead I moved the small butter dish to the centre of the table to join the line.

Despite Andrew's promise of notes, I could not resist jotting down these five points in my notebook. "I'll be with you in just a sec," I pleaded as empty glasses were removed from our table and replaced with the welcome sight of our delayed second round.

We paused while everybody refreshed his pallet in preparation for dessert.

As we drank, an over-enthusiastic waitress not only cleared away our plates, but with them the jars and pots that had been such an integral part of my education. Andrew's jaw dropped as his steaming plate of apple and blackberry crumble with clotted cream halted all conversation once more.

Noisily scraping our bowls, we could almost hear ideas reforming in Andrew's mind, and I realised that the lesson hadn't finished yet.

As that thought struck me, Daniel spoke, "Prof, look, I'm interested in hearing the rest of this. But my brain is starting to seize up. Could we continue this some other time?"

"I'd second that," said Nathan laying his credit card on the table. "Jam Roly Poly on top of five miles trekking the fields is taking its toll. Let's finish there for the day."

I awoke with a start as the grandfather clock in the main hall struck 4 pm.

I remembered little of the quiet drive back through the villages of East Kent and even less of ridding myself of muddy boots and grubby, wet gloves. Obviously, the log fire had worked its magic as I looked around at my companions in various stages of head-lolling and soft grunting. It was a sorry sight.

Trying to get up from the settee, I found myself still trussed and swaddled with thick jacket and two pairs of everything warm. In my dazed state I rolled off the cushions and landed in a cackling heap on the floor.

Woken by the noise, Daniel was the first to take in the scene and dug Nathan in the ribs as he caught sight of my helplessness.

Making our way to the kitchen and raiding the fridge, we poured ourselves long chilled drinks and stretched lazily whilst toasting our heroic achievements of the morning. Outside the winter's gloom had begun to slip quickly towards dusk.

Excusing myself, I slipped into the downstairs toilet, locked the door, turned on the light and stared at my face, tracing the scar down its full length. As I did so, I realised that this was becoming a habit – almost an obsession.

Was it getting thinner or was it my hopeful imagination?

Coming back into the kitchen, I bumped into a yawning Andrew. "I'd forgotten where we were, Jonathan."

"The last I remember, Prof," I said, "We were about to embark on the next step to create a lifelong something-or-other."

"Yes, that's right," he continued, grabbing a tall stool and leaning his elbows on the breakfast bar. "Before our stomachs got in the way, I was about to mention building a database of satisfied readers or customers."

"How big a database?" I asked, wondering what on earth I'd have to do to create that.

"At least five thousand people I'd say," he responded.

"But how do we do that?" I wailed.

"Leave that one to me. For the moment concentrate on the strategy," he replied.

I nodded, knowing that he already had a solution up his sleeve. "But what's the point of building a database like that?"

"Good question. Well, let's assume you have built that, shall we? Once you've achieved that you can talk to all those people and market further services and products to them. This converts your readers into clients whom you keep serving. And they become your Lifelong Stream of Clients. Get it?"

"Oh, right!" I sighed, still digesting the idea.

Cutting across my thoughts Daniel raised the question that none of us had considered. "So, what are you gonna call this book of yours?"

All eyes turned to me.

"I've been wrestling with that from the moment I started writing," I admitted. "I wanted to make it something like 'Ten Powerful Steps to Win Back Your Life'. But the fact is I only know seven of the laws that The Prof is teaching me. I've still three to go. So that won't work."

"You're right," said Andrew. "But what you know and what you've achieved combine to make a spellbinding story."

Immediately, I felt enthused by his certainty.

"How about 'From a Kings Cross Gutter to Financial Success in Ten Months'?" offered Nathan.

"Well, yes…" Taking a sip from my glass, I looked at him with a half-hearted smile.

He didn't seem offended and continued talking almost to himself. "Without getting too philosophical, it seems to me we live in a world that's dizzy with change. I see peoples' lives in confusion with the speed of it all. All the signs are that they're looking for ways to deal with that turmoil, the sort of turmoil you've been in, Jon. Now you can help them – one million of them – by turning your experiences into all the stuff we've discussed."

"And, Jon," interjected Daniel, "we've already told you how unusual your experience is. You can give folks some serious life-changing advice."

"It's in your hands, Jonathan. Don't throw away this opportunity to achieve your goal." Putting down his glass, Andrew tore off a sheet of kitchen roll to dab at his moustache.

The room was still. "Thanks fellas. Look, I don't wish to be a bore," I said, standing up with the intention of visiting the bathroom once more before leaving. "But I'd like to think about this alone while my poor addled brain is still functioning. I'd better get back to London. It doesn't look too friendly out there. In fact, the forecast suggests more snow."

"Are you sure you won't stay the night?" asked Andrew enticingly.

"No, really. Thanks Prof." I said. "I promised two of the guys in London that I'd give them a lift to church tomorrow. I guess I'd better not let them down."

"Church? You? And 'two of the guys'?" hooted Daniel. "I reckon that 'guys' translates to 'some nice looking girls' to make you that eager to get back!"

Suddenly the room was heavy with tension and embarrassed silence. Daniel coughed dryly.

"There's only one girl, Daniel." I said, meeting his stare directly.

"I know, mate," he answered quietly, sorrow and apology in his eyes. "We all know."

LESSONS LEARNED

- There are much less expensive ways of creating and marketing a book than going to the traditional publishers;
- Creating an eBook only costs time and a bit of design skill. The distribution cost is minimal;
- Once an eBook is created attractive versions can be Printed On Demand to sell when you're speaking to your target audiences;
- I learned about identifying a target market and the five rules that market must possess to make my book a success:
  - Rule One: A big problem or desire;
  - Rule Two: They're conscious of their problem or desire;
  - Rule Three: They're easily accessible;
  - Rule Four: They've shown that they have money enough to solve the problem or meet the desire, and
  - Rule Five: they have a history of spending money to solve that problem.

PROGRESS TRACKER

- I'm hoping that my scar will miraculously heal. But, in spite of what Daniel and Nathan say, I'm frightened that Naomi will find the sight unpalatable;
- I'm now in the 8th month of paying the IVA. I've paid back £8,000;
- I have been in my job for 11 months;
- I'm earning pro rata £90k pa;
- I last spoke to Naomi eight months ago. It hardly seems possible.

David J Scarlett

Chapter 15
Law Eight : Develop a Balanced Life

Monday, 14th January

I was in a good mood as the escalator scooped its early evening load from the bowels of London's heaving underground commuter network. Shuffling and silent we were delivered into the clattering arms of the automated ticket barriers.

My involuntary smile came from the same sense of mischief that used to accompany summer afternoon teenage escapades, when we would slip out of the school gates, praying that we wouldn't be missed.

I had been lucky today. The morning had emerged unusually bright for January, the winter sun almost warming. Or had it only seemed so because I was playing truant from my city office...avoiding the misery of Monday?

As I walked from Colliers Wood station, the growing chill of the early evening struck me. It was nearly 5 pm, and the strips of darkening clouds were backlit with crimson.

The familiar tune of my mobile phone annoyed me as I took it from my breast pocket and clamped it to my ear.

"What have you been doing, Jonathan?" It was Andrew. "I've been trying to track you down all afternoon." I laughed in response as I continued striding towards the cluster of shops that lined the High Street.

"Hi there, Andrew. I've had the most amazing day. You'll never guess where I've been, and who I've met after thirteen years!"

"Yes, I can imagine. Tell me, how was Putney? I hear the place has changed quite a bit."

I was stunned. I could hear the bleeping of the pedestrian crossing calling me to action, but I chose to ignore it. "How on earth did you find out where I've been?" I shouted over the noise of the traffic.

"Come on Jonathan," he said. "Parents talk, you know. I tried to call you at home some time ago and got talking to your mother. I've been aware of this school reunion for a couple of weeks."

"I felt too embarrassed to tell you," I said meekly. "There's so much to do, and the weeks are flying past. I thought you'd feel that I was wasting my time at something so, well, so frivolous."

"Don't be daft. We've all noticed how tired you've been looking since Christmas. You seem to be the only one not having enjoyed a decent break. You need to keep a balance, Jonathan. Otherwise you'll burn out and be no good to anybody, including your future readers."

The pedestrian crossing bleeped at me again, and this time I jogged across the road. "Look, where are you right now?" he asked.

I explained that I still had a five-minute walk and some personal shopping to grab on the way. So he agreed to call me in an hour with 'some important news'.

When the phone in my bedroom rang precisely an hour later, I was lounging with my journal on my lap trying to capture the images and emotions of the day.

"So tell me about your adventure," Andrew prompted.

Delighted to get a chance to talk about my experience I told him about the school reunion that had filled my day. I had moved with my parents from Elstree Grammar School and Hertfordshire to South London after just three years in secondary school. It was here, in Putney, that my fondest school memories had been built.

For some weeks, news had spread rapidly through the Friends Reunited™ website. People had travelled from across the UK to join in an afternoon of half-fearful rediscovery.

Friendships were renewed and earnest promises made. Photographs galore were taken and business cards swapped. Lunches and visits were agreed and secrets divulged, which added to the hilarity and helped banish haunting memories.

"So, was she there?" he asked.

"What do you mean?" I said, my voice squeaking unnaturally.

"Come on Jonathan," he said. "There is always that special somebody we hope to meet at these reunions."

"Yes. She was there," I admitted. "Jane Britton. The very first girl I ever properly dated."

"And?" he teased.

"She was lovely. Just the same." I could hear the embarrassment in my voice, fourteen years later. "And she still had that same gentleness, the same smile, the same voice." For a brief moment, I lost myself in those summer evenings once again.

His voice broke through my daydreaming. "I wonder what she thought of your injuries?" He waited while I tried to recall her reactions when we had first bumped into each other, wandering around the school corridors. There had been nothing but delight written on her face.

"Jonathan. You still there?" I was jolted back to our discussion.

"Yes, still here, Prof?" It was difficult bringing myself back to the conversation. "But I'm curious. Why all this interest in my day back at school?"

"Fair question," he admitted. "To be honest, I've been a little worried about you, as I mentioned earlier."

"I'm fine," I said, not quite nonchalantly. "This has been the most brilliant day in a ridiculously hectic month."

"No," he argued. "I don't think you're fine at all. Which is why I'm glad you took the excuse to get away from your office. And which is why we need to discuss the next of the Ten Laws."

"Which is?" I shot back.

"It's time for **Law Eight**, the title of which is: '**Develop a Balanced Life**'. Are you ready with your notepad? We have some diagrams to sketch."

I had an idea. "Why don't I write it into my journal?"

"Perfect," he agreed. "Are you ready?"

I wedged the phone between my ear and my shoulder and sat cross-legged on the duvet with my journal open on my knees.

Andrew asked me to draw four circles, each circle representing one of the four main areas of my life – Physical, Mental, Spiritual, Socio-emotional. I needed to use a double page in my journal so that the circles could be really big – about half a page each.

"We're going to look at developing your life in such a way that these four areas work together in powerful harmony," he said. "The question we will then ask is, 'How can you create a life which is fuller and much happier?'"

I had seen these four concepts discussed in books, seminars and workshops before, and I stifled a yawn. But at that moment he introduced a different view, which grabbed my attention. He asked me to make the circles – two on the left page, two on the right – all overlap each other a little so that they came together, forming a centre common to all of them. The diagram now looked like a four-leaf clover.

"We'll come back to why that's so important," he said.

He then asked me to select one circle so that we could examine it more closely.

I pointed my pen at the one marked '**Physical**'. It seemed the easiest to deal with.

"I'll take Physical, then."

"What words come to mind when you think of the physical aspects of your life?" he asked. "Write them into the circle. Just randomly, squish them all in."

Balancing the phone precariously, I scribbled and mumbled. Words such as 'body', 'energy', 'strength', 'sleep', 'health' spilled onto the page. (I also added 'injury', and leaned to my right, so that I could see myself in the dressing-table mirror.) But he pushed me to think more broadly than that.

With a little prompting I added 'organised surroundings', 'shelter', 'finances', 'job', 'diet', 'ageing'.

When I had run out of ideas, he asked, "Would you say all those items are working well in your life? For example, do you have enough energy to work effectively throughout the day? Or do you feel unusually stressed and exhausted?"

Then he asked me to concentrate on the same Physical circle whilst we discussed financial strategy. I relaxed. This was an area I felt I could handle.

"Do you have reserves to see you through difficult times? Or are you under pressure because of debt? Are you constantly worried about today's needs and the possibility of struggling tomorrow?"

"Am I supposed to write these questions down?" I asked, struggling with the speed of his ideas.

"No, no," he chuckled, "just scan the subject quickly in your mind and jot down one-word actions for those areas obviously needing attention."

And so we continued, working through each of the circles in turn.

He asked me if **Socio-emotionally** I was setting aside time to develop relationships at home, amongst friends? Or was I ignoring those who loved me most in order to focus on projects, goals and acquiring money? In the office was I investing my time in nurturing and listening to those who looked to me for leadership? Or was I using them as a resource? You know, taking from them rather than giving. Overall, was I taking time out to serve others or was I self-absorbed and self-indulgent?

These were difficult questions. I found myself squirming inside, sighing and restlessly shifting from the bed to the small table that served as my desk.

In recent weeks I knew I had been concerned with my looks: constantly re-examining my face and eye. Narcissus would have been proud.

If I thought that was unsettling, moving to the spiritual circle challenged me even further.

While I continued writing, he continued his questions. **Spiritually**: did I have a clear sense of purpose and meaning to my life? What was truly important to me, what filled my days with energy, power and direction? What did I believe in, other than the satisfying of my own wants and needs?

I reeled as I tried to grasp the enormity of each question and my inability to immediately answer. But there was more.

Was my life full of noise and busyness – he continued – or did I take time to think, ponder and meditate? And if I did, what did I hear in those moments? If I was prompted during those quiet moments, did I have the courage to follow the promptings?

For a moment I stopped writing and asked him to pause while I mentally caught my breath.

However, I also wanted to ask my own questions as we moved to the circle labelled '**Mental**'.

"Let me see," I murmured, "I suppose I'd ask myself whether I was using my gifts and talents. Perhaps I'd query whether I had stopped learning and was stagnating." As I spoke, I wrote key words into the circle: 'gifts', 'learning' and so forth.

I was enjoying the flow of thoughts. "I suppose," I said almost to myself. "I'd want to check whether I was limiting my personal growth. Maybe I'd stopped myself believing that I was capable of greater things. Perhaps I'd failed to seek sources of inspiration."

As I spoke, I touched the row of books – Jane Austen, Thomas Hardy, Daphne du Maurier, Shakespeare – above my desk, where I had lately been seeking inspiration for my writing.

"That's the idea!" he said. "Those are the questions that need answering." Then he asked me why I thought the circles should overlap each other. At that I looked at the circles, each filled with lists of ideas. The completed diagram suggested the answer.

"I presume it's because these areas of life are all interconnected?" I responded.

"Carry on," he prompted.

"Well, when one of them is not working well, then I suppose we tend to get sucked into putting it right. Just like my situation: my finances were a mess, so the rest of my life began to fall apart." Having the diagrams in front of me, I began to see my life from a new perspective.

"Ah, but the question is, Jonathan, why were your finances in a mess in the first place?"

I scanned the diagram again, and the words came from me with a groan. "Because, looking back," I said, "the emotional and spiritual circles were in a mess."

"Yes!" came his answer without any tone of judgement. "The quality of each circle is directly linked to the health and power of every other circle."

I interrupted him as I heard a call from downstairs. I excused myself briefly.

A few seconds later I was back in my chair. "Sorry, Andrew, but Mum and Dad are ready for dinner, so I'll need to wind up in a couple of minutes."

"That's fine," he said, "we're almost there. Now where was I? Oh, that's right. If you look at the socio-emotional circle, you'll realise that when our life is riddled with selfishness, our world eventually shrinks to include no one but ourselves. This affects personal and professional relationships, which eventually fall apart.

"Another example is that, when we're addicted to something, emotionally or physically, we find it difficult to give of ourselves in helping others."

This was getting difficult. I was uncomfortable as he spoke even though I didn't believe he was attacking me.

Taking a break from chewing on my pen, I tried to take up the theme. "And if I'm stressed and exhausted, it's more difficult to listen to others' needs in business or inspire them through my book."

"Exactly! The more we become aware of this relationship between the four areas of our lives, the more we take care to nurture each one . . . "

"Knowing that we will grow stronger in each of the other areas," I added.

"So that, for example," continued Andrew, "your book becomes not simply a method of paying a debt, but a way to contribute to other people's lives emotionally and spiritually."

"And my health and energy allow me to be more effective for longer each day in the office?" I queried.

"That's the idea. The result is that our life becomes beautiful because we feel balanced, fulfilled and much happier."

We had reached a conclusion. "Thanks Prof. This diagram allows me to see my life more – what's the word?"

"Holistically?" he offered.

"Yep. That's it. Is there anything else?" I asked, closing my journal and drifting over to the window to peer out into the cloudless sky. "I seem to remember you mentioning 'important news'?"

"Yes, there is. Firstly, Chrissie apologises for not calling you but confirms that they exchanged contracts on the Hertfordshire property last Thursday."

"That's great news. Thanks," I said.

"Apart from that I wanted to confirm that you're still free to come to East View a week from Saturday. D'you remember me asking if I could send the drafts of your book to someone other than Diane? Well, they want to see you – and urgently. I think you're going to find this very, very profitable indeed."

"No problem. I'm intrigued."

"But I warn you," he said with mockery on the edge of his voice. "You'll need to be down here, at East View for 7 am."

"What?" I almost screamed. "That means me getting up at . . ."

He didn't let me finish my plea. "'Bye Jonathan. See you in two weeks. Early."

I shook my head as I replaced the receiver. It had been a day full of emotion, and I headed downstairs ready for the questions bound to be fired at me over dinner.

LESSONS LEARNED

- Every aspect of our life – physical, mental, socio-emotional, spiritual – is inextricably linked;
- When one aspect is damaged, neglected or underdeveloped, it has a profound effect on at least one of the areas;
- Achieving balance in our life consequently creates a more complete, happier, fulfilled individual with far more to give to those around them;
- It occurs to me that very few people ever give room or time for these thought processes. No wonder we get our lives into such a mess!
- We tend to bumble along through life thinking that, if we just 'keep trucking' doing more and acquiring more, it will all work out in the end. And of course, it doesn't;
- Looking back, I can see that much of my life has been – emotionally speaking – quite dysfunctional. Should I then be surprised when I find myself feeling empty and confused?

PROGRESS TRACKER

- I'm still in the eighth month of paying the IVA;
- This is my fourth month of paying into a savings account;
- It's six months since I started paying into my tithing account;
- Every time I look at my scar, I wonder what impact it will have on my future.

David J Scarlett

Chapter 16
Birth of the eBook

Saturday, 2nd February

*G*rim winter had arrived. Waves of thick fog and slanting rain greeted us throughout much of our journey from East View that ridiculously early morning.

We were in Andrew's Mercedes, heading towards a village on the borders of East Sussex. Our conversation had lapsed into a comfortable silence, broken only by the rhythm of the car's wipers and the requests being played on Classic FM.

I flipped down the passenger mirror intending to look at my face and immediately flipped it back, annoyed with myself.

The thought of getting up in the pitch dark at 5 am to travel from London had caused me to invite myself to stay the night before. By 7 am it was still dark, so I was glad I had taken the initiative.

I thought back to the conversation we had had about my progress since Christmas and the interconnecting circles. It hardly seemed possible that life could have changed so much in the intervening fortnight. But, with Andrew as a mentor, I was beginning to learn that things could alter at surprising speed.

Before heeding Andrew's advice, I had forced myself to fit in a massive 70 hours' writing during December, whilst still attending carol concerts, parties and the shower of invitations from Naomi's friends to 'drop by'.

Much of early January had seen me working with Andrew's hard-nosed editor, Diane, on tidying up my writing style. A straight-talking Yorkshire lass, she only accepted the best I could give. I had grown to trust her insight concerning what would work and what wouldn't. For the last couple of weeks, she had gone away to review the whole twenty-five chapters, in her role as editorial support, coach and occasional ghost writer. It was a good job that my income had moved up a couple of notches; her bill was not going to be small!

Anyway, as far as I was concerned, the story had been told. In the process I had developed an almost reverential regard for the courage and faith of authors and their ability to face the terror of a blank page every day.

Staring out through the rain at the blackened hedges, I only mildly registered Andrew's voice interrupting the comfort of the radio.

"Mmm? I'm sorry, Andrew. What was that?"

"Finances. Money. How are they?" he asked, obviously repeating himself.

"Oh, right. Let's see. You remember that new recruitment account that came back to us? Well, that's immediately improved my monthly income by a solid 20%."

He made noises of approval.

"And I've kept up with the IVA payments, which means I've now cleared £9,000; only a mere £91,000 to go," I said, sarcasm sharpening my voice. "But, what I'm most excited about is that I've saved hard cash for the first time in my life. I admit, it's only £2,000 after five months of trying, but considering everything else that's happening, I'm feeling pretty chuffed."

"Good stuff. It's still £400 per month." His bottom lip stuck out and he nodded in his habit of approval. "By itself that doesn't sound a great deal. But – as you said – add to that your monthly IVA commitment of £1,000, and the 10% of gross income set aside for tithing; well frankly, I'm overawed," he paused and continued as if speaking to himself. "The way you talk, you don't seem to realise the extent of your achievement."

"That's probably because I'm slap-bang in the middle of it."

"Maybe so, but don't forget you still have a full three months to go. I know another £91,000 seems ridiculous in that space of time. But the best of what's possible is still to come."

"Yeah, I guess I'm always hopeful that success is just around the corner." I tried to sound positive.

"Hmmm, I'm not sure that success is what you're after," he mumbled to himself.

Just then he put on his indicator and slowed down to peer out through the windscreen. "Ah! This is it, I think."

And we turned carefully through a narrow white gateway.

With lights full on, the front of a wide, low house swam before us. I couldn't see the ends of it. Through the thick fog I thought it might have been painted pink and noticed that part of the roof was thatched.

Weaving our way past a couple of vintage cars, we were greeted by our young host, his slight figure and boyish face incongruous with his surroundings.

For such an early hour on a Saturday, he was lively beyond reason.

"Please, Andrew, come in and warm yourselves! Jonathan, isn't it? Welcome to our little homely place. Now, if I remember correctly, Andrew, it's apple and ginger tea for you. Jonathan? What's good for you?"

"Oh, caffeine, full strength for me, thanks. I need all the help I can get right now."

As he disappeared, Andrew confirmed that this bounding creature was Simon Russett. I recognised his name instantly. He was mentioned in the papers and all over the 'web', as I had discovered during my recent foray into Internet marketing. If I remembered correctly, Simon was a dot-com millionaire.

The cottage's sitting room was surprisingly spacious. Looking around, as I stretched my legs towards the open fire, I was impressed by the way Simon had retained centuries of oak-beamed character with modern functionality.

"How many sugars, Andrew?"

I was startled by the bright girlish voice and turned to see a curtain of strawberry blonde hair, peeking around the kitchen door.

"Oh, hello Janine!" said Andrew. "One for both of us, please."

It wasn't long before both Janine and Simon had sunk into the soft cream leather sofa opposite me. They turned to Andrew expectantly.

"Simon, Janine, let me properly introduce Jonathan Broom," began Andrew. "Jonathan has been through an extraordinary few months, much of which he has documented in the draft document we sent to you on Thursday."

"Yes, Jonathan," said Janine. "Simon was so moved by what he read that he took the liberty of showing it to me. I hope you don't mind?"

I could feel myself blushing and looking for specks of fluff on my trousers. "No, no, not at all, Janine. And please, do call me Jon. I'm glad that Simon liked it. I think that Andrew's probably a bit biased, and I value a second opinion."

"Well, for what it's worth, I fell in love with the story. It nearly broke my heart to read about your pact with Naomi. I don't know how you have the courage to do that. I couldn't bear to be away from Simon, especially now that we're married."

"Married?" exclaimed Andrew "You rogue! You never told me."

"I'm sorry, Andrew. I know I should have told you, of all people. But we did it overseas three weeks ago, and I thought I'd spring the surprise on you today. We do intend to have a big reception here in April. We'd love you to come."

Andrew stood up and leaned over to Simon, grabbing his hand. "I'm so happy for you, Simon. Janine is a gift. You need to treasure her."

The two newlyweds glanced at each other for a moment.

Still grinning, Simon looked at me. "Jon, I have to confess that Andrew has been working on me for months, trying to convince me to marry Janine. I have to say that the change has been a real boost for our relationship. I think we've fallen in love all over again. He was right."

Simon paused, his smile fading slightly, his gaze turning to the cushion on his lap. Then looking up at Andrew, he finished. "That's what annoys me. When it comes to big decisions, he's always right." His hand shifted from the cushion to intertwine with Janine's fingers.

Janine broke the spell. "But back to your book, Jon. Simon and I think you have a winner here, and we'd be proud to be involved. And not just for old times' sake, Andrew. I do believe, that with some drastic editing, less flowery prose and an attractive title, there's a possibility that this could be a serious seller. But we'll have to work on it," she frowned.

I could feel my pulse start to race as I spoke. "I know it's not good enough yet," I said. "That's why I'm working with Diane. But what's wrong with the title then? I quite like *The Rocky Road to Riches and Joy.*" I almost pleaded.

"Well, I agree that it will set your market's expectation that you're going to teach them a set of financial strategies. Have I got that right?" she asked.

"Yes. But they should also expect their lives to change in other ways too."

"Which is fine," she continued. "But this is an Internet-driven electronic book, an eBook, and expectations are not the same as with ordinary published books, which you can pick up at a big bookstore. The content needs to be more driven towards getting people to take action. You know like *Be Rich in a Year* or *Ten Steps to Financial Freedom.* Trying to be Byron, Shelley and Wordsworth whilst teaching them your strategies will get in the way of your message. Trust me, we need to exceed their expectations. But adding lots of frills won't do it. I'm sorry to be so tough."

My disappointment must have shown on my face.

"Also," she said.

"Also?" I exclaimed.

"Also," she continued, "there are chunks of the story that seem implausible. We'll have to trim some of those back. In fact, we've already taken a risk and, with Andrew's permission, spoken to Diane, who has done much of the editing already."

"But they are real events!" I complained. "They really have been happening."

"Jonathan, time is against you," she responded. "Your initial eBook will probably be no more than a taster of the second edition.

All I can say again is, trust me." There was that disarming smile again. "Let me work with Diane to get the title and the detail right. She's excellent at what she does, I know. Together, I'm convinced that we can quickly produce something that will sell. As we've said, the story is powerful, and the strategies meet a desperate need out there."

I looked at Andrew.

"I'm sorry we've worked around you like this, Jonathan," he said, looking worried. "But I knew that you were producing something exceptional, and I didn't wish to stop your flow of ideas. I'm sure you can use them more fully in the second edition."

The room was silent as I nodded and folded my arms.

Turning to Janine, Andrew cut straight to the point, "So what do you see in this for you?"

"Well, considering we've been working on this for a little while, and anticipating that Diane and Jon will soon be ready, we can prepare promotional copy ready for 1st March – only three weeks away. That also gives us time to prepare our group of Internet associates and affiliates. Most of our products are distributed through them, and they receive a percentage of the revenue, of course. Using their help will distinctly improve our efforts."

"What is it about the story that you think will make it sell?" I asked.

"Jon, we love the authenticity," answered Janine. "The story's great power is its truth. What do you think Simon?"

I clasped my hands tightly and looked closely at Simon.

"Hmm, yes, generally, I agree with Janine. The major weakness I see is the lack of reader involvement. You'll need to develop Executive Summaries at the end of each chapter. These should summarise the key points and prompt the reader to take specific action before moving on to the next chapter."

Janine continued while topping up our cups, "Either Diane or I can help you with those summaries, so don't panic. Apart from that I think we're onto a winner!"

I could see that I was going to be very focused rewriting the draft during the next three weeks – almost unbalanced. Ironically, I would have no time for those overlapping circles. But I was determined, and I was convinced it would be worth it.

"Jonathan, that's quite a demand on you. Do you think you can achieve all that in the next three weeks?" asked Andrew, looking worried.

"I desperately want to," I replied. "Look, could I check my diary at home and come back to you both tomorrow, say, after lunch? I could always take a couple of days' holiday. But I can't afford more than that because of the sales competition."

"Of course. I understand. I'm sorry that we have to be tight on your dates, but Simon has to schedule in another couple of large projects for March," explained Janine.

Simon stood up, prodded the fire, then, turning towards us said, "But Andrew, we haven't answered your question, 'What's in it for us?' Well, for a new, untested author and product like this, we'd need 60% of the sale price. This will be divided between us and all the distributors and so on and . . . "

"60%?" exclaimed Andrew. "That leaves Jonathan just 40% of the sale price! Can't you do any better?"

"Ah, but Andrew," Simon held up his finger. "Firstly we're talking about pure profit with none of the overheads associated with distributing an ordinary book. Remember, this is an elect-ronic book. We'll create a simple document that people can download from their PC. That avoids the normal production and printing costs. There's none of the usual advertising, wholesale or retail middlemen; no bookstore staff and prime property overheads to pay. On top of that, we're talking about reaching a potential audience of 75,000 between my Internet customers and those of our affiliates."

"Hmmm, that's a sizeable number," admitted Andrew. Then turning to me, "And if you remember, Jon, 40% is a lot more than you would get from a mainstream publisher."

"On top of which, we also have to allow an attractive enough commission for the affiliates to take action," added Simon.

"Yes, of course," Andrew nodded.

Janine leaned over, the flickering of the fire catching the excitement in her eyes. "Now, if we price the eBook at, say, $47, then Jonathan's looking at almost $19 per sale."

"Forty seven dollars!" I heard my voice rise. "That's a bit much for a book, isn't it?"

"For an ordinary book, yes. But eBooks are completely different," said Simon, sitting down on the floor, leaning against Janine's legs. "We can package them with additional bonuses to be downloaded. Janine and I already have a range of simple audio, printable and visual products that we can add, which have a high-perceived value. We can add links to other resources and websites. The meaningful added value you can plug into an eBook is enormous. Many people will view the additional items as worth more than the book. Then $47 is hardly a discussion point."

"But what can we expect from a target market of 75,000?" queried Andrew.

"Let's see." And Janine opened a folder beside her on the settee, running her fingers down one of the pages. "We'd be working on a success rate of between 2% and 10%. It's that broad a range because Jon's an unknown quantity."

Andrew put his head back and stared quietly at the ceiling whilst we all watched him closely.

"At today's exchange rate I make that somewhere between £20,000 and £100,000 for our budding author. What do you think, Jonathan?"

"It all seems a bit unreal to me right now. But, for my first shot at writing, I'd be absolutely delighted!"

"Well, that's settled then," said Andrew. "Simon and Janine, assuming for the moment that Jonathan can cope with the pressure, I believe the phrase is: 'You have yourself a deal'."

LESSONS LEARNED

- I feel as if I've burst into a new world: the world of Internet marketing!
- Now I can see the wild possibility that £100,000 could be within my grasp!
- An eBook provides an opportunity to get your products to a large audience for minimal cost.
- An eBook can be priced differently from a printed book because masses of added value can be included that is not possible in an ordinary paper/hard-back.

PROGRESS TRACKER

- The months roll on relentlessly, and here I am having paid only £9,000 of my IVA;
- Oh joy! Only another £91,000 to go, as I said to Andrew;
- I'm now earning pro rata over £100k pa;
- This month is the anniversary of me crawling back, with my tail between my legs, to being an employee. It's not so bad given the success that I'm enjoying.

Chapter 17
Law Nine : Go Beyond Success

Saturday, 2nd February

We lingered so long with Simon and Janine that we accepted their invitation to join them for lunch. Conversation wandered comfortably as we discussed their recent wedding, and the story of how, four years previously, they had started their burgeoning Internet business from a desk in their bedroom.

Eventually, following a flurry of warm handshakes and hugs, we made our way to the front door. As we stepped out, we all looked up to see welcoming patches of blue sky appearing among the thick grey cloud. Instinctively we spread our arms wide and turned our faces to the sun.

"Ah! That's better," I said.

"You have every right to feel better," said Andrew with a wink. "You, my friend, could have just hit the jackpot."

I looked around at the wet sweep of lawns, the profusion of bare trees and the dark soil, carefully prepared in expectation of March. My instinct had been right: the grounds looked about as large as East View, and I could see the outline of stables and paddocks as I scanned beyond the landscaped gardens.

On our return journey I raised another question. This one had remained buried under the excitement of the morning.

"Prof, you made a strange comment when we chatted in the car this morning. Something about 'I'm not sure that success is what you're after'. What was all that about?" We slowed down to pass two youngsters on horseback braving the chilling mists that were returning to settle on our stretch of road.

"Mmm? Now, what precisely did I mean by that? Oh, I remember! I was wondering what you'd consider to be success, given all that's going on in your life right now?"

"I'd not given it much thought," I said. "I suppose if the eBook took off and sold thousands of copies, I could achieve my target of clearing the IVA in 12 months. I mean, that would be success, don't you think?"

"That would be a start, yes," he said, not sounding convinced.

"Oh, come on, Prof! It would be a great start!" I snorted. "How many people do I know who have cleared a debt of £100,000 in 12 months flat? Frankly, none; I'd feel totally heroic!"

"Of course you would," he said with a mocking tone in his voice.

I could feel myself growing irate. "Well then, why the sarcasm? That's success isn't it?" I folded my arms as I glanced sideways at him again. "What? What is it I've missed? I know that smile, and there's something I've got wrong, isn't there?"

"Carry on," was all he said.

I was quiet for a moment. Then I snapped my fingers. "Okay, I've got it! It's Naomi, isn't it? I guess, if I ever felt I'd changed enough," I paused, "and if this scar would disappear, then perhaps Naomi would love me. And she'd want to stay with me. For me, that would be the biggest success of all."

"Tell me. How do you think you're doing?" The mocking tone had disappeared, and he looked serious. I knew he was talking about more than just money and Naomi.

I was struggling. "I wish *you'd* tell me. You see things more clearly than I do."

He smiled gently. "No. When you're ready, you won't need me to tell you."

"So that's it, then? Naomi will be my measure of success?" I made the statement with very little conviction.

The corners of his mouth turned down slightly as he gently rocked his head from side to side, signalling 'not quite'. I was about to show my exasperation when I was pushed back in my seat as we accelerated past the tractor we had been trailing.

Seeing that I wasn't in the mood for further riddles, he started to explain. "You see, what I hear is a world with you at the centre. The payment of *your* IVA. Will Naomi love *you*? The success of *your* book sales. I'm not convinced that's where your happiness, or success, lies at all."

"Forgive me. I know Naomi's your daughter and everything, but I can assure you, Naomi wanting to see me again would make me feel incredibly happy and successful too."

"Initially, I'm sure. I'm simply concerned about who you're putting at the centre of all this."

"Sorry, you're losing me," I said. I glanced at the roundabout ahead and noted that we were only five miles from East View.

"Here's a suggestion," he offered. "There's a small notepad and pen in the glove compartment. Between now and home why not try to list all the definitions and examples of success that come to mind. Then we'll continue our discussion in the office.

Doing as he suggested, I marvelled as ideas flooded onto the paper just as if the dam that had been blocking my mind had given way under the pressure. His adjusting his seatbelt and patting his stomach distracted my attention.

"Hmmm. I definitely haven't recovered since indulging over Christmas. Looks like I'm going to have to up the rate of my exercise routine. How many miles did you say you're jogging now?" he asked.

I answered nonchalantly, "Oh, I've reached a comfortable four miles, six days a week." Then I went back to my list.

Stepping out of the car in front of East View, we rubbed our hands together and looked around us, pleased to see the afternoon brightening again and the clouds shifting. A line of crows passed noisily over us, their harsh cries echoing the bleakness of the grey trees they were flying towards. We headed inside.

Relaxed and seated at his desk, he studied my notes whilst I stood and stretched, gazing out of the window. He picked up our discussion. "I agree that your first goal is to clear the IVA within

12 months. But you haven't mentioned the purpose of the second task."

"No, you're right," I said, still stretching my tense shoulders. "Let's see if I can get this right: 'To create a way to communicate with one million people, so that I help them to change their lives for the better'. I think that's accurate."

"That's good enough. The question is, who is that statement all about?" he asked.

I came over to his desk and pulled up a chair. "Who? I suppose it's about the one million people."

"Exactly. Don't you see? The focus of that exercise is not about what happens to *you*. It's about what happens to everyone else. That, Jonathan, is the beginning of true success."

I was beginning to get it.

He went on. "It's not about satisfying *your* emotions or desires. It's about giving of your time and means, to create something that is more extraordinary than you." He waited as I digested this comment and then asked. "Tell me, how much happier would you say your life is today, compared to when we first met?"

My response was instant. "Huh! There's no comparison. If you'd told me I could feel this good, in spite of not seeing Naomi, I would have said you were barking mad."

"There you go," he chuckled. "D'you remember that conversation we had about 'The Windows of Heaven' opening for you? I know you thought that was all a load of twaddle. Well, it's happening, isn't it? Why not use your gifts and talents as a way of saying 'Thanks'?"

I leaned over and propped my elbows on the desk. He was on his soapbox, and I was loving it. "Talents like yours," he continued, "carry with them an obligation not to hoard them for your own benefit. It's as if a label's attached, which says, 'Strictly for Touching Other People's Lives'."

Interrupting his flow, I asked, "So, are you saying that, until I can do that, I'll never truly achieve success?"

"That's almost it," he said with passion rising in his voice again. "I'm suggesting you go one step beyond the normal meaning of success.

Why not let your influence be felt widely? Why not live in such a way that your life becomes an extraordinary adventure with a great purpose? Why not make your life much more than a career? Make it a mission."

"You mean, like Barnaby working for his church in Germany?" The words from his letter echoed, unbidden, in my mind. Whilst I was inspired by Andrew's sentiments, I wasn't at all sure I liked some of the financial implications. Once I had got the taste of making money, I wasn't keen to give it all up and swap it for sackcloth and ashes in a hurry.

"That's exactly what I mean, just like Barnaby," he said. "He was a complete pain in the neck as a teenager, jumping out of windows, disappearing for days, tearing off roof tiles. I remember the numerous nights we heard him creeping in and throwing up after bingeing with his cronies. Then a light went on inside his head, and, before we could get over the shock, he was on his way to Germany for two years."

We both laughed at the images conjured up. He continued, "When you've made that shift inside, then, and only then, will you – what's the phrase the girls use? – 'get it'. Yes, then you'll 'get it'. And you'll begin to understand what I mean when I talk about happiness."

"I see. But that raises another question," I said, spotting a flaw in his argument. "What if all this works, and I start to earn some serious money?"

His response was immediate. "That'll be life's way of saying 'thank you' for what you're trying to do. And then you'll have to deal with something else."

"Which is?"

"Whether wealth stays with you or passes through you on its way to benefiting other people."

I was struck by the idea and, agitated, got up again to pace the floor. "'Passes through me'. What an amazing way of looking at money."

Sure, I liked the concept. But I wasn't happy about what Andrew was suggesting. I was already paying a tithe. Didn't that count? This felt one step too far to being 'holier than thou'. This was a tough one.

"So, what about…?" I paused and cleared my throat. "What about you, Prof? Are you a channel for money to pass through?" I needed to know. "Why, won't you tell me how you've managed to do it? And how on earth do you expect me to do the same?"

By this time I was talking to myself. I gravitated to the window again, not feeling the need to speak further. Andrew silently left the room.

LESSONS LEARNED

- Success is often viewed as what is being achieved by you, for you; Andrew's definition of success starts when a person reaches out, using their gifts, talents and achievements to benefit the lives of others;
- Andrew seems to have influenced everybody we meet to create more fulfilling lives.

PROGRESS TRACKER

- After the excitement of meeting with Simon and Janine, the conversation with Andrew really bothered me;
- I've worked so hard in every facet of my life to change my habits, behaviours and attitudes;
- I've taken on scary, and massive, projects because of his encouragement;
- I've given up old friendships and pastimes because of his influence;
- And now he's suggesting that I still haven't got my mind straight. He's saying that I'm still somewhat selfish. Me, who has been paying tithing, for goodness sake!
- But I have to admit that his whole view about success and happiness and putting others first has a ring of truth about it!
- After seven months, tithing has become a core part of my financial planning and there's now £2,000 in my savings account. After five months' saving; as Andrew said, that's quite an achievement;
- I have kept my promise concerning Naomi for nearly nine months. Now that the anniversary of our parting looms, how do I know that she'll feel anything after all this time? The answer is, I don't.

Chapter 18
Law Ten : Become The Mentor

Saturday, 2nd March

*T*he wind whipped Corrin's dark hair across her face. Wellington-clad, Andrew and I flanked her as we strode out of the front door after the comfort of Saturday morning's breakfast with the whole Lambert tribe. None of us saw fit to wear more than rain jackets, and there was even a sense of hope conjured by the early buds that were appearing sporadically. We walked in silence near the main drive. The grass was soaked, but for now the skies were clear and the sense of expectation came as much from Andrew's pensive mood as from the early spring sounds around us.

"What's the matter, Prof?" I ventured, my patience giving out.

"Matter? Oh, nothing's the matter. Far from it. I was considering how well things are progressing for you. For example, I'm not sure that I've told you about the discussions I'm having with the seminar organisers and speaker bureaux."

He always caught me off balance. "Seminar organisers? And what on earth is a speaker bureau? What's going on?"

He hardly seemed to notice the irritation in my voice. "During the last few weeks I have been looking at the PR opportunities that we could use to raise the profile of your book. As well as depending upon the online power of Simon's business, we could significantly raise awareness ourselves by using more traditional methods of promotion. The problem is, of course, doing that while trying to deal with the pressures of your career. I wouldn't want you to jeopardise your current position. That's what's concerning me."

I was more worried about other things and asked, "When you say 'promoting', what exactly do you mean?"

"I'd suggest speaking at conferences, Chamber of Commerce meetings, that sort of thing," he said casually. "Then there's radio, newspaper editorials. The routes are as many as our creativity, and your time, allows."

I felt myself growing overwhelmed simply trying to picture each event. "Look, I appreciate what you're trying to do; really I do. But I hope that you haven't been arranging things without checking with me." I could feel my throat tightening, my voice growing strained. "All of that sounds a bit scary to me. I wouldn't have a clue about organising things like that. And you of all people know how packed my life is already."

"Don't worry," he said, waving his hand dismissively. "Once we see the eBook achieving some success, Corrin and I can help there. The big problem will be ensuring that your employers are comfortable about your activities."

A gust of March wind shook the oak tree under which we were passing, and the heavy branches dumped their load of water upon us. Pulling my collar tighter, I replied hesitantly, "Fine, that's all very well; I can talk to my MD next week. But let's assume for the moment that they do approve. Even then, how soon do you envisage starting all this activity? Honestly, right now I feel stretched to the limit!"

"Ah. There's the rub," he said. "I've been making some enquiries, and there are two organisations who want you to speak later this month. They initially invited me to speak, but I've convinced them that you have an exceptional message to deliver. I've shown them excerpts from your book, and they're really interested. Jonathan, this could be the perfect platform for you."

"This month? You're kidding!" I exploded, horrified, and looked over at Corrin, pleading. One glance at her lopsided smile told me that they were entirely serious.

"Oh, come on! I know nothing about talking to groups like that." I was panicking. "Presentations about recruitment to IT directors and HR managers is one thing; they don't frighten me at all. But I wouldn't know where to start when it comes to promoting a book. What on earth would I talk about? And how do you expect me to find time to prepare?"

Corrin was ready with her response. "Jonathan, Dad thinks that we can negotiate with each of them to buy about 500 copies of your book; that's one for each conference delegate. He's offered them the knock-down price of £11, and they're thinking about it. These are big companies having annual conferences. If they agree, we're talking about a total of about £10,000 for your two presentations!"

"But," I exclaimed. "They won't buy an eBook, and we've got nothing printed to give them!"

"Ah, you're forgetting about Print On Demand." Andrew said. "Don't you remember? Diane is already talking to some designers to produce the cover of the printed version. She can get that done at very low cost. Then she'll get a printer she uses, specialising in Print On Demand, to produce only those books that you want. In fact, for what they're paying we can even print the name of the conference on the front cover."

"And," added Corrin, "you've done all the preparation. All you need to do is tell your story from your journal."

In spite of my annoyance, I didn't stand a chance. It wasn't long before Andrew's assurances and Corrin's smile had melted away all of my resistance, and I found myself in Andrew's office agreeing to let her tutor me in the art of public speaking.

"We've set up Dad's office with a flipchart and mock podium," she explained, nodding her head persuasively. "I reckon a couple of hours together this morning on creating structure and then speech delivery; that should do it. But I hope you don't plan to go home early. We're gathering together this afternoon, for me, Dad and Mum to be your audience for fifteen minutes. We'll make a game of it, where each of us will have to deliver a speech on a weird subject. That'll make it much more fun."

Andrew raised his eyebrows as I turned to him for an escape route. "You'd better listen to her Jonathan. You already know that Corrin was a superb teacher, before she and Nathan had children. But the reason I asked her to join us is that she's also a natural speaker. Besides which she specialised in speech and drama during her University year in America."

I was exasperated and amused. "Why the pressure today?"

"Ah, yes," Corrin continued, blushing. "Well, Dad has those two organisations he mentioned waiting for a phone call on Monday to confirm that you're available for brief slots in their seminars. They'll want you during the last two weeks of this month."

I stopped walking and turned to face Andrew, trying my hardest to glower and frown simultaneously. But the twinkle in his eyes and the innocent smile he managed to shoot back immediately broke through my mask. Soon we were all laughing at the sheer audacity of their planning and plotting. At the same time I felt myself revelling in being at the centre of the plot.

Corrin was a good teacher, very good. By the end of the afternoon, I was given a standing ovation by my completely biased audience. Even Louise was caught up in the gaiety and managed a deadpan face whilst requesting my autograph.

When the chatter had faded, I was left alone with Andrew, who seemed very sombre.

"Take a seat, Jonathan. It's been a long day for all of us."

I looked around me, still fascinated by the attic where we had played out our game. Many decades ago it had been converted into a tiny theatre, presumably for the children of the Champernon family.

I sat on the 'stage' facing him. "I'm fine, honestly. I suppose I must be on an adrenaline high right now."

"Well, I hope that I don't puncture that inflated feeling," he said, pacing slowly with his hands clasped behind his back. "Simon called this week to apologise for not checking with you before marketing the eBook."

"I don't understand why he's worried." I frowned. "I thought we had agreed to let him get on with it."

"Yes. But he didn't confirm the title with you."

I watched him, intrigued.

"They decided upon *Seven Steps To Riches and Success*." He smiled at me, waiting for my reaction.

Grimacing, I stifled an unkind comment. "Well, they seem to know what they're doing." And I shrugged smiling back at him.

In that easy style of his, he changed the subject. "You know, Corrin was right," he spoke almost in astonishment. "You do have a gift. I enjoy your writing. But considering you're a comparative novice, you're even more exciting when you speak."

"Thanks," I said, blushing. "Believe me, I appreciate your encouragement. You don't know how good it feels."

"Oh, I think I might do," he replied. "I had a mentor once, you know."

"Really? You've never mentioned him, or her?"

"I worked with him when I was much younger." He went on to describe his mentor, almost in awe. Terms like 'charismatic leader' and 'spiritual giant' came easily; a man with four sons, and weighty commercial responsibilities – European Director of Executive Development, or 'some such grand title'. "He took me under his wing, and I watched him like a hawk. Ten years later I'm still trying to emulate him."

I waited in case he was merely pausing for thought. "Sounds like quite a man," I commented, trying not to break the mood that had settled upon us.

"He was," he replied quietly. "But his help didn't come without a price."

"A price? How do you mean?" I asked.

He looked at me carefully. "He had always dreamed of giving his sons a life amongst mountains and forests. So, since his employer's headquarters were in the USA, he accepted a senior position there and took them to America. Before he relocated he held me to a lifelong promise. This promise was remarkably similar to the kind of ideas Louise and I were trying to put into practice with our promise to mentor people, only this added another twist."

"Which was?"

"That not only would I seek out those who were ready to learn what he had taught me, but that I would be their mentor. My task would be to help them take their life to a new level. Then he raised the stakes by suggesting that I find ways to mentor more than one person at a time. He challenged me to find a way to touch thousands of lives. The Ten Laws is our response to that challenge."

"Oh, I see." I stood up, as he watched me. "So that's what these last few months have been about. You know, I thought this was all about Naomi. I had no idea that you were carrying out your promise. Hey, hang on a minute . . . you challenged me to touch a million lives not thousands!"

"Ha ha!" he said, winking and clapping me on the shoulder. "With you, I was more than tempted to raise the stakes!"

I couldn't help smiling as I shook my head. Moving away from him, I started to pace back and forth across the stage, my hands thrust firmly in my pocket. Eventually, I turned and walked over to where he sat.

He rose and took my hand firmly in his. Looking into his strong face, I spoke hoarsely: "I reckon it was a good decision. And I guess you already know that I'm grateful, don't you?"

"Yes, I believe I do," he said.

"Goodness knows why you picked me," I continued. "I was a hopeless case, and I can't believe you saw much in me that you liked, let alone an author, a property developer and all that stuff. But, I guess you did."

I folded my arms, feeling awkward. "But I can't help wondering why you're telling me this now?"

"Because Jonathan, I have already taught you nine of the Ten Laws. I'm now ready to teach you the tenth and last. We're approaching the end of my part of our agreement."

"Somehow, I feel . . ." I spoke slowly, "I'm only just beginning to get my head around the stuff that you've taught me. But I can't wait to hear about the Tenth Law."

"It's simple really," he said, "but why don't we continue downstairs. You must be parched, and I can tell you what I have in mind over a drink."

As we strolled down the wide stairway from the first floor, he explained more about the speaking engagements that he had lined up. He pointed out that I would be presented as a perfectly ordinary guy, with a supremely extraordinary story, and it was precisely because of that background that the audience would be on my side.

As we settled in the bay window seats in the kitchen, he continued.

"Once the twelve months are ended and you have achieved your goals (and I'm satisfied that you will), you face a responsibility. That responsibility is to do exactly what I have done: find someone who is ready to change their life, and help them to live the 'Ten Laws of a Soul Millionaire'. Your challenge is to become The Soul Millionaire for them. The question is, do you want that responsibility?"

I hesitated before answering. "It sounds rather overwhelming. But I'd love to try. Not yet, though, eh? I'm still a novice, a Soul Millionaire in training."

I waited while he drained his glass. "Good. That's what I hoped you'd say," he nodded. "We have a great deal of work to do; we're not in sight of your goal yet. But when we are, I'll hand the baton of responsibility over to you, and you must run with it." He looked up and held out his hand. "Deal?"

"Deal," I said, with tears pricking at the back of my eyes.

Then, in an attempt to cover my embarrassment I announced, "Well, that's it then."

"That's what?" he looked puzzled.

"That's the title of the book. I've continued writing since meeting with Simon and Janine, and the latest version builds in the first nine laws."

"Well done." He sounded surprised.

I continued, ideas flashing through my mind. "But now, I have the Tenth Law. If you can give me a week or so, I reckon I can finish an updated version that we can print off in time for the conferences."

"It'll be tight," he said, "but let's see what Diane says when she sees the new chapters. Then we'll have to run it past Simon to make sure we're not breaking our intellectual property contract with him. But you still haven't told me what it is."

I looked blankly for a second. "Oh, right. The title, you mean? I was thinking: *The Soul Millionaire*. Maybe a subheading: *True Wealth Is Within Your Reach*. I folded my arms in satisfaction.

He stroked his beard. Then he smiled. "That'll do nicely, Jonathan."

LESSONS LEARNED

- There is value in mixing traditional offline marketing activities with online. In fact, there are some advantages in using a mix of the two;
- Selling products as part of a speaking engagement can create more revenue than any speaker's fee you might be paid;
- Knowing that you're going to be teaching principles and skills to somebody else increases your desire to put those principles into practice in your own life.

PROGRESS TRACKER

- So far I have paid off £10,000 of my IVA. It sounds like a lot. But it feels like a drop in the ocean;
- Add to all that another £400 of savings this month…
- That totals more than £12,000 that I could pay off if I wished. We're getting there, but too slowly!
- Andrew's loading me with tasks and projects. I'm not sure that I'm going to be able to cope with speaking as well. Or is it simply that I'm scared?
- Not long ago he was probably terrified that his daughter had picked up some predatory smart Alec. And here he is telling me that I'm special enough to stand in front of an audience and tell my story. I'm pretty gob-smacked!
- It's weird that Andrew believes that I'm capable of mentoring somebody in the Ten Laws.
- I'll be able to deal with mentoring when the year is over, and I can see if life has turned up trumps with Naomi. I have only another 11 weeks or so before my promise regarding her is fulfilled;
- I have come up with a cracking title for the latest version of my book. It is *The Soul Millionaire - True Wealth Is Within Your Reach.*

Chapter 19
In Over My Head

Thursday, 7th March

*M*y mind had drifted back to the scenes of last Saturday. It was the bleep of my PC which brought me back to the fact that – five days later – I was sitting in my office in London and still had a heavy afternoon ahead.

As I scanned my emails, I could scarcely believe how dry my mouth was.

This latest sales competition had grabbed the attention and fired the imagination of the whole national team. The prize was a week for two in a top hotel in New York, with £2,000 spending money plus tickets to Carnegie Hall and other events. Whatever else was changing in my life, the thought of being applauded as top revenue producer still held a thrill, there was no escaping that.

Ah! There it was: a memo from James Bacon, our Managing Director. James was not known to be a prolific email communicator so I guessed this had to be important. I was right.

The background hum of conversation around me dissolved.

"Come on, come on, let's cut the waffle. Get to the point, man!" I heard myself whisper fiercely as I read the emailed memo. "Who's in the frame to win?"

There I was! Up from fifth to third place. Looking at our revenue performance, there was little to choose between the top half-dozen consultants. But just ahead of me was Brian O'Connor. Not only was he by far the most hilarious Irishman I had worked with, he was the most skilled sales negotiator I had ever encountered. He would be hard to beat.

There were only another eighteen working days to go to the end of the business year. Yet even then, I wouldn't know the results of the competition until mid April.

"Hey, Jon, how does it feel to be riding high in the competition, knowing that if it weren't for me you wouldn't stand a chance?"

That was Steve Davey, the latest graduate recruit to join my team as well as the one consuming most of my management time. Unmistakeably likeable, he exuded an almost boyish charisma. If only I could get him to focus his talents on his job, he'd make quite an impact. He might even survive his probationary period!

"What a cheek!" I retorted, laughing. But before I had a chance to throw a rubberband ball at him, my phone demanded attention.

I answered robotically. Then was jolted out of my routine. It was Simon Russett. "Oh, hi Simon," I said. "Good to hear from you. Anything wrong?"

Two minutes later I put the phone down in a daze. One hundred and ninety-three eBook orders taken within the first five days! Simon and Janine must have done an amazing job on the sales copywriting. I would have been happy with nineteen orders!

Simon had suggested that sales might continue at this rate for a while. But then he assured me that they would climb once his affiliates started to use the sales material and weblinks sent to them.

Janine had been right. People did want to read my story.

I smiled, as I considered the question forcing itself to the surface of my thoughts. Hmmm, what if they had priced it higher? No, that was silly. If it had been up to me I would have charged no more than a tenner and they were charging $47. The result was unbelievable already. I pushed the thought away but grabbed my calculator anyway. Then I sat back and ran my hands through my hair, almost in shock. So this is what Andrew meant by the power of residual income!

Glancing at my watch, I realised that my meeting with James Bacon was a mere ten minutes away. Whilst I was unsettled by his request for an unscheduled meeting, I saw that this would be an ideal opportunity to discuss the book and all that went with it. For a fleeting moment I realised that the business might actually benefit from the publicity I could be giving them as their representative. They might even like to sponsor me or the book!

Before I knew it, I was in his office, quickly running through a preamble of small talk. He seemed to concentrate on discussing my plans for the future, which I felt uneasy about revealing at that stage.

"Jonathan, I want to share something with you that requires your utter commitment to confidentiality." He stood up from his desk, and moved his tall, slim frame slowly towards the long river-facing window, his hand tapping his side.

Then he turned towards me. "The position of UK sales director has become free this week. I want to present your name to the Group Board as the person to fill that slot."

My hand went to my forehead as I tried to grasp the implications of what he was saying. "What about Keith?" I stammered.

"We've had to let him go," he replied, grimly. "I'm not at liberty to go into the details, but we can speak more freely in a couple of weeks."

I was reeling. "But James, there must be others you trust; successful consultants and great revenue producers?"

He shook his head. "No. I agree, we might be blessed with more than our fair share of sales talent. But that's not what I'm looking for. There's more required of a business leader than sales skills or even good management ability. I've been watching you closely during the last . . . how long is it? A year?"

"Almost exactly thirteen months," I replied without thinking.

"Yes. That's enough time for me to observe character traits and leadership quality. There's something . . . something about you that has developed during that time. I have to say, it has impressed us all. That quality, combined with your obvious commercial awareness, is needed here. It's needed to head the sales team nationally."

I could hardly breathe, let alone speak.

"Naturally, we'd have considerable time together," he continued. "Clarifying your role, setting expectations, that sort of thing. But my commitment to you would be to act as your mentor, being available when you call upon me."

I believed him. I had noted his style of individual involvement with team managers in recent months.

Now I felt him looking at me as I stared beyond him, seeing little, and thinking furiously. I realised that, whilst I didn't feel comfortable about explaining all the detail, nevertheless he *deserved* to know about my plans, my book and about Andrew and his ideas.

"I need to talk," I began.

While I struggled to organise my thoughts, he gave instructions for all calls to be held. The next hour flew as the intensity of our conversation ebbed and flowed. I told him everything. About my bankruptcy, my Three Challenges, the Ten Laws and Naomi, of course.

Eventually we lapsed into silence, the air charged with tension as he rose from his desk again and stared at the lone seagull wheeling and swooping between the barges slung low on the Thames.

Without turning he let his thoughts emerge carefully. "Jonathan, I won't pretend that this doesn't cause some concern. But, I think we can turn your activities to our advantage, if we plan carefully. If your material is as good as people are suggesting, and your story inspiring, there's bound to be some way to create good PR for our company. Why don't we set up a meeting with Andrew Lambert – your 'Prof' as you call him – and see if we can create a win-win arrangement between us? What d'you think?"

"I think that's very generous," I responded enthusiastically. I couldn't believe that he had taken a position that I had prepared so hard to argue for. Then I paused. "There is one thing that niggles me, and I'm surprised that you haven't mentioned it."

"Which is?" he asked, looking intrigued.

"Let's suppose that my book – and all the other things that might spin from it – really takes off. What then?"

"That's what's causing me the most angst," he admitted. "Whilst you're here, I must have your full commitment. This is a multi-million pound organisation, employing over 200 people. That's a colossal responsibility. It's not something that you can play at."

He sat down and started drumming his fingers gently on his desk. There was silence as each of us waited for the other to speak first.

Eventually, James spoke: "Here's what I suggest. I need to have your honest opinion, not a view that you want me to hear to shut me up. Okay?"

"Okay. That's what you'll get," I replied.

The incentives that he suggested were almost certainly well rehearsed. Firstly, there was to be the obvious commission structure based on revenue performance with a basic salary of £50,000. My on-target-earnings would take me to £130,000 per annum. Striving for that would keep me hungry for sure. Then he suggested creating some share options, which would allow me to benefit after three years. I would be locked in with golden handcuffs.

"I would expect three years' commitment from you," he concluded. "Do you think you could handle that?"

"That's quite a commitment," I agreed. "To be honest James, my hope is that my residual income from my personal activities might at least exceed my basic salary within three years."

"Then I'd be jealous. But happy for you," he said. He paused. "So, that's what I'm going to present to the Main Board. Are we agreed?"

"Agreed," I replied, and our hands clasped tightly as he clapped me firmly on the shoulder.

He walked with me to his door. "How's your eye now?" he asked. "I don't mind admitting, you had me a little worried there."

"Yeah, me too," I responded, trying to smile.

There was a moment of hesitation, neither of us quite sure what to say next. Thankfully he spoke first. "I'll be able to let you know about the Board decision one week from Monday. That okay with you?"

I nodded.

"Good. Oh, and Jon," he called as I was about to stride away, "don't forget, when you're settled into your new position, I'd love to have a long chat with this Prof of yours. Seems quite a fella. But remember, not a word to anyone. Yes?"

LESSONS LEARNED

- There are qualities needed for leadership that are not necessarily present or obvious in good salesmanship or management;
- Internet marketing and sales have an immediacy about them that is seldom present in offline activities;
- When we feel overwhelmed, it helps to bear in mind that we can get through far more if we know that the pressure is only going to last for a short while.

PROGRESS TRACKER

- I have just been offered the position of UK sales director of a multi-million pound recruitment company;
- I thought I had enough responsibility on my shoulders already, what with the IVA, the book, and now the speeches that I had agreed to give. But this!
- 193 orders for my book. Wow! I make that £2,582 for me at today's exchange rate;
- I have already paid off £10,000 of my IVA;
- Added to my £2,400 savings. That totals about £15,000 that I could pay off if I wanted to;
- We're getting there!
- To be honest, my pressure is likely to end in about 11 weeks. Either I'm going to achieve my manic goals or I'm not. And when May is over, at least I'll know what my position is: with the IVA, with money, with Naomi.

Chapter 20
The Offers Roll In

Walking out into the dazzling morning, I closed the gate behind me and leaned against it as I reached into my coat pocket. Plugging my finger firmly into my left ear and clamping my mobile to my right, I responded to the call that I had just missed.

"Andrew," I was almost shouting, "it's Jon. Is anything wrong?" The signal was poor, and his words came in waves.

"Look, I'm sorry to bother you, Jonathan," he said, finally sounding crisp and clear. "But I have some wonderful news. I was speaking to the conference organisers for The Excalibur Life Annual Convention. They have…"

Damn! I'd lost him in the noise of a passing lorry. "Hold on Prof!" I bellowed. "Let me walk away from the main road. The noise is deafening."

Within yards the signal cleared and the noise reduced. He continued. "Now, where was I? Ah yes. The Excalibur conference organisers. I was speaking to them yesterday afternoon. Well, they asked me to call the Excalibur Financial Director urgently. And guess what? They've been glancing at the draft of your book for the last four weeks. They sound as if they might be interested in buying a branded copy of *The Soul Millionaire* for every conference delegate. They'll want it heavily discounted but Jonathan, this is a European event, and we're talking about more than 500 people."

I was amazed, and said so.

He hadn't finished. "Hang on, Jon, there's more. I've also been speaking to Williams, the publishers, and they're prepared to talk about giving you an advance for your next book, once we can show a track record of promotion and sales for this one."

I was almost dizzy with the shock. "My next what?"

Again he interrupted me. "We're talking about a £15,000 advance on your next book," he crowed with glee. "They think you'd be a perfect fit for their 'Turn Your Life Around' series. You'd get something like £5,000 upon signing the contract, another £5,000 when submitting the manuscript and the final instalment on publication."

I could feel my chest tightening with the rising stress. "Look, Andrew, with recent events, I simply haven't got time to think about writing another book."

"Jonathan, listen." I could sense that he was trying to control his excitement. "We're not talking about tackling it right now. I'm simply saying that a £15,000 advance – albeit in three staged payments – speaks volumes about your ability as a writer. It's a project 'in the bag' that we can come back to, once the pressure is off you this summer. Think about it!"

I started arguing, but he was quietly persistent, his soothing voice calming my confusion. "Trust me on this. They believe you have an outstanding talent. They're prepared to invest in you when the time is right, believing that you're a profitable commodity. They believe in you, and so do I."

"But I thought you said that mainstream publishers only gave a 7% royalty on net receipts. Is this really worth it? Financially I mean? I can get ten times more doing it the way we are doing it now." The thought of writing another book was daunting enough, but making so little for each book that was sold seemed ludicrous.

"You wouldn't be doing it for the money, though the advance is not insignificant," Andrew said quietly. "You'd be doing it for all the other benefits."

"Such as?" I scuffed the earth at the edge of the pavement with the toe of my shoe.

"The fact that Williams will see your book gets into all the high street bookstores and the libraries. They will do you a press campaign, get you on the radio and the telly and you, Jonathan Broom, will become a household name." He went quiet and let that news sink in. "And the more of this book you sell mainstream the more you will sell of the other products, for which you are getting that 60%."

"Right," I said. The penny dropped.

It was then that I realised that I hadn't explained the situation at the office, and the commitment that my promotion would require. Quickly, I summarised my meeting with James Bacon.

"I'm just not sure how I can fit everything in," I said, feeling the panic rise within me. "Right now, the last thing I want to be thinking about is writing a new book."

"You're right," he said quietly. "That's wonderful news, of course. But the pressure will be enormous. Why don't I ask Williams to give you more time? Leave it with me. Maybe we can come back to this in nine to twelve months?"

"That sounds more like it," I said, able to breathe again. "At least give me time to get into my new job. But let me think about the whole thing before you call."

We agreed that I needed to collect my thoughts and look at my new commitments. I would call him with any decisions on the following Wednesday evening.

"Incidentally, what are your plans this weekend?" he asked.

I explained that I was on my way to Elstree to see Matthew's progress with the refurbishment, hopefully to give him some help, if only for a day. Before closing I remembered that Louise had been trying to reach me and asked him if he knew what she wanted.

"Yes, I do," he confirmed. "She was calling to arrange details of the speaking engagements we discussed. They'll be prestigious milestones to have on your CV. Why don't you two talk about that when you call on Wednesday? Oh, one more thing. I know how busy you are. But, whatever you do, you need to leave the last two Friday afternoons of this month free for speaking. Can you arrange that and let me know tomorrow morning?"

I gulped. "Probably," I replied. "I just need to pass it by James, but it should be fine. I'll need to make the time up over the weekend though. This is a pretty crucial period in our sales competition."

I turned my phone off, in a daze once more. The last few days had been a whirlwind of news. I felt as if my head was about to explode.

I called on Wednesday, as promised.

True to his word, Andrew had finished negotiating with Williams. "I've agreed with the publishers that they wait nine months before committing you to another book. Meanwhile, Excalibur has signed an agreement to purchase 617 books, to be delivered on the day of the conference. They pushed me down to £6 per book because of the pre-conference commitment. But, since the cost of our Print On Demand is only £3 per book, that's still 100% profit.

All Diane has to do now is ensure that she gets the right wording and logo for the cover from Excalibur. Then she needs to get that many books printed in time."

I relaxed a little. "That's brilliant! Thanks Andrew."

For the next two weeks I could concentrate on the sales competition and my first two speaking engagements. What was interesting was that James Bacon was supportive of my efforts and had asked me for Andrew's number to discuss it with him.

Then he went on, "What's needed now is for you to keep your eye on the end game. May I give you some counsel?"

"Go ahead," I said, not that he ever needed encouragement to give out advice.

"Keep reviewing your objectives each night so that they stay crystal clear in your mind. Review them and consider them as you write your journal. That way, disappointments or obstacles won't push you off course."

I could see how that process might help. "I'll try to remember that," I agreed.

Then he passed me to Louise.

"Oh, hello Jon." By now, I was growing used to her clipped manner, and was no longer awed by it.

"Andrew has mentioned your good news. Well done! Forgive me for being brief, but I need to help Jessica collect the children shortly. Do you have your diary with you?"

"Of course!"

"Good. I've confirmed your first speaking engagement – or keynote, as it's called – for 3 pm on the Friday. That's enough time for them to wake up again after lunch. The second one is slightly more difficult: it's at 4 pm when they're likely to be rather tired. What we need to do now is discuss the audiences and their expectations. Okay?"

I had already started digesting a couple of books from Andrew's library, including *The Ultimate Business Presentation Book* by Andrew Leigh, which proved useful. Now I was going to need more inspiration than even a book could give me.

I barely got a wink of sleep that night, fretting about my first keynote speech. Yet, I knew it wasn't just that which was keeping me awake. I was scared, not because something was going wrong, but because so many things were going right, and at such an alarming rate. Even my scar had healed to a fine pink line – a mere trace of the original mess.

The fear that gnawed my stomach was: when everything was this good, it was bound to collapse.

LESSONS LEARNED

- It sounds as if I'll receive more income from pre-selling the book than from the fee for speaking. What a great idea of Andrew's;
- It seems that the medium-term revenue power in a book is not the profit made from selling it, but the opportunities and credibility that it creates.

PROGRESS TRACKER

- The offer of a directorship. Share options in the company. Book sales going alarmingly well. A major publisher wanting me to create a new book. Then two public speaking assignments. No wonder my head is spinning!
- If we pre-sell 617 books at £6 each, that's another £3,702!
- I've paid £10,000 of my IVA;
- As at today there's another £5,000 available (from savings and the eBook) if I need it;
- Still a long way to go!

Chapter 21
The Roar of The Crowd

Friday, 22nd March

*A*s I started to prepare a strategy to hand over some of my recruitment accounts, the pace at work became furious. On top of all this, Steve and I were focused on filling vacancies with our biggest clients. The week disappeared in a blur.

Before I knew it I was in a limousine outside one of the Gatwick Airport hotels, squeezed between Andrew and Louise with Daniel driving and Nathan keeping him company in the front.

Nathan took my arm as we clambered onto the wet forecourt. "You'll be fine. You'll be really great."

I turned to look at Louise. She smiled and nodded encouragement and, for a split second, I thought I saw Naomi's face.

She leaned towards me and said quietly, "You're a natural speaker, Jon.

Now, all you have to do is be yourself and tell your story. We'll be there, in the front row. If you ever feel uncertain, just look at us. Alright?"

"I think so," was all I could muster.

As we stepped into the hotel lobby, the Welcome Board announced the evening's event: 'Excalibur Life, Annual Sales Convention'.

Apparently, this was an all-day event, and I was the penultimate speaker.

I wondered what they were expecting.

The conference centre was packed. Earlier, Corrin had explained that Excalibur was renowned for their sales and management training.

As I endured the next couple of hours, I might have become nervous, had I not been caught up in the energy of the two speakers before me. They were good. They were very good. One had divided up the entire audience into groups according to what colour represented their character. Another, almost blind, spoke of how he had climbed Everest in spite of his disability. I was definitely not in their league.

I was so engrossed that I was startled by the announcement of my name. Daniel's hand squeezed my arm, and I looked to catch his wink of encouragement.

Then I rose to start what seemed like an eternal walk up to the steps and onto the main platform.

My introduction had been flattering, and the applause more than polite. My 'speaker's credentials' impressed even me. But there was no time to gloat. I was busy holding my jellied knees in place and taking conscious steps forward so as not to trip.

Finally, I turned to face the sea of expectant faces. I had decided to avoid worrying about distractions like PowerPoint presentations. I wanted to talk from the heart, like Andrew had encouraged. Shifting the microphone slightly, I carefully opened my folder onto the podium.

My voice echoed towards me across the vast space.

"I want you to imagine the most miserable of lonely, God-forsaken nights in the red light district of King's Cross, London. You've just lost your business, your home . . . and you're looking for somewhere to sleep."

Then I spoke about my mad, self-indulgent gambling days, which had led to that night of deep despair, about not seeing Naomi and about lessons on the Thinking Bench.

I told them about the incredible family who had taken me under their wing and then proceeded to share their secrets, their special time together, their friends and their colleagues with me.

I urged them to find a mentor in their life. I talked about mixing with the best people we can, about pushing ourselves to the limit of our comfortable knowledge, about rising to a challenge, even when we don't see the outcome.

I explained about facing personal weaknesses, about how sacrifice is far more fulfilling than the eventual emptiness of gratification, about letting go of ego and arrogance and about keeping a journal.

On I went, led by an instinct to expose my soul to a concert hall full of complete strangers.

My throat was hoarse with emotion as I closed my folder.

There was a split second of silence, and then the room erupted. Whistling, whooping, cheering, and applause – such applause!

Then my confused eyes registered a blur of movement through the glare of lights below me. The movement spread like a rolling wave, as row after row stood up shouting their approval.

I could feel myself, open-mouthed and grinning in amazement and amusement.

A standing ovation.

For me!

I can't recall much of what happened after that except that I was being steered by my elbow from one group to the next.

I remember being asked to sign some copies of my book. I remember also handing out business cards without considering for a moment how they got into my pockets.

All I clearly remember is sitting in the limo afterwards, unable to speak as we purred through the traffic.

"Jon, open your hand," commanded Louise somewhat seriously.

Obediently, I prised open my clenched fist. Then I stared at the slip of paper that she dropped onto my palm.

Trying to focus in the dim light, I gasped. "A cheque! Good heavens, **five thousand quid**! What's that for?"

"That's from Excalibur Life," Louise said in controlled triumph. "That's for telling your story and for the books that they ordered. It should have been exactly £5,202 – £1,500 being your speaker's fee. But I wasn't about to argue the point. We'll have to sort out paying Diane for the cost of printing next week."

"I can hardly believe it!" I exclaimed.

"Believe it, Jon Boy," came the teasing response from Daniel, our chauffeur.

"And it happens all over again next Friday," beamed Louise. "Be as open as you were tonight, and you can expect a repeat performance. We're hoping to pre-sell at least 400 copies to them too, but if they don't bite we can arrange to sell them to the audience during the conference. In that case we can push the price up to £10. I know that the pre-sell printed copies sell for far less than that, but, hey, even at £6 a pop, you can't grumble if it's guaranteed, eh?"

"Tell me," I looked at her. "Will I ever stop shaking like a leaf as I stand to speak?"

"I'm not sure you want to, Jonathan." Andrew had been silent for most of the night. "My experience is that the minute the adrenaline stops pumping, and the butterflies stop fluttering – that's when you lose your edge." He paused for a moment and exchanged a glance with his wife. "Shall I tell him or will you?" he whispered. Louise cleared her throat.

"Are you ready for more good news?" she began and then, without waiting for my response, continued. "As you have noticed, your story is selling well both as an eBook and as a book. The next step is to open it up to more channels still. People have started to talk about it to their friends and that means other people now want to buy it too. And that means we have to make it easy for them."

"And?" I asked, uncertain of what else I was going to have to add to my already busy life to make this happen.

"It's okay," she laid a reassuring hand on my arm. "You don't have to do anything. Simon and Janine will take care of it all."

"And 'it all' actually means?"

"Diane is going to hand the new version of *The Soul Millionaire* back to Simon and Janine and they will convert into a range of different formats. Then it can be sold via online bookstores like Amazon and for all those eReaders out there. Now, I know Amazon and the like will be taking a chunk of the profits, but this will easily be compensated by the volume you will shift. In fact Simon told me that since he and Janine started making their most popular titles available for eReaders they have doubled the number of books they sell!" She folded her arms and sat back in her seat, clearly pleased with her announcement.

"Is there a catch? I mean, it all seems too good to be true?" I asked. "Am I going to have to post books off to everyone who buys it on Amazon?" I could picture my parents' dining room filled to the gunnels with boxes of books and my heart sank.

"Goodness no! All the distribution is taken care of automatically. No one has to post a thing. The only catch, if there is one, is that while tonight I was able to give you the money there and then, when you sell things online via Amazon it can take a few months for payment to come in. I'm afraid you're unlikely to receive it until after your year is up, Jonathan." She shrugged.

I went quiet while I took all this in. I'd been so busy of late I'd hardly noticed the new trend for eReaders and I'd been so bowled over by the direct sales we'd been making I'd clean forgotten about the biggest bookshop in the world – Amazon. That the money might be delayed didn't seem so vital. It would be there for the future and that was important too.

The chattering died down as we wove our way towards South London and home. The evening's experience had given me a boost of confidence, such that I felt able to excel in anything. But, in the aftermath, I felt drained. Trying to absorb what Louise had told me was just a step too far. But, as Louise had said, I didn't need to actually do anything myself to make that happen, so instead I'd just accept it and trust it was the right thing to do. I mean, how could it not be?

My mind drifted ahead to the sales competition at work. Although I was now privilege to many things, even I was being kept in the dark about who was likely to win. The announcement would not be made until the next National Conference on 12th April.

The euphoria of that evening lasted all the way through my sleeplessness and was only heightened by an early morning phone call from Simon Russett. eBook orders had started to escalate, and he had received another 312 since we last spoke! Not only that but he reckoned that he'd soon convert *The Soul Millionaire* into the right formats for Amazon and eReaders and the book would be on sale online in less than a month.

The dream was beginning to come true.

I had hardly finished showering when Mum's voice reached me from downstairs. I strolled to the phone and was confronted with the voice of a somewhat breathless Chrissie.

"Jonathan, I'm sorry," she announced. "It's Matthew. He's awfully sick. In fact he's in hospital right now. It's food poisoning. We're supposed to have the refurbishment complete by Monday for the estate agent to inspect. But now I'm going to have to postpone that.

"Jon, it's nearly the end of March. I just don't see how we're going to meet your deadline for the end of May."

LESSONS LEARNED

- Speaking on a subject that you're passionate about can be the most effective presentation of all even if you're not a skilled public speaker;
- Heavily discounting a book or other product to an audience who have come to listen to you anyway is an excellent way of securing revenue;
- When audiences have listened to you and like you they often want to go away with a part of you. A book or other product provides that opportunity and can often create more income than the fee for speaking;
- Once people start to talk about your book or product, other people will want to buy it too, so you have to make that easy for them. For a book to be widely available, it must be distributed via the internet.

PROGRESS TRACKER

- Given the cheque for the speaking engagement, plus the additional orders for the eBooks, I calculate that I have added £9,175 to my assets;
- I reckon that, once those eBook orders turn into real cash, I would have about £14,000 in total to pay off my IVA;
- All my books are going to be available online via Amazon and in eReader formats too. In time, that will give me even more passive income;
- Having already paid off £10,000, I make that another £76,000 to find from somewhere;
- Of course, I have to remember to pay the costs of producing the Print On Demand books;
- Chrissie's call was such a blow;
- Everything seemed to be going so well. The premonition that I had felt ten days ago seemed to be coming true;
- On the other hand, aren't I making a small fortune on the eBook sales?
- Come on Jon! Where's your faith? Andrew would be dismayed, even hurt, that I'm harbouring such negative thoughts, when so much has happened, which other folk would see as being nigh-on miraculous;
- I have only another eight weeks or so before I can contact Naomi.

Chapter 22
The Secret

Friday, 29th March

*L*ouise was right. The next Friday was a carbon copy of my debut.

The management convention of Centre Space UK was just as packed and every inch as enthusiastic.

This time my support team included Corrin and Jessica, rather than Nathan and Daniel, who had stayed at home to take their turn with bedtime routines. I was blissfully aware of being flanked by beautiful women and felt like a celebrity as I caught the envious glances of the other speakers.

Yet I was still surprised when Louise handed me the cheque for £4,300 in the car. As we neared my parents' home, Andrew's phone interrupted our tired silence.

Within seconds he turned to me grinning gently. "Jonathan, I think you'd better take this."

It was Janine. What she had to tell me about sales of my eBook left me stunned. I was still shaking my head in disbelief as we pulled up quietly outside our house.

Everybody in the car craned his or her neck to stare at me, questioning wordlessly.

"Janine says I've had orders for a more than 1,000 eBooks this month. And they'll advance £10,000 in two weeks against the receipts. This is ludicrous!"

Andrew laughed, "And this is only the beginning, my man!"

Arriving at our house, I staggered onto the pavement and waved goodbye as they sped off, their cheering voices mingling with the noises of the night.

As I turned to open the door, only one thought disturbed my excitement. It was the meeting that I faced tomorrow, a secret that I could share with no one.

It wasn't difficult to conjure the image of Tiffany Belmore, the young lady I was so eager to see again. Bright, witty; I could hear her confident voice, her slight Australian accent. She possessed a sharp, quick mind, natural poise and unquestionable beauty.

As I sank into bed, sadness tinged my thoughts. I was about to do something that I had to hide from the Lamberts – not an easy task with a family that had been so supportive. But, they, of all people, could not be allowed to discover who I was meeting – or why.

LESSONS LEARNED

- The success enjoyed in my first speaking engagement wasn't a fluke;
- I've hit upon something big in my story and my book! Andrew was right. People are eager to hear real stories of rising from failure to success;
- I'm getting a taste of walking in the limelight, and it's not difficult to see how the adulation of the crowd could become addictive.

PROGRESS TRACKER

- My confidence in meeting my target is soaring in spite of the bad news about Matthew's food poisoning;
- I'm getting hooked on this public speaking routine! What a tremendous buzz I got out of tonight as people stood to applaud me;
- My one worry now is my meetings with Tiffany. What we're doing feels so important that I can't stop now even if it means hiding everything from Andrew and Louise;
- We've had 1,016 orders for the eBook this month! I make that £13,594 at today's exchange rate;
- I have received two cheques totalling £9,300 for my speaking engagements and Print On Demand book sales;
- Add to that my £2,400 savings, and I've accumulated £25,294 in theory;
- I've also paid off £10,000 of my IVA;
- So, all of that added together totals £35,294 so far;
- I have exactly two months to go and just under £65,000 to find;
- Of course, I need to remember to deduct the Print On Demand costs, which will amount to about £3,250;
- Yet all my financial concerns are nothing compared to the fear and anticipation gripping my stomach as I consider the approaching day when I can contact Naomi;
- Come on, Universe, I need another miracle!!

Chapter 23
When The Student is Ready

Monday, 1st April

I noticed his empty desk as soon as I entered the office on Monday morning. It was 10.15 am, and I had already attended a breakfast meeting with a client. So where on earth was he?

I turned, questioningly, to Sophie, one of our recruitment resourcers.

She had anticipated my thoughts. "Steve's upstairs in one of the meeting rooms. He's waiting for you."

As I opened the door, I saw a forlorn looking figure seated with elbows propped on the table, his head buried in his hands. As he looked up, I could see how pale his face was. This wasn't unusual for a Monday morning. But it was the haunted look in his hollow eyes that struck me.

He managed a feeble "Hi!" then buried his head again. Sitting down opposite him, I remained silent. After a short while he uncovered his face and continued staring at the table.

"I'm in trouble Jon. I'm in a mess."

I waited as the silence hung between us.

He continued, filling the void, "Last night. I, er, I was in hospital. I was so scared. I never want to go through that again. I felt myself passing out, and I thought I was dying."

He took a sip from his glass of water and coughed. Starting again, he avoided eye contact. "I don't know why I do it. Go over the top, I mean. You know, the drinking and the parties during the week. All that stuff. Fact is, I'm not as happy as everybody thinks."

He looked at me, his brow furrowed. "Jon, it's just an act."

He caught my smile. "Okay. Maybe I don't fool anyone," he went on. "It's the same every week. And I know you all think I'm goofing off all the time. I can tell you're fed up with me forgetting everything from day to day. But, honestly, Jon, I was scared last night."

He paused. This time the silence was long and painful. "I don't want to do this anymore."

"You want to leave?" I asked.

He replied quickly, "No, I don't mean the job. I mean, I don't want to live like this. I want to be different. I want to, I want to be like, I s'pose I want to be like you. Sort of get my life together. I'm not really sure what I want. But first I want to – you know – say 'I'm sorry', I guess."

I waited to see if there was more to come. But he looked at me expectantly.

"What do you want me to do, Steve?" I couldn't force myself to get annoyed.

"Show me," his voice pleaded. "Teach me what I can do to live with, well, with some point to it all. How can I put it? Some – I don't know – some direction."

I could see that he was genuine. But I wondered if he had what was needed to make a change.

"It's not going to be easy. Keeping promises is not your greatest strength."

"Yes. I know, but …"

"And nothing miraculous is going to happen overnight," I added.

"Yes. I know all that, it's just …"

I interrupted again, "And there are a number of things that I won't tolerate any longer."

"I know," he whispered.

"But I have an idea," I smiled. "To be precise, I have ten ideas. They're likely to take you some months to learn about."

"I can take that. As long as you don't give up on me," he pleaded again. "I need this job. It's one of the only things I can rely on to keep me sane."

I looked at him until his eyes shifted back to the table. I continued. "Here's what we'll do. We'll meet every week on Friday at 9 am sharp. When we meet we'll…" Well you can guess how the conversation progressed. And no, I did not expect him to call me Prof! Strange, before I believed I was ready, here I was living the Tenth Law!

The next morning was taken up by a strategy meeting with James Bacon. It was hard work, and the list of tasks seemed endless. But we had quickly homed in on those changes needed to take the organisation to the next level, and to make it internationally.

One of the decisions to be made in the coming weeks was my replacement as Regional Manager. James wanted my input before he made a decision.

I began to learn that popularity was not going to be part of my reward package. There were some unpleasant tasks ahead. Such is leadership.

Nevertheless, the announcement of my appointment would create an interesting stir at the upcoming National Sales Meeting, mid-month.

As I returned to my desk, Steve immediately thrust a message in my hand.

For the first time, its details were perfect. Time, date, spelling. Tiffany wanted me to call.

My breathing grew shallow as I tapped in the number.

"Hi Tiffany. Thanks for tracking me down. Yes, I'd love to pop in to see you. This Saturday is fine, but I'll need to make it early. I have to be in Sussex by lunchtime. Does that fit in with you? Yes, it's important for me too. You're right, I am excited. Does it sound that obvious?"

As I put the phone down, I gently punched the air with a sense of euphoria. I looked up to see Steve staring quizzically at me. I chuckled, reading his mind about what he thought he had overheard.

I pointed at him. "You've a list of projects on your pad, mate. I'd suggest you get stuck in." Within seconds he was on the phone.

LESSONS LEARNED

- I once heard the saying 'When the student is ready, the teacher will appear'. I thought that was a bit corny, but it seems pretty accurate to me, given today's experience.

PROGRESS TRACKER

- Today I became The Soul Millionaire Mentor;
- Everything that Andrew said would happen has 'come to pass', as he would phrase it;
- Only six more weeks to go before I've fulfilled my commitment not to talk to Naomi for a year. She's home for the Easter hols; only a short drive away, yet I still don't know what's happening in her life. I wonder what she's doing tonight?
- I have been in this job now for 14 months;
- This is my ninth month of paying into my tithing account;
- My savings account now holds £2,800;
- I have paid £11,000 of my IVA;
- I have 'a mere £63,000' left to pay off.

Chapter 24
The Ghost of Easter Past

Saturday, 6th April

Memories flooded back as I followed the curves of East View's newly tarmacked drive. It had been a long year since that morning last Easter when I had driven with Naomi down this same route.

I chided myself as I noticed the tenseness of my chest yet again. Yes, Naomi had been here only the night before. But, no, she was unlikely to be back again until the summer. Having celebrated Easter with her family, she had promised to spend a long weekend helping at a youth convention on the south coast.

Andrew was waiting for me at the main door. As we ambled towards the 'Thinking Bench', he pointed out the explosions of blossoms beginning to appear. Once or twice we stopped as he caught an early skylark throwing its song at the sky.

When the grey clouds passed, the sun was tantalisingly warm on our faces. Soon we were seated pleasurably on the bench with me emulating his outstretched legs by habit. He had brought his guitar with him – the first time I had seen it outside of the music room. For a few minutes I enjoyed listening to his strumming and humming as he tried out a new song.

The notes died away as he leaned the guitar against the bench. "Before we plunge into the day, I thought we could take stock of what has happened since we first met. Would you mind?" he began.

The idea appealed. "No, not at all. There's so much to recall. I'm not sure where to start."

He didn't look at me. His eyes were closed, and I thought I caught the hint of a smile playing around his mouth. He stayed silent, leaving me space to think and talk.

"I guess it's over to me then." I took the cue, "Well, this week has seen me attempting the Tenth Law of The Soul Millionaire. I started life as a mentor, teaching the First Law to Steve, at work.

"Now that I've started working on that Tenth Law, I can honestly say that I've tried to live by everything you've taught me. Doing that is probably the toughest thing I've ever done. Nearly as tough as…"

Here, my voice trailed to a whisper, and I stayed silent trying to compose my thoughts.

"I know that Chris Charles was gob-smacked when I told him that I'll soon have accumulated an additional £26,000 to pay off the IVA early. Eleven months ago he didn't share your belief that I could clear it within less than four years. He thought you were barmy. Frankly, I did too."

His smile broadened.

"But now? Now, I admit that I believe extraordinary things can happen.

"Yeah, maybe even miracles, as you call them."

Watching the herd of Jersey cattle ambling towards the horizon, I let my words drift gently away.

"What else?" he said quietly.

"Then there's keeping my daily journal, which led to the book, didn't it?

"Your nagging has definitely paid off there. I didn't think I could write until I re-read the journal.

"Which brings me to Simon and Janine and nearly £14,000 in eBook orders. I can't believe what they've achieved, and so quickly! And if it weren't for them, I wouldn't have been able to create the revenue for the Print On Demand books. I reckon that I've earned about £6,500 on those so far."

"I assume you've taken into account the printing costs for those POD books?" he asked.

My heart sank. "Blast! I'd almost forgotten that. That's a big hole in my budget. If I recall my calculations, that's a whopping £3,250! Great! I was beginning to feel everything was coming too easily. I was right!" I leaned forward and picked up a small stone to throw in anger.

"Come on Jonathan," said Andrew, sounding surprised, "look at the possibility of a £15,000 author's advance from Williams – even over a period of nine months – that's amazing! And don't forget all the extra money that'll come in from your eReader and Amazon sales."

We were distracted by the companionship of a robin hopping in front of us fearlessly. It stopped to our left and tugged at worms from the loose earth that had been turned over in preparation for the spring.

"I suppose you're right," I continued. "I guess I should be grateful for what's happening at work. The promotion has come as a real shock; I feel the weight of my new position already. But what a brilliant opportunity!"

I mulled over what I had just said. An idea was beginning to form.

"And, you know, nine months ago I started paying tithing into my deposit account. What did those verses from the Bible say would happen? 'The windows of Heaven'? Well, I have to admit, they've been well and truly opened up for me."

The silence was comfortable between us.

"Anything else?" he asked.

"I can speak!" I exclaimed. "Well, of course I can speak. But those audiences looked spellbound. I couldn't believe the power of holding an audience in my hand. It was intoxicating! All of that thanks to Louise and Corrin, and your encouragement."

"No. I think Corrin brought out what was already there," he said quietly.

"I wonder what else you're feeling and thinking," he murmured.

"Surprised, I suppose," I responded immediately. "I'm thinking about my recent reaction to Easter, particularly on Sunday. I spent some time talking to Naomi's friends about their feelings. I suppose I'm comfortable with the thought that there's a . . . well . . . somebody there who's involved in my life."

"Hmm, that's interesting. A paradigm shift, huh?" There was laughter in his voice. "There's one thing you've forgotten, isn't there?"

"Which is what?"

"I haven't heard you mention Naomi for quite some time."

"What can I tell you, except that I think about her constantly? I'm going to be open with you, Prof. Every time you teach me something new, I do it wondering what she'd think of me. Maybe that's not what you want to hear. But that's what I do."

"So, how do you think she would feel if she knew?"

My laugh was a shade hollow. "If she cared, I think she'd be proud."

"So do I," he said, stroking his beard thoughtfully.

I broke the mood. "So what do you have in store for me today? What mighty mountain to climb, Prof? What raging river to cross?"

I was soon to find out when Louise joined us after lunch.

Andrew had built a cinema room, mainly for the grandchildren, and as we entered it, Louise pointed out the video camera and carefully arranged three chairs ready for our discussion.

"Jon, it's all right. Don't panic," she began. "The only reason the camera is there is to help us review your behaviour under the pressure of an interview. We're not filming you for a documentary or anything like that. You're only going to be on the radio."

"Only? I'm petrified! How could you do this to me?" I wailed.

"Be a brave boy, now. This won't hurt a bit." I was never sure if she was joking. "We're going to try to get you onto one of the BBC 'Money' programmes starting with local radio. We're aiming for a slot in May, if possible, so we have some time to practise. I'll pretend to be the programme presenter and conduct the interview. I'll watch for your ability to respond cleanly and confidently to questions. Okay?"

I'm sure my eyes didn't roll back in my head. But I could have sworn that Louise could read my mind as I thought 'Oh, great!'

To be honest, Louise proved to be skilled in putting me at ease, and an hour sped by with only the occasional need for me to dab at the beads of sweat on my upper lip.

Taking me from the point of losing my business, she encouraged me to move smoothly through the principles of financial organisation, discipline and control until we finally reached the rules and laws around creating Residual Income. Here I started to feel passionate, and it wasn't long before I was waxing lyrical about the benefits of creating a book and all the opportunities that could lead to.

I was exhausted when we'd finished.

"Hmmm," she mused. "We still have some work to do. But I'm sure you'll polish up with some practice."

"Well, thanks a bunch, Louise. I'm flattered, I'm sure!" My hand shot to cover my mouth; I was getting a touch too familiar these days.

The next thing I knew, she was punching me on the arm and struggling to contain her laughter.

Andrew intervened, "Come on you two. That's enough torture for one day.

I have a date with Nathan in the Jacuzzi. I deserve it. Why don't you join us?" he nodded to me.

He opened the door onto the patio, stepped outside then turned and popped his head back in. "Oh, by the way, Jonathan, I think I've found two more speaking engagements, if you want them. I think one's for this month, the other is some time in May. Can we do some diary planning once we've turned into prunes?"

I used the rest of that day to start thinking through the different products that I could create from the eBook. As I reviewed my notes that evening, I realised that touching one million lives with my story had changed from becoming a crazy dream to more than a possibility.

I was on my way.

LESSONS LEARNED

- Lack of faith in ourselves is largely what limits us in creating magnificent lives;
- The power of a mentor – someone who can see more clearly and much further – cannot be believed until you've experienced it;
- There are many things that are true and that work, even when we don't have empirical evidence to support our belief. Tithing is one of those.

PROGRESS TRACKER

- Just over five weeks to go before I get to contact Naomi;
- And exactly eight weeks to go before my self-imposed IVA deadline.
- After paying for the POD book costs, and if I used all of my spare cash resources – including the eBook money expected from Simon – I would still have £66,000 of the IVA left to pay off;
- The cycle of seasons is almost complete;
- I look back at the pain of last spring and marvel at my feelings today.
- As I think back over these last 12 months, I feel as if the person that first arrived at East View no longer exists;
- If this story had not happened to me, I would have considered it little more than the rather twee product of someone's fevered imagination. But it's real!
- And within mere days, I'll know whether all of my waiting has been in vain.

Chapter 25
A Private Triumph

Friday, 12th April

*T*he day of the National Sales Convention came with deceptive speed.

As we filed into the conference centre, my mind was elsewhere. Chrissie Field had phoned the night before with a 'Good News, Bad News' report.

By calling in favours from some of Andrew's contacts, she had managed to get the refurbishment complete in time for viewing by the Estate Agent. Knowing her, I can't say that I was surprised. The bad news was that the first offer she had received was £20,000 below the asking price, which annoyed her intensely. She had no intention of considering it. So the outcome still hung in the balance.

I could feel my most important financial opportunity slipping away from me. I felt sick.

You'd think that I'd be filled with optimism, having phoned Simon earlier in the morning to check on the eBook numbers. He had explained that our hopes rested on his affiliates now that they had been given the promotional material to send to their tens of thousands of subscribers. He had pointed out that some of them would also be vying for Internet traffic using the search engines. This meant that the target market could be far more than the original 70,000 envisaged.

I had listened, unfeeling, as he jubilantly explained the latest sales figures: an additional 1,014 orders creating a potential £13,000 or more in revenue. One week ago that would have set my adrenaline pumping. Now, I felt as if I was imprisoned in one of my childhood dreams, trying to run – being chased by a dark, faceless being – but not moving an inch.

Seven weeks to go, and if I counted this £13,000, there was still £53,100 to raise. I felt completely impotent, having tried all the ideas that I knew. Even with the latest piece of good news, I was convinced that events were now out of my hands, and all of my excitement and energy were ultimately wasted.

Drawing a deep breath, I tried to slam the door on the insidious hopelessness and fear coiled in the dark recesses of my busy mind. That fear was this: even if the finances were perfect, I was unable to stop myself entertaining the possibility that nothing I was doing would bring Naomi back to me.

With this battle going on inside, I had difficulty making sense of the scene around me. Yet, I welcomed the noise of chatter that invaded my thoughts, and instinctively looked around for my two most obvious rivals in the sales competition. Simultaneously, we all spotted each other, nodded and gravitated into a huddle, the banter cheering my mood a little.

For the rest of the morning, I struggled to concentrate on each announcement and presentation even though James conducted the meeting with his usual charisma.

"...announce the appointment of our new national sales director..."

I came back from my meanderings with a jolt, I had almost completely lost the thread! I was lucky that he'd paused teasingly to force the emotion in the room to a peak.

"Jonathan Broom!"

I wasn't prepared for the reaction across the room.

Endless bodies came up to me in a blur of backslapping and a babble of congratulations. I had no idea that I was known outside of the London office. I suppose that I expected jealousy. But I saw none in the faces around me.

Over the noise James called, "Jon, why don't you join me at the front on the stand?"

So I did. Filled with renewed confidence on the platform (thanks to Corrin and Louise's tutoring) I slipped straight into an off-the-cuff speech that had them all hooting with laughter. "James had to offer me this job," I pointed out. "He said I was causing far too much havoc dealing with our clients. I think he's exaggerating just a little. What I want to know is, what's wrong with wearing a wig and pink braces to a client meeting?"

But there was a serious side to my comments. "As I take on this role, I feel that, together, we're ready to make some changes." The jovial murmuring calmed. "I intend to review the way that teams work, so that each of us can be more effective and cut the time spent in the office, for example. In addition, there's a need for you to take part in influencing the direction of the company."

"That sounds wonderful in theory," piped up one of the Birmingham consultants, a sharp edge to his voice. "But how are you going to make that work in practice?"

"Yes. Good point," I responded. "Well, I see an opportunity to set time aside for planning and networking between teams. I see regional involvement in raising our PR profile, including helping with local charity projects." There was a general murmur of assent.

"Look. I don't want to take up our time in this conference," I continued. "Let's discuss these ideas gradually over the next three months and see if we can make them work to benefit all of us in a measurable way. What d'you think?"

The response was favourable and so, taking my seat, I handed the meeting back to James.

Lunch was a sumptuous affair with the menu doing its best to focus our attention on New York. I had a chance to mix widely, soak up the ribbing and joking that came my way and survey the teams that would now report to me.

What we didn't expect in the afternoon was the elaborate and ostentatious build up to the announcement of the sales competition winners.

Videos of New York city… a superb Frank Sinatra sound-alike, with the obvious rendition of the classic song from Ol' Blue Eyes. As he finished, he was joined by a New York cop, who took the microphone to the sound of Hill Street Blues. His accent was spot on.

" . . . a week at a luxury four star hotel in the heart of New York . . . Limousines to take you to and from the airport…Champagne and flowers on your arrival . . ." our New Yorker crooned into the microphone.

We interrupted with whoops, whistles, catcalls, Mexican waves – the noise rising with every element of the prize.

"I shall continue. Tickets to Madison Square Garden, Carnegie Hall, the Statue of Liberty…"

Someone at the back broke out with his own version of 'New York, New York'.

". . . a night-time tour of the city, a guide to take you around the art museums, Rockefeller Center, St Patrick's Cathedral . . . more tickets for a Broadway show. And finally . . ." He paused for effect. "£2,000 spending money to spoil yourself rotten!"

And with that the drum rolls began.

". . . pleasure to announce the winner of the semi-annual National Sales Competition."

Silence.

"The winner is . . .

"Meees-ter Jon-a-than Brrroom!"

I yelled and threw my hands in the air as the room erupted. I could hardly believe my own excitement. I had worked so hard for this but had no idea that I had finally won.

As I stood, the chant and the foot stomping started. "Fix, fix, fix . . ."

I can remember little else after that except pumping the cop's hand and holding aloft my plane tickets to New York, knowing in that instant that I couldn't go. My priority right now was to avoid disappointing Tiffany.

Coming home late and jubilant from the Convention, I found Dad in his favourite place – still pottering in the kitchen. Hearing me enter, he turned to speak. Clapping my hands firmly on his shoulders, I stared at him straight faced and stern.

"Dad, I have a problem," I announced. "I've been told I need to go to New York City in four weeks' time. It's going to be a week of unadulterated pleasure. The problem is, I've got two tickets. What d'you think I should do?"

"Well, the first thing that comes to mind is a week of romance with a beautiful girl. But from what I understand, the girl you might be thinking of is not the sort of girl that would go with you for a week's fling in New York. Am I right?" he said.

"Yep. That's the sort of girl she is. And anyway, I've agreed not to see her," I replied. "Frankly Dad, I wouldn't want her to change for me. Which leads me to a sad conclusion." I paused and looked at him seriously. "I'm sorry to say, the only solution I can see is that…you're just going to have to go in my place."

"What?" he shouted, as his eyes widened.

"…And you're going to have to find a beautiful girl to go with you! Life's tough isn't it?"

I started to laugh as his jaw dropped and realisation spread in a grin across his face.

Behind me I heard Mum's squeal, as Dad looked at me in amazement and burst out, "What on earth do I say to an offer like that?"

"How about promising me that you'll have a good time," I said, grabbing his hand and squeezing tight.

And, as his eyes filled, he hugged me hard before he realised what he was doing.

LESSONS LEARNED

- Could I ever have achieved today's success without help from Andrew Lambert?
- Saying 'Thank you' means so much more when you've worked long and hard to say it;
- I wish I'd known years ago what a great feeling it is to give and not to take all you can.

PROGRESS TRACKER

- Who would have thought 12 months ago that I'd be packing my parents off to New York in May?
- It's a pity about the low offer for the property in Elstree. But I'm willing to believe that Chrissie can pull something out of the bag. She's agreed to continue handling the problem whilst I pick up the reins of my new job;
- The eBook sales have created another £13,379 in orders.
- If that turns into cash, I would have sufficient to pay off just short of £53,100 from the IVA;
- It's exactly seven weeks to go before my self imposed IVA deadline;
- I have been in my job now for 15 months;
- This is my tenth month of paying into my tithing account;
- The deadline approaches rapidly before I can choose to call Naomi.

Chapter 26
Is This Goodbye?

"Tiffany, you know that I'm deadly serious about this. Coming here today, this is what's keeping me going. I'm having a really tough time right now. Look, I have to dash. I promise I'll call you on Monday, and I'll be back next weekend after my trip to Leeds. Can it wait that long?"

The visit had been too brief. There was a great deal left to talk about, and I knew that I needed to get back to her quickly.

"Jonathan, I'll wait. You know that. Look, I know you're busy. But please don't leave it longer than that."

We said our goodbyes. "I promise. You're the best," I called over my shoulder as I strode to my car.

"Thanks for the Belgian chocolates. They look delicious," she called after me.

The meeting with Tiffany played on my mind for the next couple of hours so that I hardly registered my journey to East View. After a year I was driving on 'auto-pilot' and arrived nicely in time for lunch.

"So how are your parents?" asked Nathan as we settled into our meal.

"Hmmm. At first we were worried because Dad had a struggle booking the time off work," I said between mouthfuls. "But Mum's gone into organisational overdrive. You'd think they were emigrating, with all the activity she's started."

I caught a raised eyebrow from Louise. "If my family's anything to go by," she said, "I can just see your dad arriving at the airport late and half naked unless your mother packed the cases and tied up all the loose ends of their trip."

Andrew joined Nathan and me as we nodded in submission. "Men, eh?" we muttered in chorus.

I stood up to help Louise begin clearing the dishes as Jessica made room on the table for some homemade lemon and chocolate cheesecake, accompanied by Louise's speciality – upside-down apple pie.

"Talking about loose ends," said Andrew. "Has Chrissie updated you on the latest news about the property in Elstree?"

"The last I heard before travelling on business last week," I replied, "was that she'd received an excellent offer. I think that was just after our Convention in April. She was hoping for completion just before Mum and Dad returned from New York."

"Oh dear." He looked worried. "Then you haven't heard the latest news?"

My heart sank. "Go on, let me have it."

"She'd mentioned some problems with the solicitor only yesterday and hadn't been able to reach your mobile to discuss it. I think you'd better call her. It doesn't look as if it's going to be a quick fix solution, either. There seems to be a query about right of way and land demarcation between three properties. Yours is the property slap in the middle." He looked at me, his laden spoon hovering near his mouth.

"Oh, damn!" I snarled, dumping my napkin onto the table. Chatter around the table stopped instantly apart from a splutter of laughter from Daniel. I looked instinctively across to Louise whose eyes were locked onto mine whilst, next to her, Corrin concentrated hard on her plate.

"I'm sorry, people," I moaned apologetically, "but that's all I need! I've got to have the cash from that sale to meet my target. There's only four weeks to go until the end of the month. That'll be the end of the year for me, and I'm not even close to my goal." My cheesecake lost its allure as my stomach dropped to my boots in despair.

"Well, how short of your goal are you?" asked Jessica, just settling down after making sure that we had all satisfied our eyes with the desserts.

"Good question." I started to calm down. "Let's see. After our sales convention last month, I still had £53,000 or so to go. That included the value of everything else that had been saved or sold."

Here, I turned to Louise again. "But when you and Andrew helped me to sell the Print-On-Demand books after that third conference, I think we made – what was it?"

"One hundred and twenty four books at £10 per book," Louise said, a little too crisply.

"And, you received £1,500 again as a fee." Andrew rescued me from facing Louise alone. "I make that a total of, let me see, £2,740."

"Yes, that's about right," I continued. "I've got to remember to subtract the cost of printing those books. However, if we add to that the eBook orders in the last two weeks of April."

"So how much was that?" interrupted Daniel, examining his spoon licked immaculately clean.

"According to Janine, Simon rewrote the sales script and sent it again to all of their Internet marketing partners and affiliates."

"And?" asked Daniel, impatiently.

"She reckons additional orders are worth about £14,000. And at the end of this month they will get the first figures in from Amazon and the eReader sales. Simon's been watching the book's Amazon sales ranking go up steadily and lots of purchasers are posting five star reviews so that's a good sign it's selling well," I smiled, beginning to warm to the exercise and calculating furiously as I spoke.

"So there's that money to look forward to and 14 grand!" exclaimed Daniel, leaning back to undo his belt a little.

"Jon, that's incredible," enthused Jessica glancing at Andrew. "What do you think, Dad? How's he doing?"

"This is getting tantalising. Jonathan," he answered. "We're talking about a balance to clear of just under £37,000."

"Yeah. Now you know why I'm so upset about the property," I whined. "Twenty thousand quid sitting on some solicitor's desk."

As we strolled across the gravel and onto the grass, I realised how much I had come to cherish this place: this mansion, these gardens, these spinneys; the swathes of fields and the richness of trees, together carrying memories of families and seasons; the rabbits fleeing and the early summer noises; this man beside me with his inexplicable generosity and insight.

Andrew pointed to the large trampoline, slightly tattered but enduring children, frost and rain.

"I've discovered," he said lazily, "how comfortable it is lounging on this thing. If you lie on your back and stare at the sky, it feels as if you're floating."

"As good as the Thinking Bench?" I asked as we clambered unsteadily onto the frame.

"Aaah! Now there we have some memories, don't you think?" he sprawled, yawning, onto the softly rocking, black surface where I joined him. "Tell me. Did you ever sort out the mystery of why Chrissie knew you when you met last year?"

I was caught off balance by his question – and his sharp observation – and turned to look at him. "Why? What did she say?" I asked.

"Nothing," he said. "It's merely one of those curiosities that has puzzled me all these months."

I spoke carefully. "Yes. We sorted it out. She's quite an exceptional lady. She's helped me to lay a ghost to rest and move on with my life."

There was a moment of silence between us.

"Moving on?" He sat up and let his gaze wander to the horizon and back to me. "You seem to have done quite a lot of that over the months. What a journey this has been, eh Jonathan?" He paused. "I realise you're not home and dry yet. But, what an adventure!"

He paused again, his face beginning to look pained.

I felt uncomfortable. "What's the matter, Andrew?"

He sighed before answering. "Well, I've been thinking. I've taught you exactly what we set out to do. I suppose I've grown to feel – what can I say – proud of you. Louise feels the same. The mentoring relationship has that effect. The problem is – how can I put it?"

He ran his nail across the surface of the trampoline raising goose bumps on my skin.

"If you and Naomi don't, well, hit it off again; if you've become strangers in this year. What then?"

I couldn't answer him. So we left the subject hanging between us.

LESSONS LEARNED

- When life takes you through a wilderness, it also places people in your path who can show you the way;
- Sometimes life's twisting path severs wonderful friendships. It hadn't occurred to me that my close relationship with Andrew could end;

PROGRESS TRACKER

- This week, I have paid off another £1,000 of my IVA (that makes exactly £12,000 paid so far – £1,000 per month as promised);
- Add to that another £400 that has gone into my savings account;
- The last speaking engagement in April created a cheque of £2,740 in fees and post-speech book sales;
- In the last two weeks of April, eBook sales created another £13,960 in orders;
- Together, those figures have brought the outstanding debt down to just over £35,000;
- Amazon and eReader sales are doing well, and I should get some idea of how many are sold at the start of next month;
- It's exactly four weeks to go before my self-imposed IVA deadline;
- I have been in my job now for 16 months;
- This is my 11th month of paying into my tithing account;
- My intention is to call Naomi next Saturday!

Chapter 27
Conspiracy and Hope

Friday, 10th May

The regular Friday morning hour with Steve Davey had developed into a time of intense learning and growing friendship.

He was hungry for information and new views on life. Part of the freshness and exhilaration in the relationship was his ability to question whatever I tried to teach him. During this time I discovered how bright he was and sensed that this young man possessed the capacity to carve himself an enormously successful life.

But this morning I realised how eager I was to break from our meeting and make my call.

I remained in the meeting room after dismissing him and was immediately on the phone to Tiffany. The conversation between us was brief and breathless. She sounded excited, and I felt elated.

"Jon, this is what we've been waiting for. Soon you won't need to keep things a secret anymore," she said. "I'll meet you there when you get back tomorrow."

I glanced at the phone lead, wrapping itself tightly around my hand. "I can't wait. Oh, and Tiffany . . ."

"Yes, what is it?" she asked.

I sounded anxious. "How can I thank you for what you've done?"

She laughed. "I'm sure I'll think of something very expensive." And we laughed together.

Saturday 11th May

As we drove through Croydon the following morning heading towards the airport, I glanced from time to time at my dad. He hadn't stopped smiling all morning. Behind us sat Mum lounging as if in regal splendour and enjoying the comfort of the Mercedes that I had hired for the day.

I thought back to the previous evening and my latest triumph as I spoke to an audience of over 600. Another large convention, this time an American company distributing products throughout Europe using network marketing. The atmosphere was electric throughout the evening, and I was one of those called in to kick off a weekend of razzmatazz.

Only Andrew accompanied me that night. The Lamberts figured that I was getting an old hand at this and didn't need all their emotional support. However, after counting the 'back-of-room' book sales, the cheque and cash I took home totalled just short of £3,000. Again, I had to set some of that aside to refund print costs.

At Gatwick we had an hour to kill after completing their check-in, which gave us a rare opportunity to talk.

As we sat down, Mum looked at me carefully, and I waited.

"I've looked at the calendar. If I'm not mistaken it's almost exactly twelve months since you said goodbye to that lovely girl of yours – Naomi, isn't it? Forgive me for prying, but how are you feeling?"

"To be honest, Mum, I'm both excited and scared," I said. "I'm probably one of the few that haven't a clue what she's doing or what her feelings are. I intend to contact her during the week ahead, but goodness knows what she'll say, and, to be honest, I wouldn't be surprised if it was 'Get lost!' Even if she doesn't, what happens when she sees my scarred face?"

"Is that what you expect?" she asked, sounding surprised.

My response came out more curtly than I had intended. "Mum, I'm not stupid. I understand what the Lamberts believe about relationships, marriage and all that stuff. They've been incredible – almost adopting me. But, when it comes to marrying into their family – well, I'm not part of their religion. So, although I've missed Naomi like crazy, I haven't a clue whether she feels the same for me. And even if she does, how long could it last?"

For a few moments she was quiet. Looking at me, her cheeks coloured as she responded. "Jon, I won't pretend I wasn't pretty appalled when you came back home. To be frank, you seemed a bit of a mess. But, before I step on that plane, there's something you need to know." I felt my hands clench and my back tense. "I'm telling you this: you've changed, Jonathan. My word how you've changed."

And the shadow of a smile played on her lips. "You've softened at the edges. There's a bit more to you now. Your head has shrunk, and you've grown up. You're less full of yourself."

I was expecting a 'but' at any second. "And this trip!" she continued. "This has to be the most generous thing you have ever done. And what's more, I'm sure there's no hidden agenda; no clearing the house for an all-night party."

I couldn't help smiling at the memory of how easily she had pre-empted my plotting as a teenager.

Her smile disappeared momentarily, but her eyes softened as she spoke. "Naomi's a stunning girl, looking at her photos. So, I agree, it's more than likely that she's found somebody else – or at least she's been lapping up a lot of attention. A whole year's a long time, and it would be natural, don't you think? *But*," and here she paused and reached for my hands, "my instincts tell me that she's still got a torch burning for you. And I'm as certain as I can be that you'll get to see each other again. When you do, I hope she sees in you what I now see."

"How can you be so sure she still feels something? Do you know something I don't?" I asked, my hopes rising.

She tapped my cheek softly and smiled. "Let's just put it down to female intuition, shall we, honey?"

Before I could respond Dad came over and hovered by us. I looked up at him from the airport settee and took his outstretched hand. For only the second time since I was a child, we hugged again.

Tiffany was waiting for me outside of the apartment just as we had arranged. The door of her Mercedes SL350 was open, and she was sunning herself as she leaned lazily against the leather upholstery.

Her smile widened as she saw the outsize bunch of flowers that I had ordered from the local florist. A wry smile played on her lips as she hid her pleasure with difficulty.

Easing herself gracefully out of her seat, she led the way to the front door and ushered me into the long, sunlit hall where the smell of fresh paint and apple scent caught my senses.

"How long do you have?" I asked, glancing at my watch.

Moving ahead of me on the parquet flooring, she called out, "just two hours for everything. Then I have an appointment followed by some pampering time before I head to the theatre."

Following her into the kitchen, I noted the sunlight playing across her hair as she checked inside the units lining the length of the wall.

"Look Tiffany, there's something I must do before we carry on. I need to make that phone call."

Standing up from looking inside the oven, she turned to face me. She looked serious.

"You're right. You'd better make that call now; otherwise, we won't know where we are, will we? I need to know if there's any point in taking this further."

I found the nearest door, which happened to be the main bedroom and instinctively walked to where the sunlight streamed through the net curtains.

Shutting the door firmly behind me and leaning against the window-sill, I started dialling on my cell phone. The numbers swam in front of me, and my heart was thundering against my rib cage.

"Hello. Is that you, Naomi?" The strangled voice I mustered didn't seem to belong to me.

As she answered, her brightness seemed to contrast my tension. "Hello, Jonathan. Of course it's me, silly. I've been waiting all week."

"You have? How did you recognise my voice? It's been twelve long months."

"Oh, c'mon Jon. Did you really think I could forget so easily?" she sounded annoyed.

"I guess not." My well-rehearsed speech floated out of my reach. "I can't believe you were waiting for my call. I assumed you would be going out with someone else by now. Don't tell me you've been a hermit."

She sighed and hesitated briefly. "Look! I must be honest with you," she said. "I won't pretend I've had a miserable, lonely time. But, on the other hand, I couldn't resist keeping tabs on you, month by month."

I was startled. "What? You mean you've been checking up on me through your dad?"

She laughed. "No, no. Dad has to keep so much confidential stuff from us because of his counselling and all that, so he tends to say very little at all. No, it's your mother who's 'the mole'. She's a sweetie."

Then scenes from Mum's kitchen flashed back to me: moments when I caught her guiltily finishing telephone conversations as I burst in.

"So, those calls she was hiding. That was you on the line! The two of you plotting together. Well, who'd have believed it! You sneaky lot!"

There was laughter in her voice now. "It was the only way I could keep an eye on you without making you break your promise."

I lapsed into silence trying to take in what all this meant.

"Naomi, I," my practised nonchalance stuck in my throat.

"What is it, Jon? And why are you whispering? Where are you phoning me from?" she asked.

Quickly I changed the subject. "Naomi, it's been a year. Can we not . . . I mean, why don't we . . . you know . . . meet? Won't you come home next weekend? I want to see you again." I felt like an incoherent, fumbling teenager.

"I'd like that," she replied as if she had anticipated the question.

"You would?" I stammered. "I mean, of course you would. Well, that would be wonderful, wouldn't it?"

Now she wasn't hiding her laughter. "Yes, I believe it would. Look Jon, I need to go now. I've promised my flatmates that I'd join them for a badminton tournament. They're waving at me right now."

"Why don't I call you tomorrow?" I asked, trying to sound relaxed, my heart hammering. "We could arrange where to meet – ideally away from prying eyes at East View."

"Oh please do," she said, with mock formality, teasing my inadequate acting.

"Goodbye, then," I said, delaying the moment.

"Goodbye. And Jon, thank you."

"For what?" I asked, confused.

"For making me so proud of you."

"Oh, right. Yes. That's fine. Erm, I'll call you tomorrow then." I was floating, and she was gone.

The next hour or so wasn't easy as I tried to be attentive. But Tiffany was masterful at holding my attention. We only had until the following Saturday, and she knew it.

LESSONS LEARNED

- When you let go of short-term gratification and incorporate principles of integrity, honour and selflessness into your life, happiness is the result;
- Women seem to run circles around men in their plotting and planning;
- Never underestimate a woman's ability to see through the shell of a person and glimpse the possibilities within.

PROGRESS TRACKER

- In seven days all that I had dreaded and hoped for, the months of waiting – everything – will come to an end;
- Then I can be honest and open with everybody about Tiffany and my time with her;
- Theoretically, the outstanding IVA debt is down to just under £33,000;
- It's exactly three weeks to go before the IVA deadline;
- Three weeks to make £33,000! Aaaaargh!

David J Scarlett

Chapter 28
Coming Home

Saturday, 18th May

So it was that I found myself walking, nervous and disorientated, through a field of long, undulating grass, towards Naomi's tall figure standing beside a silver Mercedes. As I approached, the car sped off, and we were alone.

The sun was behind her and glowed through and around her, creating an ethereal silhouette. Slowly, she started walking towards me, and we both wandered towards the lake, which glittered in the late spring sun.

Still paces apart we stood silently, unsure of what came next. Throwing her raincoat from her shoulders, she gently lowered herself down onto the grass, her waist-length auburn hair touching the budding stalks, her white cotton dress spread around her.

I sat carefully, within reaching distance.

And so we spoke: of days past; of fretful nights; of questions and pain; of laughter and triumph; of friends and adventures; of new hopes and old memories; of coming home.

As the sun journeyed towards its rest, she never questioned why I didn't attempt to touch her. I couldn't explain why I felt it was too soon, not even to myself.

And in a comfortable moment of silence, I said what I didn't think I'd have the courage to say. "Naomi. I've missed you." My throat was tight, and the words sounded strangled.

Her fingers froze as she stopped plucking ears from a tall stalk of grass and raised her face to look at me, pain momentarily showing in her eyes. "Don't you think I know that?" she whispered.

I traced the edge of a button on her raincoat, and the back of my hand felt the softness of her hair as a breath of wind caused it to ripple and shift across the meadow flowers. Such a simple sensation, yet I could hardly breathe with the wonder of her closeness. My voice shook as I matched her whisper. "Then please, tell me that we won't be apart again; not just yet. Say you'll give me a chance to stay with you for a while longer – for a few weeks at least."

Studying the tiny petals settled on her palm, she answered, "I'd like that. I'd like that very much."

"I've so much to tell you, but…"

"Shhh," she said, and my words evaporated as slowly she raised her hand, and with sadness in her tear-filled eyes softly traced the line of my scar. The sensation of her fingers on my cheek so shocked me that I grasped her hand, holding it to my face, and pressed her palm to my lips.

Dusk began to fall as we said an awkward farewell in the driveway of East View.

I hesitated as I opened my car door and called to her.

"Will you be able to travel up to London next Saturday? I wouldn't ask you unless it was important. There's something I need you to help me with. I can pick you up from East View – say, after breakfast."

"That sounds intriguing. I can't think of anything keeping me at university next weekend. But it had better be good," she warned with a smile.

It was the following Wednesday at the end of my first meeting with the northern regional team in Manchester, when I responded to the message to call Steve Davey.

Waiting for one of the London secretaries to track him down, I looked once more at the cheque that I had drawn the previous day from the building society. The figure was substantial, and I was looking forward to paying this accumulation of my tithing to the church I'd been attending with Naomi's friends. It was a very satisfying feeling.

Steve's voice broke into my thoughts. "What is it Steve?" I asked.

"Look, Jon, I know you didn't want to be disturbed, but I think you need to return this call. It's from Mr Lambert; he says it's urgent."

It wasn't like The Prof to contact me in business time. Anxiously, I returned his call.

"Jonathan, thanks for coming back to me so promptly," his voice was unusually sharp. "I understand that you're taking Naomi to London on Saturday. Is that right?"

"Well, yes. I didn't think you'd have a problem with that. I wanted to…"

"Jonathan, I'm sorry to be so blunt. But you need to be here on Saturday morning, just after breakfast. Something has happened, and I think you had best be at East View."

I was furious. Now I'd have to change the meeting with Tiffany that I had looked forward to for so long.

I called her in a panic; she was none too pleased. The timing of our meeting had been carefully planned, and we were both on edge about what was going to happen.

I waited tensely for her return call to confirm whether she had been able to rearrange her diary.

LESSONS LEARNED

- The wilderness hours and uncertain adventure of the journey adds to the sweetness of the arrival.

PROGRESS TRACKER

- My head is spinning trying to understand the emotions of the last few days. All of my fear and pride was washed away in the healing tenderness of Naomi's eyes;
- It seems almost incomprehensible that she is as happy as me that we're together again;
- What's really strange about Andrew's phone call today is that it's made me mad with him for the first time since last April;
- Two weeks to go before the IVA deadline.

Chapter 29
The Creation of The Soul Millionaire

Saturday, 25th May

I had tried to argue with Andrew, but he was adamant that I rearrange my Saturday schedule. I was genuinely annoyed because what I had prepared for Naomi in London was the culmination of months of work and negotiation.

Yet, strangely, my annoyance had turned to worry by the time I knocked on the familiar front door of East View three short days later. I could still catch a whiff of breakfast bacon and smiled at the thought of what I had missed.

Naomi answered, which should have been a delightful surprise. But her mood was sombre, and her eyes flitted everywhere avoiding mine.

"Come in, Jon. We need to go to Dad's office. He's waiting there."

As I pulled off my shoes and tossed them towards the shoe rack, I couldn't help noticing how very quiet the house seemed.

Then I registered that Naomi knocked on Andrew's office door and waited for an answer. That was strangely formal behaviour.

She stepped aside avoiding my outstretched hand. My heart sank as I pushed the door open and stepped into the room.

The blast of sound that hit me was so disorientating that I couldn't focus on any single face or body around me. I was physically rocked back, my stomach lurched and my vision swam, trying to take in what was happening.

"Surprise! Surprise!" came the bellowing chorus.

Around me confetti bombs exploded to fill the air.

In my confusion I saw streamers popping and snaking towards me.

There were bursts of whistling, whoops, hoots and clapping.

In amongst all this stood Andrew, beaming and leading the applause.

There were Nathan and Daniel, whistles in mouth, blasting noisily. Jessica was there laughing and holding Corrin's hand, arms raised above their heads and each pumping an ear-splitting air horn.

Even the children were jumping up and down, caught up in the delirium.

I noticed Louise, more animated than I had ever seen her, bursts of laughter refusing to be stifled.

I began laughing with her as my senses feasted on the crazy scene. This was mad!

Then my eyes took in faces, which were entirely out of context, and I had to concentrate hard to place them. Simon and Janine were applauding and mouthing something, which I couldn't understand in the confusion. What were they doing here?

Beside them stood Chrissie and Matt, with him looking in good health.

But who was this? I couldn't believe it! There, standing sedately, hands behind his back, stood the stout figure of Chris Charles desperately trying not to smile.

I realised by now that I had not closed my mouth since I'd stepped through the door. As I tried to regain my composure, I turned to where Naomi now stood.

Her eyes were fully on mine now, her face radiant. And tears rolled down her cheeks.

Out of the corner of my eye, I saw Andrew lift his arms a little, and the room fell silent.

Instinctively, we all turned to face him.

"Jonathan, welcome," he said. "You're probably wondering what this is all about."

"Well, the thought had crossed my mind." The words came in a slur of tongue-tied embarrassment.

There was a ripple of laughter as they settled down into the chairs placed around the room.

"Gathering everybody here in such a hurry was quite a task, I can tell you," he said, scanning the sea of faces around him. "But, I realise that you and Naomi need to travel to London, so I'm going to get to the point."

"Hear, hear!" piped Daniel.

The Prof shot a glance to Daniel, who put his hand to his mouth, still grinning. Then he continued. "First, I'd like to invite some brief announcements from those around me. Then I'll conclude with my own comments. Simon and Janine – you first."

Janine rose, holding an envelope tightly in her hand.

"Our news is simple, Jonathan. As you know, we've recently deposited April's revenue into your account amounting to about £27,000. Well, now we have a cheque here for May's eBook revenue. It's still selling like hotcakes. The cheque is for £26,496, representing about 2,000 sales."

A round of applause greeted this announcement, and, with a noticeably shaking hand, I took the cheque, unable to speak.

Then Nathan spoke. "Whilst you've been strutting your stuff as a speaker and radio star, we've had cameras recording your every move. So, Daniel and I have been talking with Simon and Janine about ways of repackaging your talks, and your book in addition to the Amazon and eReader versions we've done already. We'll be creating CDs, DVDs, videos and podcasts, together with transcripts…"

"…which Simon and I will be able to distribute all those versions of *The Soul Millionaire* to an even broader market," finished Janine. "We estimate we could approach other Web Masters to reach an audience of over 250,000."

Then it was Chrissie's turn.

"I know that I told you about Matt's illness. What I didn't tell you was that a whole team of guys from Andrew and Louise's property contacts came to the rescue. When they heard what had happened and what was at stake, they reorganised their schedule. They threw themselves into the project, and it finished in double quick time." Matthew pushed his arm through hers.

"Having to pay them obviously cut our profit margins. Also, the contracts have not been exchanged yet. But we're confident that we're just a couple of days away from solving the legal problems and closing the deal. If anything goes wrong, we have buyers champing at the bit, ready to take them off our hands.

"So, subtracting your £1,950 that we put up for the balance of your deposit, we're happy to present you with a net cheque of £11,550."

I looked square in Chrissie's eyes. "Thank you so much. I'm not sure if I can ever repay you. Especially…"

"Hey, fella. We made a nice profit from the deal. Don't feel sorry for us." She came towards me, and we embraced.

"And you're not the person I knew all those years ago," she whispered. Then tapping me on the cheek, she stepped back and took her place beside Matthew.

"If I remember correctly," cut in Andrew, "you had about £33,000 to find after your last speaking engagement. I make our cheques total £38,000. I reckon that takes you well and truly 'out of the red' for the first time in twelve months."

Then Chris Charles stood up and walked towards me.

"Well, Jonathan. I'm not sure what to say. I'm flabbergasted by what you've achieved. I recognise that these cheques will take time to clear. But if you can organise a bank transfer for £100,000 before the end of next week, then I think we can honourably say that you'll have achieved your goal, and that's truly astonishing!"

He shook my hand with gusto. As he took his seat again, the room fell silent. Andrew stood.

"Now it's my turn." He walked towards me and turned to face the others. Standing squarely at my side, he rested his hand firmly on my shoulder.

"Jonathan and I met just over one year ago. I'm sure we both remember it well." Glancing at me, he said, "you'll remember I set you three challenges, and I distinctly recall your reaction."

"Frankly, I thought that you were a bit of a lunatic. What you wanted was ridiculous, impossible," I said shaking my head.

"Yet you took them on anyway almost without knowing why." I felt his hand tap my shoulder again.

"The first challenge was to clear your renegotiated debts, not in four years but in one." He looked across to Chris, whose eyebrows promptly raised.

"Today that goal is in sight. By Friday it will be real." There were murmurs of approval around the room.

Again he looked at Chris. "We'll need to meet with Chris and the accountants to discuss the taxes due on what you've received today. But we have a few months to clear that up.

He hesitated, looking through the people in the room into the distance in that way he had of gathering his thoughts.

"The second challenge was, yes, to create a way to communicate with one million people, with the aim…"

I finished the sentence with confidence, "… of inspiring them to change their lives."

Louise interrupted, "That's right," she said. "Corrin has informed me that your interview on last week's BBC radio programme probably reached their average audience of 1.3 million. When your next book eventually reaches the bookstores, I believe that will begin to spread your story even further."

"Thanks Louise, that's amazing news," responded Andrew. "Finally," he said, stepping away from me and moving to face Naomi. "We come to the third challenge – the most painful of all.

"I asked this young man to stop seeing my daughter. In fact, to cease all communication with Naomi for a period of twelve months and then more."

Naomi folded her arms and, with a small cough, looked directly into his face, her eyes filling again.

Taking his gaze from her, he turned to look back to me, "which, to anyone with an ounce of passion in them, must have seemed painful and pointless beyond reason."

Then, his voice thickening, he pointed at me. "But you did it. You achieved the seemingly impossible. My belief is that in years to come, you'll see this as your most magnificent achievement. It's been a triumph of love over passion."

Still unable to move, I thrust my hands deep into my pockets and tried not to look in Naomi's direction.

"Because of that one decision," his voice grew as he raised his index finger, "you've both grown in a way that would not have been possible otherwise. Now each of you knows that whenever you make a commitment, you have the strength to keep it no matter what the temptations."

I knew in that moment that he was right. Blow me, he was always right!

Louise took a couple of steps towards him, her hands now behind her back.

Looking at me, he continued, sounding somewhat pompous. "So, it is now my duty, on behalf of the Lambert family," (I thought I caught Daniel chuckling) "to present you with this."

And as he lifted his hand, Louise's arm swung forward, revealing a large golden medallion swinging on the end of a maroon sash, which she gave to Andrew. Turning towards me, he placed it carefully around my neck and stood back to admire it.

"Jonathan Broom," he announced, "you have earned yourself the title of 'The Soul Millionaire'."

There was more. "This medallion is part of that title. You will soon discover that there are a number of us across the country, pledged to help others free themselves financially and then to live astonishing lives."

Slowly each person stood, and I looked around me as this extraordinary circle of friends applauded me once more.

As the applause died down, one by one they all unbuttoned their jackets to display their own medallions. All the Lambert family, Chrissie and Matt, Simon and Janine, everyone, they were all Soul Millionaires too.

Now I understood once and for all why I had been so fortunate, why everyone had been so magnanimous and why it had all felt so very right.

With mixed emotions we drove away from the house, and I took one last glimpse in the mirror, expecting to see the whole family still gathered at the main door, jostling as they waved us off.

Naomi let out a cry of surprise as I stabbed my foot on the brake and jerked to a halt. Quickly unbuckling my belt, I pushed open my door and stepped onto the drive, turning once more to face East View.

What had caught my attention was the sight of Andrew, left standing alone in the shadow of the front porch, his arms at his side.

I stood very still, somehow sad and uncertain. Whatever the future held, something had now come to an end. As we stared at each other, his only movement was to bring his right hand to touch his beard.

Very slightly, almost imperceptibly, he bowed his head.

I did the same.

He raised his arm a little as if about to wave, and I thought I caught a wry smile. Letting his arm fall, he stepped from the porch onto the gravel and slowly walked over to the grass, hands in his pockets. The dew still lay thick and there was a blanket of mist inches above the tips of the grass. I continued gazing as he walked towards the morning sun, passing a tall fir and skirting a gnarled oak, then over to a bench settled in its shade…

Three hours later Naomi and I came to a halt in front of a block of nine new apartments set well back from the road. The drive had seemed to take forever, and we burst out of the car with relief.

For the first time in twelve long months, I took her hand. Standing still, I looked at the Mercedes already parked in front of us and smiled at the surreptitious arrangements that had worked so well. I stared as the driver's door opened and couldn't help grinning as the elegant blonde emerged slowly and faced me, her eyes laughing as she took in the scene.

"Tiffany," I said, my voice wavering, "let me introduce you to someone very special. This is Naomi Lambert. Naomi, meet Tiffany Belmore our, ahem, 'Special Agent'."

Naomi looked completely flustered, particularly as Tiffany stretched out her hand in greeting, a delighted smile taking over her face.

"Naomi, you have no idea how lovely it is to meet you," Tiffany said, looking genuinely pleased. "Jon has talked about you incessantly for two months."

"Oh, really?" replied Naomi. "I'm sorry. I'm a little confused. But I'm not sure what's happening. Jon hasn't let me in on this secret yet."

"Oh, he will," the twang in her voice contrasting starkly with Naomi's very Sussex accent. Smiling and turning to me, she added, "Or rather, we will. Come on Jon. Everything is ready. Let's go in."

Naomi shot a questioning look at me as we started to walk down the path to the first ground-floor apartment. "You'll see," I whispered, entwining my fingers with hers.

Within seconds Tiffany was opening the blue door of Number One, Passmore Court.

Turning, she handed me the key. "I think this is your privilege, Jon."

"Thanks Tiffany. Thanks for everything. I promised you I wouldn't let you down."

"You didn't," she nodded and smiled. "You made it. You both made it."

Looking at us both, she said, "He's quite a guy, this one. Look after him."

With a brief kiss and hug, she said goodbye to Naomi, winked at me, and within seconds she was driving back down the hill towards the High Street.

Taking Naomi by the hand, I entered the hall and walked carefully along the parquet flooring. Slowly I turned right and opened the door to display a spacious but empty lounge.

"Pray enter my mansion, ma'moiselle."

"Jon, this is lovely." She wheeled around in the centre of the room, her arms thrown out as she spun. "But I don't understand."

"This is now my new home," I said triumphantly. "Tiffany has worked patiently with me for a couple of months. She helped me find it, arrange the mortgage, everything." I paused, waiting for her to stand still.

"It had to be perfect because it had to please you," I continued.

"What do you mean?" she looked at me questioningly.

"Look," I wanted to move towards her, but I stayed still, hoping to relieve the tension between us. "I prayed that you would agree to see me again, maybe even more than that. So I bought this," I said, stretching out my arms.

"It was touch and go because I had to set aside £10,000 for the deposit and various fees. And I had to hide all that from your family."

She frowned a little.

"It has two bedrooms. Come and see." I held out my hand to her. We walked slowly from room to room. She was very quiet, and I couldn't help feeling unsettled.

Soon we stood in the centre of the lounge again. This time I took both her hands in mine as we faced each other. I noticed again the high cheekbones and the unusual hazel colour of her eyes. I also noted that those eyes sparkled with the excitement and the fire that I had first noticed many, many months ago. Through the large, curtainless windows, the early afternoon sunlight struck the red hues of her hair, setting it ablaze.

Looking at me she repeated what I had said a few minutes before. "You said, 'maybe even more than that'." Then squeezing my hands tightly, she asked, "Why can it not be something much more than that? Why can't you say it, Jon? Surely, it's okay to say 'we can be married' you know."

Now I was a little confused. "I don't understand. We're still almost strangers! And I'm not one of you. I don't believe what you and your family believe, you know that. How can you be so certain about marriage? And do you honestly think Andrew and Louise would agree, just like that?"

"What are you talking about?" Now there was irritation in her voice. "How maddening can you be? It's far from 'just like that'. We've waited a whole year for each other. Don't you think

I've thought about this long and hard?" She spoke with an edge of pain.

"But your parents?" I blurted. "And everything you believe in?"

"Oh come on, Jon," she said, crossly, "Do you think I'm naïve enough to imagine there won't be difficulties. For goodness sake, I've spent hours talking this through with my parents. But can't you see, you've changed so much? Isn't it good enough, me being proud of you?"

She let go of my hands and folded her arms, holding herself. "Is there something wrong with me feeling like this? Or are you telling me that you're scared of wanting to commit to me for that long?"

I could think of nothing coherent to say. And it was then that I could hold my emotions back no longer. I felt my lips tremble, and before I knew it, tears were pricking at my eyes. I took a deep breath to compose myself.

Soon, I felt her cool hand resting on my forehead and softly brushing across my hair.

"I'm sorry," I gulped down some air. "This is so ridiculous. I guess it must be relief. This has been so tough, so long. I never thought I'd get through it. But, now it's over. I've done it. I've done it." I sniffed hard, desperately trying to find a tissue in my pocket.

"'It's over'? What do you mean, 'over'?" Her voice rose an octave.

"Jonathan Broom, let me tell you something. This story is only just beginning!"

JONATHAN'S JOURNAL ENTRY

So, now you know my story.

Now you know a little more about money, and the power it has to both bless and destroy lives.

Now you know that true riches grow, not from having more, but from becoming more.

Now you know that even someone like me can crawl back from the edge of disaster and change at the very deepest level.

Now you know that ordinary people can rise to achieve extraordinary things.

Now you know the power of love to draw a man to his greatest dream, his highest purpose, his finest character.

Now you know the power of faith when others refuse to give up on your potential.

Now you know that there are people who roam the earth constantly looking for opportunities to touch other lives, giving those lives the support and love that we all crave.

Now you know that in this world, where very few stand up and say, "This is what I stand for, and this is the line that I will not cross," there are amazing young women like Naomi Lambert. And now you know what it takes to be worthy of somebody like her.

With all of this in mind . . .

Now you know what it takes, and how it feels, to become . . .

A Soul Millionaire!

David J Scarlett

The Ten Laws of a Soul Millionaire

Law One

Develop The Mind of a Soul Millionaire

A Soul Millionaire recognises a number of truths.

There are many, but here are four:

The First Truth

We can achieve extraordinary things when we give our lives to a purpose much bigger than ourselves.

The Second Truth

A Soul Millionaire uses wealth to lift lives.

The Third Truth

A Soul Millionaire takes responsibility.

The Fourth Truth

A Soul Millionaire learns to understand and respect money.

Your Notes

Law Two

Create The Big Picture

Element Number One

is a question:

How huge and audacious is the task or goal
you have set for yourself?

Element Number Two

Describe your three-year vision.
The secret is to paint it with strongly descriptive words.

Element Number Three

Write it in the present tense.

Your Notes

David J Scarlett

Law Three

Take the Leap of Faith

Practice 'Tithing'

Save ten percent of your gross income.

*Start by depositing your tithe into a savings account
until you're sure which church or charity you wish to give it to.
It's the spiritual intent that counts.*

Your Notes

Law Four

Create Freedom Not Wealth

Achieving Financial and Time Freedom is so Much More Powerful than Gaining Wealth

Avoid the burden of trying to amass a large pot of money. Instead, learn to create sufficient streams of income.

Your Notes

Law Five

Become the Financial Master

Step Number One

Learn to value money.

Step Number Two

Track every item.

Step Number Three

Trim back.

Step Number Four

Decide how much you're going to give away
and how much you're going to keep.

Your Notes

Law Six

Residual Income Is King!

The FREEDOM Formula

F   **Five, Free, Force** - will you be able to break free from your business venture or project within five years? Also, correct timing of a business increases its force.

R   **Residual Income** - create something which continues to pay income year after year.

E   **Employee-Free** - employees can be the heaviest financial burden and highest consumers of time and energy. Think . . . could you outsource routines and projects?

E   **Essential** - the more 'essential' the need for your product or service feels to your target market, the greater your chance of success.

D   **Differentiate, Desire** - the desire and passion for what you do will shine through and influence those around you, to help you achieve your dreams.

O   **Organised** - your business must lend itself to being structured into a repeatable process.

M   **Multiply** - Could you create an army of affiliates who would be happy to distribute your service or product to your market for a share of the revenue?

Your Notes

Law Seven

Start to Live On Purpose

There are four sectors where we live out our lives:

Roosters
Eagles
Chickens
Magpies

The Eagles sector is where you should be
directing your energy each day.

Look Through the Lens of The Week

Plan by the week, not by the day.

Your Notes

Law Eight

Develop a Balanced Life

Physical, Mental, Spiritual, Socio-Emotional

These are the four areas of our lives
which are all inextricably linked.

*Achieving balance in our life consequently creates
a more complete, happier, fulfilled individual
with far more to give to those around them.*

Your Notes

Law Nine

Go Beyond Success

Success starts when a person reaches out,
using their gifts, talents and achievements
to benefit the lives of others.

Your Notes

Law Ten

Become The Mentor

When the Student is Ready, the Teacher Will Appear

Knowing that you're going to be teaching principles
and skills to somebody else increases your desire
to put those principles into practice in your own life.

Your Notes

David J Scarlett

Five Rules of Marketing and Publishing Success

There are five primary conditions for success in marketing and publishing:

Rule number one
The readers in your target market
must have a painful problem or burning desire

Rule number two
The readers in your target market should be
conscious of their problem or desire

Rule number three
You need to be able to access your market easily

Rule number four
Your readers must have available funds to deal with
their problem or desire

Rule number five
Your readers must have a history of spending money
to solve the problem, or fulfil their desire

Your Notes

About David J Scarlett

David J Scarlett knows a little about being on the wrong end of money. Raised largely in a convent-based children's home in Hertfordshire . . . Broke and homeless by the age of 28 . . .

Nobody is more surprised than he is, that he finds himself coaching and mentoring small business owners, entrepreneurs, professional advisers, non-profit organisation chairmen and corporate executives . . .

Appearing on BBC radio, giving money-wise advice . . .

Sitting on panels to judge other entrepreneurs' inventions and business ventures . . .

Co-authoring with business and financial giants Brian Tracy, Robert G Allen and Mark Victor Hansen – who, between them, have sold 150 million books . . .

Or being paid to speak at business seminars and conferences internationally.

Describing himself as "for many years, one of Financial Services' more ineffective Advisers", David understands what it is like to experience embarrassing business failure as an entrepreneur. He learned the hard way about ego, poor financial control and uncontrolled business growth.

Eventually becoming a respected Financial Planner in the City of London – David developed into a financial mentor for IT directors and wealthy families. Finally, he mastered his craft to such an extent that he created revenue streams enjoyed by only the top 1% of Financial Planners in the UK.

A work-in-progress husband and sometimes-getting-it-right father of four amazing children. An ecclesiastical leader, with extraordinary responsibilities, far beyond his natural capacity.

Now it's your turn to benefit from this business leader who has learned the secret regarded as the Holy Grail of all small businesses . . . the creation of Predictable, Recurrent Income.

And finally, discover how you can evolve so that money becomes your craftsman's tool – a reflection of the fineness of your character and emotional maturity – with which you shape, influence and bless the world around you.